Business *for* Advanced Secretarial Students

Carol Carysforth

650 CAR

Heinemann Educational Publishers
Halley Court, Jordan Hill, Oxford OX2 8EJ
a division of Reed Educational & Professional Publishing Ltd

OXFORD   MELBOURNE   AUCKLAND
JOHANNESBURG   BLANTYRE   GABORONE
IBADAN   PORTSMOUTH (NH) USA   CHICAGO

First published 1996
99 98 11 10 9 8 7 6 5 4 3

A catalogue record for this book is available from the British Library on request.

ISBN 0 435 455400

Designed by Jackie Hill

Typeset by TechType, Abingdon, Oxon

Printed and bound by Biddles Ltd, Guildford

Dedication

This book is dedicated to Eleanor (Ellie) – the new light of our lives – with the wish that her ability to learn will match her ability to charm, her intellect will rival her beauty, her achievements will equate to her dreams and throughout her life she will neither fear nor favour anyone.

Acknowledgements

My personal thanks are due to the many secretarial students to whom I have taught business and management subjects – and who have helped to refine my approach to these subjects. Their input and feedback has constantly informed my own teaching and enabled me to develop an appreciation of the areas which they find particularly difficult. It is for future students of these subjects that this book has been written.

In addition, my thanks are due to all my colleagues, friends and family who have, as always, been so helpful and supportive. In particular, Maureen Rawlinson, my friend and colleague, for her advice and expertise on employment law; Margaret Berriman at Heinemann for being brave enough to criticise (constructively) much of the first draft; Jan Nikolic for her perserverance and attention to detail; and to all those at Heinemann who continually inspire me with their enthusiasm and energy. Finally, as always, grateful thanks to Mike – my researcher, companion, friend and husband – without whom this book (and this year) may have been possible but not nearly so enjoyable!

The author and publishers would like to thank the following for permission to reproduce photographs and other copyright materials:

Action Images
British Airways
Camera Press
Controller of HMSO
Impact/Peter Arkell
Marks & Spencer
Philip Parkhouse

Contents

Introduction

This book has been written to introduce you to the way in which businesses are structured and organised, the environment in which they operate and how this affects their organisation and operation as well as the people who work in them. In today's rapidly changing world there are numerous challenges that businesses have to face and conquer – economic factors and problems, political agendas and legislative changes, competition from world markets, ever-changing technology, stakeholder demands and concerns for the environment – to mention but a few! All of these factors affect managers and their administrative staff – whether at the level of trainee administrator or top-flight PA.

A knowledge of this business environment is an essential prerequisite for anyone hoping to make a career in business. Without this knowledge it is impossible to understand or appreciate many of the decisions made every day. This is not to say that understanding necessarily means agreement – in many cases the ability to evaluate critically is a healthy sign – because knowledge and understanding are essential before informed comment can be made.

Understanding business, as a topic, often seems a formidable task for students, especially those who are studying on a full-time basis and do not have the practical experience to help them put new information into context. For that reason, this textbook is not written in the traditional, theoretical way. Instead it takes everyday examples from the business world to help to explain what happens and why it happens.

Your job is not to read this book from cover to cover, as you would a novel or short story! Use it firstly to inform you on a topic, secondly, to check understanding, thirdly, to point you to how to develop that knowledge.

You should find the format easy to follow.

- Each chapter starts with an introduction which gives you a brief overview of what it contains. This will help you target those chapters which are particularly useful for the examination you are taking.

- Each contains **discussion points** to introduce you to the idea of discussing and debating topical issues. Current news items may provide other opportunities. Try to separate fact from opinion and not to jump to conclusions.

- Towards the end of each chapter, the **keywords** are highlighted – so you can check that you clearly understand all the main concepts.

- At the end of the chapter you will find a section designed to give you **examination practice.** Four different question formats are given – your tutor will be able to guide you towards those most useful for the examination you are taking. Generally, short-answer questions and case studies are favoured by the RSA, whilst definition questions and essay topics are preferred by the LCCI. However, practice on any style of question is useful!

- Finally, at the end of the book is a brief chapter aimed at helping you to think *across* issues which are common to many chapters. This chapter is designed to develop the skills of analysis and evaluation – both of which are vital for good grades in level 3 examinations.

A final word! **Do** gain knowledge and information outside this one book alone – through newspapers, television, radio and through the many resources in your library. Buy a **good** Sunday newspaper each week (even if you can't afford a daily one) and watch at least *some* of the news on television during the evening. Don't walk out and make a cup of coffee as soon as the news focuses on business or the economy! Don't be afraid to ask questions and to listen to the answers.

Although your main aim is obviously success at the end of the year, I hope that at least some of the information you learn you will remember for much longer. Hopefully, it may even stimulate you to take more than a passing interest in what is going on in the world around you. Above all, enjoy your studies – you are about to learn more about the world around you and how it operates – and this can only be beneficial both in your professional and personal life.

Carol Carysforth
September 1996

The world of business

We floated the company in 1986 – part of your job will be helping to organise the AGM.

We decided to opt for a private limited company rather than a partnership because we didn't want to risk having unlimited liability. You understand what that means, of course?

He's thinking of starting a franchise – its a safer bet than going it alone.

Jo worked there until the demerger. She then became part of the management buyout team.

Did you read that the local authority has been granted unitary status? How will this affect us?

Introduction

In common with virtually every other country in the world the UK has a **mixed economy.** This means that some goods and services are provided by private individuals and organisations – known as the **private sector** – and others are provided by the state – known as the **public sector.**

In Britain, in common with many other countries, there has been a move away from public-sector provision. A starker example, perhaps, is Russia which is trying to adjust to a **free-market economy** – where a considerable proportion of goods are now produced by the private sector for a profit. Until relatively recently, the state made decisions relating to what goods should be produced, how many and by whom. Today this system operates in very few countries – China and Albania are two examples.

The economic success of countries such as Germany and the United States, both of which have a large private sector, has meant other countries have followed suit. In Britain there has been a consistent move away from the provision of goods and services by the public sector since 1980. The aim of this has been to

- increase consumer choice

- reduce the costs of operating the public sector – which are borne by the taxpayer

- increase competition. It is generally agreed that prices fall when there is a greater choice for consumers.

The government has largely achieved this through a mixture of deregulation and privatisation policies. Both are discussed later in this chapter.

When you start work you will be employed in either the private or the public sector. The form of organisation may vary, as may its legal status. As a potential employee, it is important that you know about these differences. This chapter is concerned with the various forms of organisation to be found in both the private and public sectors in Britain today, the differences between them and the major changes which have affected them.

Competition = lower prices

If you want to cross the Channel for your holidays, it will cost you much less than a few years ago. Why? Because of the price war taking place between Eurotunnel and the ferry companies. Until Eurotunnel opened, ferry operators had the route to themselves. All offered roughly the same type of fares. To gain customers, in early 1996 Eurotunnel announced bargain prices – particularly for day trips on Le Shuttle. The result was ferry companies immediately vowing they would match any discounts. Which must be good news for day-trippers and holiday-makers alike.

● The private sector

The private sector comprises businesses which are

- owned and controlled by private individuals – often called **entrepreneurs.** These are individuals who bring together all the necessary ingredients to run a business – sometimes called the factors of production. In economic terms these are land, labour, capital and 'enterprise'. The 'enterprise' can more easily be understood as imagination and vision. Richard Branson is an excellent example of an entrepreneur with these qualities.

- usually operating with the **main objective of making a profit or surplus at the end of each year.** The entrepreneur is therefore also a risk-taker – risking savings and financial investment in the business (known as **capital**) to make a profit.

Other objectives can include the following:

- to grow larger – McDonalds has this as its stated objective. It has grown from one UK restaurant in Woolwich 21 years ago to over 650 at the beginning of 1996. It plans to double this number over the next five years and become one of the UK's biggest employers by the year 2000.

- to increase sales or **market share.** This is the 'slice' of the total market for a product which is held by a company. As an example, the global music industry is worth £24 billion. This is shared by BMG with 13 per cent of the market, Sony with 16 per cent, Polygram with 14 per cent, Warner with 14 per cent, EMI with 13 per cent and MCA with 4 per cent. Small independent producers make up the rest of the sector.

- to provide a commercial service for customers.

- to provide a service or help others (this mainly applies to charitable organisations – see page 18).

There are several different types of private enterprises you need to know about. These are

- **sole proprietors**

- **partnerships**

- **limited companies**

- **multinationals.**

In addition, you should also know the difference between these organisations and those with charitable status, as well as other variations which exist in the business world, such as franchises.

Basically, all private-sector businesses can be divided into two types – **unincorporated** and **incorporated.** Although there are fewer regulations governing unincorporated enterprises, there are certain drawbacks – as you will see below.

Unincorporated enterprises

There are two types of unincorporated enterprises – **sole proprietors** and **partnerships.** Legally, there is no distinction at all between the owner and the business – they are one and the same thing. The owner enters into agreements, hires staff, makes contracts, owns property – all *in his or her own name.* If the owner gets into debt, then he or she is *personally responsible* and may have to sell personal assets such as a house, car or furniture to make reparation (pay the debt). This is known as **unlimited liability** – the owner's liability for the debts is unlimited up until his or her personal assets have been sold, at which point, if money was still owing, the owner would be declared bankrupt.

However, on the positive side, the owner of an unincorporated business has few rules and regulations to worry about.

- He or she can set up in business at any time, without permission, providing he or she is trading under his or her own name. Only if another name is going to be used must the owner register this first and obtain permission.

- He or she can decide when to cease trading. The business can be wound up at any time. Should the owner die whilst the business is still trading, then the business would die with the individual.

- He or she can submit basic accounts to his or her accountants. These are always kept private and do not need to be **audited** by a licensed accountant – but must be complete enough to satisfy the Inland Revenue. Auditing books means they are checked in detail. This is discussed on pages 9–10.

The owner will be charged with paying **income tax** on any profit made. This is usually paid twice a year direct to the Inland Revenue. After paying income tax the rest of the profit belongs solely to the owner.

Sole proprietors

Many types of businesses are run by a sole proprietor – or single owner – even though he or she may have several employees. Examples include newsagents, grocers, hairdressers, sub-post offices, plumbers and decorators. Only businesses which need a small amount of capital are suitable for a sole proprietor as he or she is personally responsible for financing the business. Bank loans can be difficult to obtain for a small business – even if a good business plan has been prepared which forecasts the income, expenditure and potential profit of the enterprise over the next 12 months. Lack of finance often limits expansion possibilities.

Advantages
- It is easy to set up with few legal formalities (though the Inland Revenue must be informed).

- Quick decisions are possible – there is no one else to consult so plans can be put into effect rapidly.

- The owner is independent and is his or her own boss.

- The owner can keep all the profit after paying any tax due.

- A personal service to customers can be provided because the owner will get to know their individual likes and dislikes.

- **Bad debts** (ie unpaid debts) can be avoided because the owner will know who is credit worthy and who is not.

- There is the minimum of paperwork (but more if turnover, ie the value of sales, means the business must be registered for **Value Added Tax (VAT)**).

Disadvantages

- Long working hours and little time off.

- The owner earns no money if the business is closed because of holidays or sickness.

- Capital can be difficult to raise.

- The owner's heir(s) may be liable for inheritance tax upon his or her death.

- Small-scale businesses normally have higher costs than those operating on a large scale as they cannot achieve **economies of scale.** These are financial savings made through operating on a large scale (see pages 27–8).

- The flair of the owner may be for a particular skill – he or she may have little financial or management expertise.

- The owner has the problem of unlimited liability for debts.

Partnerships

A partnership is an unincorporated enterprise. Legally, the maximum number of partners is 20 (fewer in the case of a bank). Going into partnership means that the responsibilities and problems of running a business can be shared. Cover is possible during sickness and holidays and each partner can specialise in a different skill. A typical example is a solicitors' firm – where different specialisms can be family law, conveyancing, litigation, probate and criminal law. Partnerships are most often found amongst the professions, such as barristers, accountants, doctors, dentists and vets. In many cases the professional body which controls them does not allow its members to operate with corporate status (see below) as it holds that its members must be personally and professionally responsible for the decisions made.

A partnership is formed when each partner signs a Deed of Partnership which sets out details of the business relationship such as salary, share of profits and the name of the firm. However, there is no obligation to sign a Deed of Partnership. All partnerships are governed by the Partnership Act 1890 which assumes that all partners are equally and jointly liable for debts unless a Deed of Partnership has been drawn up which provides different information.

Advantages

- It is easier to raise capital as each partner makes a contribution.

- Problems can be shared and discussed.

- New ideas and skills can be introduced.

- The business affairs and financial accounts are still private.

- Responsibility and working hours can be shared.

- **Specialisation** is possible. This means that the partners can agree to concentrate on the jobs they are good at – this increases the services offered and usually means jobs are carried out more cost effectively.

Disadvantages
- Partners may not agree on an important issue.

- Profits must be shared.

- All partners have to be consulted about decisions – which can reduce speed of response.

- The actions of one partner are binding on everyone.

- The death or retirement of a partner means that his or her investment must now be repaid into his or her estate. For this reason, it is usual for life assurance policies to be taken out which will pay out this money to protect the finances of the partnership.

- The partners still have unlimited liability for their debts.

Limited partnerships
These are rare in Britain, but can be set up if someone is willing to invest capital in a partnership on the understanding that he or she has limited liability. This means that the limited partner can *at most* only lose the amount of his or her investment.

However, under the Limited Partnership Act 1907, two rules must be followed.

- All partnerships *must* have at least one ordinary partner with unlimited liability.

- The limited partner *must be* a **sleeping partner.** This means that he or she cannot take an active part in the business.

The largest partnership in Britain

John Lewis, which owns 22 department stores and 111 Waitrose supermarkets, is a partnership! Its 34,000 staff are officially described as 'partners' – even though they don't actually control the company, they do elect half the board. Because there are no outside shareholders all the profit is available for reinvestment and the payment of an annual staff bonus. In 1994 the company made a profit of nearly £93.5 million and allocated £43 million to paying a bonus to all staff of 12 per cent of salary or six weeks' pay.

Discussion point

1   You have a friend who is a qualified motor mechanic. He is thinking of opening a garage business and working for himself. Decide the qualities you think he would need to make a success of the business.

2   Identify two examples of professional partnerships in your area. Discuss how they may take advantage of the potential for specialisation within the firm.

3   Value Added Tax (VAT) is levied on the sales of all items except those which are exempt (eg education) or zero-rated (eg food).
    a   Find two other examples of exempt and zero-rated items.
    b   Find out the current rate of turnover allowed before a firm must register for VAT.

Incorporated enterprises

In an incorporated enterprise the business is a distinct legal entity – with a separate legal status from the owners (ie the **shareholders**) and the **directors.** At this stage you should note the difference between shareholders and directors. The shareholders are institutions or individuals which have bought shares in a company in return for a dividend and in expectation of the shares increasing in value. The directors are executives who receive a salary to run a company. They may, or may not, have shares in the organisation.

Having a 'separate legal identity' means that the business itself owns land, employs staff, engages in contracts and agreements and can be held liable for its own actions in law. If, for example, you slipped and broke your leg in your local newsagent, you would sue the proprietor; if you did the same thing in a department store such as Debenhams, you would sue the company – not the manager! On the same basis, if the directors or shareholders of a company leave or die, then this makes no difference to the company itself – which will continue to exist until it is legally wound up.

The business must be run in accordance with the requirements of the various Companies Acts – the most recent of which were passed in 1980, 1985 and 1989. These control the actions both of the company and the directors – who can still be held personally liable if they are guilty of offences such as negligence, fraud, theft, misconduct or deliberately misleading shareholders. Most companies must produce accounts which are audited by independent registered auditors (usually a firm of accountants) before being submitted to the Inland Revenue – although the rules are slightly different for small and large companies (see Figure 1.1). The auditors' job is to check all the accounting records and then confirm whether

Turnover	Requirement
Less than £90,000 a year	Exempt from audit
Between £90,000 and £350,000 a year	Compilation report
Over £350,000 a year	Statutory audit

Figure 1.1 Audit requirements

the accounts provide a 'true and fair view' of the financial situation. If the auditors do not agree with the financial records (for instance, if some are missing or inaccurate), then they may issue a 'qualified' report. **Corporation tax** is paid on the profits.

However, the most important concept so far as shareholders are concerned is that of **limited liability** – which is why incorporated enterprises are known as limited companies. The capital for limited companies is raised through issuing shares (types of shares are discussed in chapter 3). However, people would not be willing to invest their money if they were going to be personally liable for all the debts of the company! The concept of limited liability therefore is that the shareholders' liability for company debts is limited to the amount of their investment. A limited company cannot, therefore, go 'bankrupt'. If it amasses debts which cannot be repaid, then it will go into liquidation – at which point the shareholders (and probably several creditors as well) will lose their money. Liquidators (or receivers) will be appointed to dispose of the assets, repay money where possible (the Inland Revenue always has the first claim!) and formally wind up the company.

There are two types of incorporated enterprises.

- **Private limited companies.**
- **Public limited companies.**

Because the regulations affecting them are different, each is considered separately below.

Private limited companies (Ltd)
Many private companies are formed from partnerships or family businesses. They are under the control of a small number of people or family members who are both directors and also majority shareholders. The basic rules relating to private companies are as follows.

- The name must be suffixed with the initials 'Ltd'.
- There must be a minimum of one director.
- There must be a minimum of two shareholders.

Measure	Small company	Medium-sized company
Turnover	Not more than £2 million	Not more than £8 million
Balance sheet total	Not more than £975,000	Not more than £3.9 million
Employees	Not more than 50	Not more than 250

Figure 1.2 Company size definitions (Companies Act 1989)

- Shares cannot be advertised to the public and can only be sold by private agreement. They are not available on the Stock Exchange.

- Under the Companies Act 1989, small and medium companies can submit modified accounts (see Figure 1.2) although shareholders must receive full accounts.

- All company accounting records must be kept for three years but company accounts do not have to be made available to the public, therefore the affairs of the company are still private.

The Littlewoods empire

One of the largest private companies in Britain (if not *the* largest) is the Littlewoods empire. This £1 billion company – which controls a variety of operations from football pools to a mail-order catalogue is owned and controlled completely by 32 members of the Moores family. However, all has not run smoothly in the Littlewoods empire. Family feuds and revolts by younger members (who wanted to sell the business) were in the press throughout 1995 – and resulted in a variety of **takeover** approaches. Their dissatisfaction was possibly triggered by the fact that profits were down in all

Littlewoods divisions in 1995. In leisure operations (eg pools and 'spot the ball'), profits fell from £26.3 million to £23.7 million. In retailing, sales rose but profits fell from £77.3 million to £57.3 million with a sharp increase in bad debts, apparently due to the recession with householders finding it difficult to pay their bills. The company now plans a major restructure to transform the business over the next five years – and to change the company's **Articles of Association** to give a clearer separation between ownership and management (see below).

Public limited companies (plc)
Public companies tend to be much larger than private companies – with shares being traded daily on the Stock Exchange. Shareholders are

institutions or private individuals with a separate identity to the directors. Whilst the directors may own shares, many are simply salaried managers paid to run the company.

The basic reason for 'going public' or **floating** the company is to enable additional capital to be raised by asking members of the public to buy shares in the company. The capital may be required to finance expansion, to assist the company to move into new markets or to diversify its product line – all these factors are discussed in more detail later in this chapter. However, to protect investors, public companies are carefully vetted by the Stock Exchange before a quotation is allowed.

There are several additional regulations relating to public limited companies.

- A public company must be so registered with the Registrar of Companies – otherwise it will be considered to be a private company.

- The name of the company must be suffixed with the initials 'plc'.

- There must be a minimum of two directors and two shareholders.

- The company must have a minimum authorised share capital of £50,000.

- The company can appeal to the public to subscribe for shares, by issuing a **prospectus.** This is simply an illustrated brochure containing the accounts of the company plus a description of the company's activities.

- Shares may be issued and exchanged through the Stock Exchange.

- The company must hold an Annual General Meeting each year to which all shareholders are invited.

- The company must prepare a balance sheet, profit and loss account and other accounts as specified in the Companies Act 1989. All company accounting records must be kept for six years.

Types of shareholder

Most shares in British companies are owned by **institutional investors** and *not* private individuals. This is despite government encouragement to individuals to invest more on the Stock Exchange – particularly in newly privatised companies. Institutional investors include banks, insurance and investment companies and pension fund-holders – in other words, large corporate investors with vast funds which they have to look after for their own investors, customers or members.

Formation of a company

Anyone wishing to start a company must go through a standard procedure (see Figure 1.3) which will result in the preparation and submission of certain key documents to the Registrar of Companies. The main documents you need to understand are the **Memorandum of Association** and the Articles of Association.

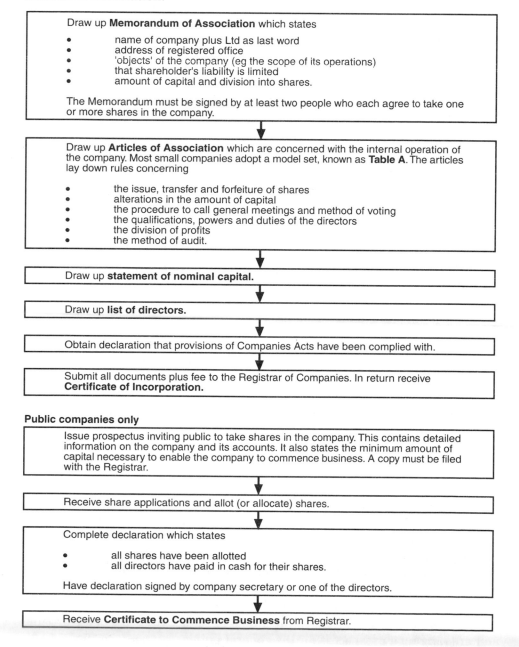

Draw up **Memorandum of Association** which states

- name of company plus Ltd as last word
- address of registered office
- 'objects' of the company (eg the scope of its operations)
- that shareholder's liability is limited
- amount of capital and division into shares.

The Memorandum must be signed by at least two people who each agree to take one or more shares in the company.

Draw up **Articles of Association** which are concerned with the internal operation of the company. Most small companies adopt a model set, known as **Table A**. The articles lay down rules concerning

- the issue, transfer and forfeiture of shares
- alterations in the amount of capital
- the procedure to call general meetings and method of voting
- the qualifications, powers and duties of the directors
- the division of profits
- the method of audit.

Draw up **statement of nominal capital.**

Draw up **list of directors.**

Obtain declaration that provisions of Companies Acts have been complied with.

Submit all documents plus fee to the Registrar of Companies. In return receive **Certificate of Incorporation.**

Public companies only

Issue prospectus inviting public to take shares in the company. This contains detailed information on the company and its accounts. It also states the minimum amount of capital necessary to enable the company to commence business. A copy must be filed with the Registrar.

Receive share applications and allot (or allocate) shares.

Complete declaration which states

- all shares have been allotted
- all directors have paid in cash for their shares.

Have declaration signed by company secretary or one of the directors.

Receive **Certificate to Commence Business** from Registrar.

Figure 1.3 Formation of a company

However, do not think that this is necessarily a long, drawn-out procedure which involves solicitors and several weeks of form filling! Company registration agents exist which will enable a potential director to create and register a private company on the spot. If you wish, look in your local *Yellow Pages* for the nearest one to you and read more about the services they advertise!

Before a company can register its name, a search is undertaken to check that it will not be operating with a name which would cause confusion. For instance, you would hardly be allowed to set up in business as Barclays Ltd! However, if you were trying to set up a small secretarial agency, you might be allowed to use the same name as another small agency operating at the other end of the country because it is unlikely you would be dealing with the same customers or suppliers.

A company which wants to become a public limited company has to go through additional procedures as shown in Figure 1.3. Normally the prospectus is drawn up by an investment or merchant bank which will also recommend the price at which the shares should be offered for sale. Deciding the correct price is critical.

- If the price is too cheap, then the issue is likely to be **oversubscribed** – more people will want shares than there are shares available. If this happens, then the company will lose out on capital it could have acquired. High demand for shares on the first day of trading is likely to result in an immediate rise in price.

- If the price is too high, then the issue may be **undersubscribed** – this means that shares are left unsold. If this happens, then the company cannot succeed in its flotation. For that reason the investment or merchant bank usually **underwrites** the issue. In other words, it guarantees to buy up any remaining shares.

Directors, of course, can buy shares. However, they must pay in cash. Otherwise, of course, they may promise to buy shares (to make it look as if all the shares have been sold) but not actually do so.

Placing shares

As an alternative to offering shares for sale, an organisation can arrange for shares to be placed, ie sold to City institutions. This is the case with Harvey Nichols, the upmarket fashion store in London's Knightsbridge, whose owners, Dickson Concepts of Hong Kong, are selling up to 49.9 per cent of their holding. In this case, the merchant bank or organisation arranging the deal contacts well-known institutional investors and offers them the shares within a nominated price range. The aim is to reduce the costs of advertising and drawing up a prospectus for the general public.

The flotation is Orange

One of the largest flotations in 1995 occurred when Orange, the UK mobile communications group, decided to 'go public' by selling 25 per cent of its ordinary shares on the stock market. The company was valued at over £2.2 billion and invited offers for shares at between 175p and 205p. The aim was to raise £577 million from the offer to repay two outstanding debts. The flotation also benefited the staff – all 2,500 of whom received 50 free shares – and the underwriters and advisers who were involved – and who gained by £41 million!

Investors had to guarantee a minimum investment of £1,000. However, huge demand saw the allocation of shares scaled down – some institutions receiving none at all and some private individuals (mainly customers) receiving only a percentage of the shares they applied for. Those who saw their bids accepted were happy to see the shares rising to 242.5p on the first day, with the shares ending the day at 237.5p – valuing the company at £2.9 billion. Continued success depends upon continued growth of the mobile phone business in general and Orange's market share in particular.

Discussion point

1   Companies have to publish how many shares each of their directors own and any dealing by directors in company shares. This is given in the financial press each week. Why do you think this is necessary and what would heavy buying or selling of shares in a company by its own directors perhaps tell you?

2   Draw up a table which shows the differences between the legal and financial status of the different forms of business discussed so far. Use the following format to help you. Check your finished work with your tutor.

Type of organisation	Legal aspects	Financial aspects
Sole trader		
Partnership		
Private limited company		
Public limited company		

Variations on the enterprise theme

Not all enterprises can be described properly simply by referring to them as being incorporated or unincorporated, owned by the public or owned privately. For instance, how would you explain the structure and differences between

- a sole proprietor and a franchise operation

- a private company and a charitable trust

- a holding company and a conglomerate

- a public company and a multinational?

The aim of this section is to give you an appreciation of the variations which exist, how and why they have occurred, and the key differences between them.

Franchises

Franchise operations are probably the fastest growing sector in British business. Benetton, Prontoprint, Wimpy, Kentucky Fried Chicken, BSM and Body Shop are all examples of franchises. In each of these cases small shops or outlets are run by a **franchisee** who has been given permission to operate the business by the **franchisor** – the organisation which owns the copyright and controls the product or service being sold.

The franchisee has the responsibility of the day-to-day organisation of the business with the incentive of keeping most of the profits. However, he or she has to raise most of the capital and pay an initial licensing fee plus a share of the profits to the franchisor for the use of the trade name.

The franchisor may give advice on marketing and company operations, supply raw materials or named goods, provide shop displays and expert advice to the franchisee. In addition, most franchisors allocate exclusive rights to a specified area to one franchisee.

In some operations franchisees may sell direct to the public (eg Tupperware) or be allocated the franchise by an organisation which provides its own service to the public (eg a florist or hairdresser in a hospital or hotel). In this case, the franchisee is given permission to run his or her shop on the site of the main organisation.

Franchises in Britain are overseen by the British Franchise Association (BFA) which operates a code of conduct for its members.

However, franchise operations are not restricted to the retail trade. Another example is in the soft-drinks trade. Coca-Cola, Pepsi and Seven-Up all franchise the bottling and canning of their drinks to independent companies. Another example is CableComms, a cable company which holds franchises to supply cable to homes in certain areas and regional television companies, such as Granada, which have the franchise for that area from the Independent Broadcasting Association.

Franchising in the 1990s

Each October the NEC in Birmingham hosts the National Franchise Exhibition at which potential franchisees can see what is on offer – and many people have taken up the opportunity to start their own business in this way. Today there are over 20,000 retail franchise outlets employing over 200,000 people. Their annual sales (or turnover) is forecast to be almost £20 billion by the year 2000. Their continued growth has been forecast because of the worldwide decline in employment in manufacturing and the increase in employment opportunities in the service sector, together with the growth in the popularity of self-employment.

Caring to franchise

The latest type of franchises have been formed in the caring professions. A company called Community Careline Service is a franchise business offering private care to people in their own homes (eg the elderly and those with special needs). Another care franchise operation is Abacus Care, which provides home care and nursing staff for public- and private-sector enterprises. Other franchise companies are offering childcare – by providing day nurseries near commercial centres or business parks – such as the

Alphabet Zoo which provides indoor playground centres for young children. All these are seen as growth areas because of the increasing number of elderly people, the needs of working mothers and the decline of care services provided by the NHS, the social services and local education authorities. However, some people consider that such services should not be offered for profit on a private basis but should remain the responsibility of the state.

Discussion point

1 A friend of yours has been a sole proprietor for several years. She is now thinking of changing to become a franchisee.
   a Why do you think she might be tempted to make this change?
   b What benefits and drawbacks do you think she would find?

2 As a group, discuss the advantages and disadvantages of providing caring services as a franchise operation and the degree to which you consider such profit-making operations should be encouraged.

Charitable organisations

Charities operate with the aim of helping other people and promoting special causes. They don't exist to make a profit as such – their aim is to raise money from which is deducted their own expenditure on administration costs. The remaining surplus is spent on the cause they sponsor. Many people consider it very worthwhile and fulfilling to work for charities – either as a paid employee or as an unpaid voluntary worker.

Today many charities operate on a very sophisticated basis, with professional public relations staff and fund-raising directors. They advertise in the national press, become involved with telethon appeals, operate computer mailing lists and send direct mail shots to potential benefactors. The structure of a large charity is shown in Figure 1.4.

There are over 170,000 charities in Britain that have **trust status.** A trust is a relationship in which a **trustee** is responsible for holding funds or other assets which have been given for the benefit of others. A charitable or public trust can be set up for one of four purposes.

- For the relief of poverty, eg Oxfam.

- For the advancement of education, eg an examinations board or independent school.

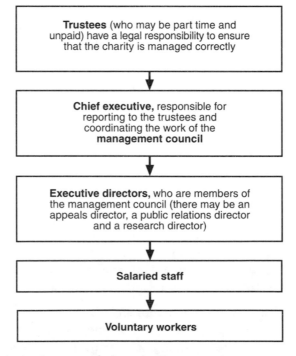

Figure 1.4 Organisational structure of a large charity

- For the advancement of religion, eg maintenance of a church or other place of worship.

- For other purposes, eg conservation or environmental charities such as Greenpeace and Friends of the Earth.

Most charities have to be registered with the Charity Commissioners who, under the Charities Act 1992, have general powers of supervision over their administration and the power to investigate if there is any suspicion about fund-raising or fraud. In addition, charities must be properly governed and regulated and keep accurate records. If a charity went bankrupt because of incompetence or if funds were used for non-charitable purposes, the trustees may find that they are both legally and financially liable.

Daylight robbery?

An argument has been raging as to how much charitable giving has been hit by the National Lottery ever since Camelot announced it was making profits of £77.5 million before tax (£51 million after tax – almost £1 million a week). Its five shareholders shared an £18.4 million dividend for the year and the chief executive and the executive directors all collected bonuses.

In 1992 (pre-National Lottery) approximately 80 per cent of people were donating money to charity. This figure fell to 64 per cent in early 1996. According to the National Council for Voluntary Organisations, the total amount donated also fell from £440 million in 1994 to £339 million in 1995. However, the government's 1995 Family Expenditure Survey shows that charitable giving is virtually unchanged with the average donation remaining at £4.10 per household. This compares with an average of £2.20 spent on the lottery each week.

Many people console themselves that much of the Lottery money goes to charity anyway. Over £1.41 billion was raised for good causes by the National Lottery during 1995. Discussions are now centring on a requirement for Camelot to pay a proportion of its profits to charity every year – given that it has a unique monopoly position to run the Lottery. There are also arguments that laws relating to bingo clubs and betting shops should be changed to give them more power to compete for customers with the National Lottery.

Discussion point

1 What is your view on the National Lottery: do you think that the Lottery itself – or the scratchcards issued by Camelot – reduce charity spending?

If possible, find out information on any surveys which have been carried out, eg by the Department of National Heritage or the National Council for Voluntary Organisations. You may also find it useful to discuss with your tutor how organisations with opposing interests may use the same statistics to produce different arguments!

2 OFLOT, as the Lottery regulating body is known, has been criticised for allowing Camelot to keep excessive profits. What is your view? If you represented OFLOT what would you recommend should be done? (See page 40 for more information on regulatory bodies.)

Holding companies

Holding companies are limited companies which have acquired the control of another company through buying its **ordinary shares.** Each ordinary share carries one vote. Therefore if the company buys enough shares it can effectively gain control. Theoretically it would need to buy 51 per cent of the shares to control the company, but in reality far less than this can give effective control (as many small shareholders never bother to vote).

If the holding company owns 51 per cent of the shares or more, then the smaller firm is known as a **subsidiary company.** If the shareholding is less than this, then the firm is usually known as an **associate company.** A useful book – *Who Owns Whom* – gives the name of many holding companies together with their subsidiaries and associates, and may surprise you. For instance, did you know that Heinz owns and controls Weightwatchers, that a group called Pearson owns a variety of operations from the *Financial Times,* Penguin and Longman educational books to Alton Towers, Madame Tussauds and Thames TV and that Whitbread owns TGI Fridays, Pizza Hut and David Lloyd Leisure – as well as the Beefeater and Brewers Fayre pub restaurants?

The aim of growing larger is to increase market share and to gain economies of scale (see pages 27–8). However, holding companies are sometimes criticised for aiming to have a **monopoly** position – which is considered against the public interest. Technically, a monopoly exists when there is only one supplier of a particular item. Camelot, for instance, holds a monopoly position because no other organisation is licensed to run the National Lottery. If there were, then Camelot may have to increase its prize money to attract or retain customers. In reality, the term monopoly is used when one organisation has such a large market share that it can dictate the price of goods or its service to its customers. W H Smith, which sells one book in every four, was accused of abusing its near-monopoly position when it demanded much larger discounts from publishers and insisted on being allowed to buy books on a sale or return basis.

By buying shares in a company which is struggling to be profitable, and whose shares are therefore cheap, quite a sizeable company can be bought for a relatively small amount of money. This has tempted some to buy a company for **asset-stripping.** In this case the company is bought cheaply and the assets are sold off for cash, the firm closed down and the staff made redundant. Another example is when a company is bought by a large organisation which then breaks up the business and sells off all those parts which are not as profitable as the others. Such actions are usually frowned upon but are not necessarily illegal.

A holding company which owns and controls several diverse operations (such as Pearson) is often known as a **conglomerate.**

The ups and downs of conglomerates

A business which increasingly looks like a conglomerate is the Virgin Group of companies, the brainchild of Richard Branson. The company was floated in the mid-1980s but since then Richard Branson has returned it to private company status (see page 33). The company operates in five main divisions – covering communications and media, retailing, travel, investments and hotels.

Joint ventures have been set up with retailers and computer organisations to promote Virgin products abroad in areas as wide-ranging as Japan, China, Australia, the USA and the Far East.

On the other side of the coin, Trafalgar House, a large conglomerate formed in the 1960s was struggling in the 1990s. The company owned a variety of companies in construction, engineering, shipbuilding and leisure – famous names included the Ritz hotel and the Cunard shipping line. The recession of the 1980s saw the company with an assortment of unrelated businesses – some of which suffered when property assets were devalued in the early 1990s. The conglomerate made moves to sell several of its assets – Express Newspapers was sold in 1983, and the Ritz hotel raised £75 million in 1995. This was not enough to save the group, which eventually sold out for £904 million to a Norwegian company Kvaerner early in 1996.

Multinational or transnational organisations

The largest organisations in the world are enterprises which own or control **production facilities** in more than one country. In reality, companies with only sales offices abroad are not classed as multinationals – the term is usually reserved for companies which operate on a global or worldwide basis. Examples include oil companies, pharmaceuticals companies, car producers, media corporations and computer hardware and software giants such as IBM and Microsoft. It is estimated that by the year 2000 the world's largest 250 multinationals will produce about half the world's output of goods.

The size of multinationals makes them extremely powerful – a fact which has both benefits and drawbacks.

Advantages

* Multinationals can afford to invest in comprehensive research and development programmes, eg in drugs and agricultural developments which can be to the benefit of everyone.

* Multinationals may set up production plants in poorer countries. This helps the economy and the standard of living of people in those countries by bringing in capital, new skills, enterprise and expertise.

* Global trading assists international understanding and friendship.

* Expertise and experience can be brought in from all over the world, eg in the development, problem-solving and trouble-shooting required for oil exploration programmes or for the production of films and music.

* A large multinational operation pays taxes in each country in which it is producing and is expected to abide by national economic, social and political policies. Its operations bring in revenue and provide employment for local workers.

Disadvantages

* In some cases the resources controlled by a multinational can be larger than those of the country in which it is operating. This can make it difficult to ensure the multinational is fully accountable to a particular government as it can operate in its own interests rather than in the interests of the host country. As an example, Shell's net income of £4 billion in 1995 is comparable to the national income of countries such as Kenya or Jamaica.

* Multinationals may be accused of setting up operations in countries where labour is cheaper, when they are not working with advanced technology. In addition, they may be accused of setting up complex operations in countries which lack strict safety codes because this cuts costs. The US company Union Carbide was accused of this after a gas

leak at Bhopal in India, which killed, blinded or severely maimed thousands of inhabitants.

- Multinationals can set their own terms and conditions for operation before moving into a country – and only set up there if these are agreed. Some years ago Ford refused to open a factory in Dundee unless there was a no-strike agreement. When the unions would not agree, Ford expanded in Germany instead.

- Multinationals can keep their taxes down by declaring their operating profits in countries where corporation tax is low. This is done by adjusting the price at which one subsidiary 'buys' goods from another (see Figure 1.5).

- If a country is heavily dependent on a few multinationals, then the threat to switch resources to another country can be serious. This is a threat to a country's national sovereignty if it can be 'held to ransom' in this way.

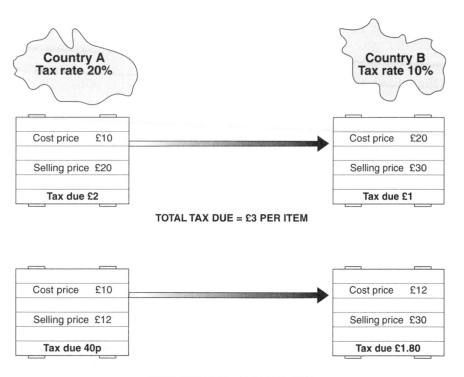

Figure 1.5 Transfer pricing

Multinationals in the 1990s

Cadbury-Schweppes, the well-known British company, is working hard towards its own global expansion programme. In 1994 it invested £10 million in a Chinese chocolate factory, £15 million in Poland, £12 million in Argentina, made sizable investments in India and in Mexico where it bought a mineral-water company. It now operates in over 190 countries and in 1995 had worldwide sales of £4.77 billion. Apparently Dr Pepper is particularly popular in Russia!

The largest British multinationals include

- British Petroleum (1994 turnover £47.7 billion)

- Unilever (1994 turnover £35 billion)

- Shell UK (1994 turnover £25.3 billion)

- BAT Industries (1994 turnover 17.9 billion).

You are almost certain to have heard of BP and Shell! You will find the Unilever name on many household brands including Persil washing powder, Sunsilk shampoo, Dove soap, Bird's Eye frozen food and Liptons tea (it even sells OMO in China!). BAT makes most of its money from tobacco, but also operates in financial services, owning companies such as Allied Dunbar and Eagle Star.

Famous European multinationals include Benetton and Nestlé.

The Japanese in Britain

Many Japanese multinational car companies have set up in the UK, such as Nissan which opened in Sunderland in 1994. These companies have been motivated to move to Britain to avoid high **import tariffs** or **quotas** on cars imported into the European Union (EU) from other countries. A tariff is an additional amount charged on imported goods. A quota is a limit on the number of goods imported. By manufacturing within the EU, Nissan can sell more cars in the European market because they are more competitively priced and not subject to any limit on the quantity of sales.

Discussion point

Economists vary in their views on monopolies. Some consider them to be against the public interest as their control of the market means they can charge what they want for their product. Because consumers have nowhere else to go for the goods, they have to pay high prices. Other economists disagree. They argue that *all* companies have to be competitive in the long run – otherwise they wouldn't survive. If a monopoly charged ridiculous prices, then other companies will see the high profits the monopoly company is making and want a share of the action! Moreover they would undercut the monopoly and take away their customers. Therefore, no company can remain a monopoly for long.

1   What is your view? In the brewery trade the trend has been towards 'big is beautiful' (see below). Today the brewery trade is dominated by four large producers – Scottish Courage with 31 per cent market share, Bass with 23 per cent, Carlsberg-Tetley with 16 per cent and Whitbread with 12 per cent of the market. Bass and Carlsberg-Tetley may combine in the future, but as this would result in one firm having almost 40 per cent of the market, it is likely any takeover would be referred to the **Monopolies and Mergers Commission** – which usually investigates any mergers which would result in more than 25 per cent market share for one company.

   a   Do you think that the large brewers will be able to dominate the market and dictate prices in pubs and supermarkets?
   b   What factors do you think might operate to stop them doing this – particularly in supermarkets?

2   The government's Beer Orders attacked the traditional tie between breweries and pubs, where breweries owned pubs and controlled what was sold. Why do you think the government was wary of this link?

The impetus for change

The business world is never static. Various factors interact which either affect individual organisations or industries in general. These are apt to create trends towards either growth in size (such as in the brewery trade) or contraction. Growth is often achieved by **mergers** or takeovers. Organisations concentrating on contracting or reducing their operations – are often said to be **demerging** or **downsizing**.

The factors which force business to change may be **external** or **internal**. You can read more about this in later chapters.

'Big is beautiful'

Some companies make enough profit and/or have enough financial backing to invest in growing larger, year by year. You have already read about the growth in Richard Branson's empire, Virgin, and McDonalds' plans for growth were given on pages 4–5.

However, a quicker route to growth is by taking over another company. The more usual method is to find another organisation which operates in the same market – and either merge with it or take it over.

Amalgamation, mergers and takeovers

An **amalgamation** occurs when two or more companies consider there will be mutual benefits if they combine. In this way potential trading opportunities can be maximised.

The term merger is often synonymous with amalgamation. A merger takes place when businesses (usually limited companies) unite to create a single organisation. Mergers are usually amicable and arranged for the joint benefit of those involved.

In contrast, a takeover bid can be amicable or hostile. This is where one person or organisation makes an offer to buy shares in a company with the aim of gaining control. In the case of public limited companies, the bidder is expected to observe the City code on takeovers.

The offer bid may be conditional or unconditional. The bidder may offer a price for the shares but make the offer conditional upon receiving enough shares to gain control. Once these have been obtained the offer may then become unconditional.

Whilst it is usual to gain control with fewer than the technical 51 per cent required to control the vote, if a person owns a minimum of 90 per cent of the shares he or she can apply for a court order entitling to purchase the remaining shares at a price agreed by the court. Equally, the shareholders may insist that their shares are bought. The aim of this is to protect minority shareholders whose wishes may be ignored because they do not have enough power to be influential.

Merger mania in the financial sector

First banks, then building societies, then insurance companies. By the year 2000, will the British public have only a handful of companies offering financial services? First Lloyds Bank launched a successful takeover bid for TSB – although the latter continues to operate under its own name. Abbey National plc took over National and Provincial, and the Sun Alliance and Royal insurance company agreed to merge. The combined group intend to reduce costs by using a joint head office and uniting various other functions. They consider that the new company – Royal Sun Alliance – will save costs of more than £200 million a year and be able to take on developing markets, such as China, more effectively in a combined operation.

When the insurance merger was announced the result for shareholders was share price increases – not only in the two companies concerned but throughout the insurance sector – as investors scrambled to guess who might be next.

Economies of scale

Economies of scale are the main reason why companies wish to become large. You may have noted the cost savings predicted by the merged Royal Sun Alliance company! These may result from an increase in the scale of production in the firm itself, in which case they are known as **internal economies.** There are also advantages to be gained when the industry as a whole increases in size. In this case, they are known as **external economies.** This is when the size of a particular industry brings benefits for all the organisations that operate within it – such as plentiful, skilled labour. External economies are even more pronounced if an industry is heavily localised. This is the major reason why industries often set up in an area (eg computer firms along the M4 corridor or in silicon glen in Scotland) and why they may be unwilling to relocate into areas of high unemployment despite government incentives.

As an example of an internal economy, the organisation which can afford the resources to buy the optimum number of machines benefits from one type of technical economy – that of 'the principle of multiples'. This is easily illustrated in the discussion point on page 29 – and if you can remember how to work out the lowest common denominator, then you should be able to calculate the answer quite easily! Figure 1.6 shows both internal and external economies of scale.

Internal economies	
Technical	Increased specialisation
	Optimum number of machines can be purchased for output
	Can afford advanced technology eg robotics
	Lower unit costs possible (eg double decker bus cheaper to run than single decker)
	Some facilities only compatible with large output, eg automated car assembly plant
Marketing	National advertising affordable
	Expensive promotions possible, eg national competition, free gifts, 'saver' schemes
	Marketing costs cheaper per unit of production
	Can afford specialists, eg advertising agencies
Financial	Cheaper capital available
	Access to more sources of finance (see chapter 3)
	Can afford bulk buying which reduces costs
	Can employ specialist buyers
	Can operate just-in-time system with suppliers (see chapter 6) to retain flexibility/reduce storage costs
Other	Can invest in research and development to stay ahead of market
	Can offer good working conditions for staff

External economies	
Labour	Local skilled labour force
	Specialist training courses offered at local colleges
Ancillary services	Subsidiary industries in the area cater for major industries
	Specialist smaller firms provide cheaper supplies because they are able to mass produce for industry as a whole
Networking	Research centres can be set up as joint ventures
	Formal and informal contacts between companies and employees
	Trade associations and trade journals cater for needs of industry
Other	Service industries in the area develop expertise in relation to needs of industry
	Size of industry increases political lobbying power (eg food or tobacco lobby) because of taxes paid/employment provided

Figure 1.6 Economies of scale

Discussion point

1   You are production manager for an organisation producing chocolate bars. Four machines are involved in the process.

   • Machine A mixes the chocolate. Its capacity is such that it can mix enough chocolate for 3,000 bars each hour.

   • Machine B moulds the chocolate. This machine has the capability of moulding 6,000 bars per hour.

   • Machine C cooks the chocolate. It is only capable of handling 2,000 bars each hour.

   • Machine D wraps the chocolate. This machine can handle 5,000 bars each hour.

   Assuming you have the resources to buy as many of each machine as you wish, what would be the smallest optimum number of each machine you should purchase to ensure that no machines are ever idle and there are no bottlenecks in the production process? Discuss your answer with the rest of the group.

2   As a group, identify all the possible economies of scale which are likely to be
   a   achieved as a result of a building society or insurance company merger
   b   enjoyed by a supermarket chain as compared with your local grocer's shop.

Integration

The quickest way a company can increase in size is to amalgamate with another company. This process, whether by merger or takeover, is usually referred to as **integration.** There are three types of integration – **horizontal, vertical** and **conglomerate.**

If you owned a company, how would you know with *which type* of company you should amalgamate? For instance, if you owned a brewery, would you be better amalgamating with other breweries or would it be of more benefit if you bought a chain of pubs or hotels and controlled your own outlets? As you have already seen, in the brewery trade companies have done both – Scottish and Newcastle took over Lion Brewery in the 1980s before it took over Courage. Earlier you read about Bass's intention of taking over Carlsberg-Tetley. In addition, Whitbread has links with Heineken. On the other hand, you also saw that many large breweries own pub and food chains – such as Whitbread's Brewers Fayre and TGI Fridays.

Much depends upon your intentions. If you amalgamate with other firms *at the same stage* of the production process as yourself (eg two breweries, two building societies or two insurance companies), then this is known as **horizontal integration.**

You would do this if you wanted to

- increase your market share and achieve market domination
- enable rationalisation of capacity, particularly when demand is falling
- achieve a greater degree of specialisation (eg by discarding low-selling or specialist brands)
- obtain economies of scale.

However, there are disadvantages, for instance:

- your proposed amalgamation may be investigated by the Monopolies and Mergers Commission – especially if it is likely that your market share will be too large.
- as the organisation grows in size, you may suffer from **diseconomies of scale** (see below).

If you amalgamated with a firm at a *different stage* of the production process, then this is known as **vertical integration.**

The production process is in three stages: extraction (primary production), manufacturing and tertiary services, including retailing.

Backward integration refers to amalgamation with a firm which operates at an earlier stage in the production process (eg an oil refinery amalgamates with an oil producer which operates its own oil wells).

Forward integration refers to amalgamation with a firm which operates at a later stage in the production process (eg the oil refinery amalgamates with a garage chain).

The different types of integration are shown in Figure 1.7.   ·

Your aims in this case would be

- to achieve economies of scale, eg by obtaining supplies more cheaply
- to increase market share by securing your own market outlets and dictating the standard at which they operate
- to prevent any problems with supplies – vertical integration backwards means the organisation will get its materials at the right time, right place, right quality and quantity

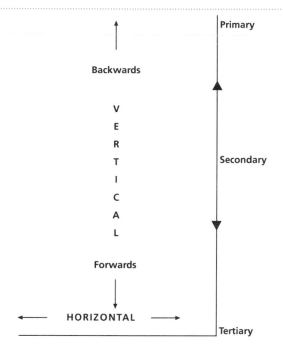

Figure 1.7 Types of integration

- to prevent problems with the sellers of your goods – vertical integration forwards ensures that the goods are sold at the right time, place, quality, quantity and price

- to prevent suppliers or sellers making a large profit.

Disadvantages, however, can include the following.

- The cost of maintaining supplies can be disproportionate to the benefits. It is often cheaper to **contract out** the supply of goods (see chapter 3).

- Contracting out also means greater flexibility if the demand for supplies changes.

- Technology can mean the need to maintain natural supplies is outdated. Many companies, such as Dunlop, which produced rubber-based goods, owned their own rubber plantations in Malaya. When synthetic rubber was invented they were left with an outdated and costly investment.

- It can be difficult to ensure quality provision across a whole range of services – from extraction to retailing.

- A variation away from the core business can mean problems if there is a lack of expertise in running the new area.

- Diseconomies of scale.

Conglomerate integration occurs when the amalgamation is neither substantially vertical nor horizontal – indeed it may appear totally disparate. The major aim is that of **diversification,** ie expanding or varying the range of products offered, to reduce the risks of trading – particularly if the organisation believes that the potential for future growth for existing goods is limited. Another reason may be to even out trade cycles which affect the demand for certain types of products. For instance, if the housing market is depressed, an organisation involved in construction may diversify into other areas. (Conglomerates were discussed on page 21.)

Restructuring electricity

History was made in the electricity industry when Trade and Industry Secretary Ian Lang blocked two takeovers in the electricity industry – and overruled the Monopolies and Mergers Commission which had ruled that the takeovers could go ahead on a conditional basis. The two large generating companies, National Power and PowerGen, had wanted to take over two electricity distribution companies – Southern Electricity and Midlands Electricity. Ian Lang's decision was based on the fact that to allow the takeovers to go ahead would reduce competition and be against the public interest.

Discussion point

1 What type of integration were National Power and PowerGen aiming for? Was it
   a horizontal integration, or
   b vertical integration?

2 What case *in favour* of the takeovers do you think the generators may have put forward?

3 Why do you think Ian Lang considered the takeovers might be against the public interest?

'Small is beautiful'
Despite the perceived advantages of large-scale operation, about 50 per cent of manufactured output of the western world comes from factories employing fewer than 500 workers and about 80 per cent of UK factories employ between one and 50 workers.

Small firms will always exist for several reasons.

• There are disadvantages and diseconomies to large-scale production (see Figure 1.8).

• Small firms bring economic benefits and governments often encourage small enterprises for this reason. They breed new ideas and new leaders and, jointly, help to reduce unemployment to a greater extent than large companies. If you think about it, even the largest organisations started as small companies!

• There are market limitations on mass production – some products are only ever demanded on a relatively small scale (compare the demand for wet suits to that for toothpaste!), luxury goods are produced in small quantities for prestige markets (eg designer clothes and Gucci luggage) and some areas demand a personal service (such as hairdressing or beauty therapy). Customers' demands for variety 'fragment' even large industries and allow small firms to operate in areas as diverse as toiletries and computer software, jewellery and furniture. This is known as **imperfect competition.**

• Legislation and other restrictions are fewer for small traders and many people prefer to be independent. The owner may have no desire to cope with a large-scale operation but simply want a reasonable income and a quiet life. He or she may wish to remain in control of the business and consider flexibility is better maintained if the company stays small.

Find the common denominator!

If someone asked you what Richard Branson and Andrew Lloyd-Weber had in common, you might struggle to think of anything! The answer? Both *bought back* their company from the Stock Exchange and therefore converted it back from public limited company status to private limited company status. The reason? Both were dissatisfied with having to make business decisions which would please both the City and the shareholders – they wanted the freedom to do their own thing. Anita Roddick at Body Shop has similar ambitions. She wants to buy back the company to convert it to a charitable trust. Whether she will be able to raise enough finance to do so is not yet known.

Technical	Each organisation has an optimum maximum size where costs per level of output are at a minimum. Growing larger would initially increase costs (for more space or equipment) until the next most optimum size level is achieved.
Financial	As a company increases its demands for resources (eg materials, labour etc), it may create a scarcity of supply. This will increase the price (for instance, for specialist workers or materials). The company may have to make financial or management decisions in the interests of powerful shareholders or to suit the City, rather than in company interests (see chapters 3 and 4).
People	Personal contact may be lost with staff and customers. Flexibility for individual customers may be difficult or nonexistent. Division of labour results in monotony, boredom, abseenteeism through demotivated workers. Large numbers of staff may be difficult to control. Morale of staff may be low if they do not identify with the organisation, its objectives or management (see chapter 7).
Managerial	Departmental heads may become competitive rather than cooperative. There may be lack of communication between departments and between management and staff. Increased size is apt to result in increased procedures and systems and an increase in bureaucracy and paperwork (see chapter 5). Directors of large public companies may operate more in their own interest than in that of the shareholders (or owners) (see chapter 4).

Figure 1.8 Diseconomies of scale

Management buyouts

A 1980s innovation was that of the **management (or worker) buyout** (MBO). A buyout occurs when the managers or employees of an organisation buy their existing company and take it out of the hands of its existing owners with the aim of running it themselves. This is often done to protect jobs if a large parent company is in financial difficulties (eg Coloroll). In 1989 over 500 MBOs took place involving a total of £7.5 billion, either as a result of conglomerates getting rid of smaller or less profitable subsidiaries or as a result of the government's privatisation policy or action by local authorities (see page 45). During the 1990s this level of activity has continued with about 550 MBOs taking place each year.

The problem for managers or employees wishing to buy up the company is usually that of raising the capital. Usually the money is raised through a combination of personal funds and bank loans or overdrafts. Larger buyouts may be financed by **venture capital** – where the lender takes a share of the company equity (ie ordinary shares) in return. A **leveraged buyout** (LBO) is one in which a large proportion of the capital has been raised by borrowing from a financial institution. Repaying this debt can cause problems for the new owners, particularly if interest rates rise, and can reduce potential investment and expenditure on new equipment, research and development and advertising.

The strength of the management or employee team is that they usually have an in-depth knowledge of the organisation and are very committed to its success – both financially and personally. The drawbacks can include limited prospects for growth and no potential for economies of scale.

Buying out a newspaper

In late 1995 the management team of Reed Regional Newspapers bought the company from its conglomerate owners Reed Elsevier for £205 million. The capital was raised with the help of KKR, a New York-based investment institution.

The company has a good track record of 'free' newspapers. Revenue is derived from advertisers, and the management team hopes to increase distribution levels and therefore revenue and profits in the future. However, instead of pleasing its conglomerate owners in the future, it is KKR which will be inspecting its accounts and checking the company is on target.

Despite this, many have been successful with several MBOs going on to float the company on the Stock Exchange. In 1989, Silk Industries, a silk manufacturing firm, was bought out by its management. It has prospered since then and was floated in June 1995.

Note: an innovation in the 1990s has been that of the **management buy-in** where an outside team of owner/managers come in to run and put money into a company if there is no suitable expertise within the firm. By this means, teams of successful managers can search for companies which they can re-organise and turn round for profit.

The trend in the 1980s

Generally, the 1980s saw a trend towards an *increase in size*. Computerisation, international communication and distribution systems saw an increase in **globalisation** with many companies aiming for world markets and achieving rapid growth by either merging with or taking over their competitors. Their aims were

- the monopoly motive or the desire to obtain a greater share of the market and therefore greater market power

- the wish to achieve greater security through diversification

- the desire to achieve economies of scale.

The trend in the 1990s

Increases in size
In some industries the trend towards increasing size and globalisation is still strong. In 1995 there were more takeovers and mergers than in the previous record year of 1989. However, whereas takeovers in the 1980s were motivated by a desire by large organisations to buy up underperforming companies in a variety of industries and either **restructure** these (see chapter 5) or break them up, in the 1990s there are different pressures for growth. The first is to obtain savings in cost (ie economies of scale) in areas such as marketing or research and development. In other cases, some owners have been tempted to sell before there is a general election when tax regulations may change. Overall, mergers and takeovers have been confined mainly to three areas: pharmaceuticals (where finance for research and development is essential), finance, ie banks and building societies (where there are major cost savings in a policy of growth), and electricity (see Figure 1.9).

Decreases in size
However, rapidly changing markets have meant that some large organisations have found it difficult to respond quickly to changing consumer demands. Whilst increased competition has put greater pressure on companies to reduce their costs – so they can sell at more competitive

Sector	Organisations	Value
Pharmaceuticals	Glaxo acquired Wellcome	£9.1 bn
	Rhone-Poulenc acquired Fisons	£1.8 bn
Finance	Lloyds Bank acquired TSB	£4.9 bn
	Dresdner Bank acquired Kleinwort Benson*	£1.0 bn
	Swiss Bank acquired S G Warburg*	£4.9 bn
Electricity	Hanson acquired Eastern Group	£2.4 bn
	Scottish Power acquired Manweb	£1.1 bn
	Southern Company acquired SWEB	£1.1 bn

*For investment banks, see chapter 3.

Figure 1.9 UK takeovers, 1995

prices in some industries – this has meant that some conglomerates have decided to streamline their operations through a process of demerger. Other companies have deliberately streamlined their operations through **delayering** and **downsizing.** Both these concepts are discussed in later chapters.

A demerger occurs when a large (usually conglomerate) organisation decides to split up its operations. Examples in the 1990s have included Thorn EMI, Pearson, ICI, Racal, Hanson and British Gas. The aim is to focus the business on key activities. As an example, Thorn EMI owned both Thorn rental businesses and the EMI Group – which includes EMI and Virgin record labels, HMV record shops and Dillons bookshops. The management considered that Thorn was always overshadowed by the 'glitz' of the music business and undervalued on the Stock Exchange and therefore the companies would be worth more separated than together. Thorn would be free to expand in Europe and EMI can concentrate on developing its record labels. The cost of the break-up and reorganisation required is likely to be in the region of £130 million.

Demergers are not confined to the private sector. British Gas has planned to float off its gas supply business and gasfields to create British Gas Energy. Its gas pipeline system will be operated by TransCo International. However, the investors, who control 51 per cent of the voting shares, will not be asked for their approval until the AGM in April 1997 (see also privatisation on page 47).

Discussion point

In 1996 BP and Mobil – two multinational oil companies with assets of
£3.2 billion and annual sales of £13.3 billion – announced their intention
to form a joint venture. The aim is to pursue efficiencies and growth,
and annual cost savings of up to $500 million a year are expected within
the next three years. BP is to operate the joint fuel ventures and Mobil
the joint lubricant ventures. About £400 million has been allocated for
restructuring operations – everything from the refineries to the retail
sites will be combined, with Mobil petrol station workers converting to
BP style uniforms and working under a new BP/Mobil logo.

Why is the change considered necessary? Mainly to gain economies of
scale – the bigger the volume of petrol and lubricants sold, usually the
greater the efficiencies possible. Sixty per cent of the savings are aimed
to be achieved by eliminating duplication and 15 per cent from
economies in purchasing. Both companies have been operating over
capacity since the UK retail petrol market stopped growing and
supermarkets started selling petrol. Originally, the only major petrol
retailers in the UK were Esso, Shell, BP, Texaco and Mobil. Today cheaper
petrol can usually be purchased at Tesco, Sainsbury's or Safeway. The
joint venture enables BP and Mobil to increase its market share to 12 per
cent of the fuels market and 18 per cent of the lubricants market.

However, whilst the venture may be good news for shareholders, it is less
likely to be beneficial for employees or customers. Over 3,000 workers
worldwide are likely to lose their jobs in the restructure and fuel prices
could start to rise again as the main companies dominate over 75 per
cent of the British market.

1   Identify the types of economies of scale from which BP and Mobil
     may benefit.

2   The entry of supermarkets into petrol retailing broke the **oligopoly**
     which had previously been in force. An oligopoly exists where a few
     large firms are responsible for the total supply of a particular
     product or service. One example is commercial banks – where the
     'big four' (NatWest, Barclays, Midland and Lloyds) control 80 per
     cent of the market. Another example is oil companies.
     a   Why do you think an oligopoly is usually considered to be
         against customer interests?
     b   Why does the joint venture of BP and Mobil mean that petrol
         prices may rise again?

The public sector

In Britain the term public sector relates to the provision of goods and services by **the state.** At its broadest, the public sector relates to all those areas of economic activity in which the government is involved and particularly concerns those organisations which are directly funded by the state.

The role of the state in Britain

A public corporation is an organisation owned and controlled by the state. Sometimes this is confusing because of the similarity with the term 'a public limited company'. Traditionally, the state owned a considerable number of different enterprises such as British Coal, British Steel and British Gas. Today many have been transferred into private ownership through **privatisation.** This is discussed later in the chapter.

Not only does the government still own a few public corporations, it also owns a major part of the country's natural resources, such as oil and gas. Private companies are only allowed to extract these under licence. This enables the government to retain control whilst not actually undertaking the activity itself.

Whilst the size of the public sector has declined in relation to public corporations, it has arguably expanded in other areas. It allocates licences not only for natural resources but also for commercial radio and television and grants licences or franchises to private television companies such as Granada. The government is the largest customer in Britain buying supplies daily for schools, hospitals and defence establishments. It is also a huge supplier of goods and services – from education and health care to housing and roads. At local level it can provide investment to assist private enterprises and enter into partnership with the private sector to promote regeneration and development schemes – such as London Docklands.

Finally, the government is concerned with regulation. This not only includes criminal and civil law but also relates to those laws which regulate the behaviour of organisations within the workplace – such as employment law and health and safety legislation. At a different level, there are regulations relating to private-sector businesses and their relations with society. Examples include environmental legislation and consumer laws. Again, the government may choose to licence a regulatory body to monitor the operations of a particular profession or industry, such as the Law Society or the British Medical Association. This is sometimes described as self-regulation.

The objective of the public sector

The public sector relates to publicly funded organisations, which receive their finance through taxation raised by the government. You would therefore be working in the public sector if you were employed

- in a **central Government department,** eg the Home Office or the Treasury – in this case, you would be a civil servant

- by your **local authority,** eg a metropolitan council or county council – in this case, you would be a local government officer

- by a **public corporation** or a nationalised organisation, eg the BBC and the Post Office

- by any other organisation funded by the government, eg as an administrator in a school, college, university or hospital.

The total amount spent on the public sector, eg in running government departments, providing services such as the National Health Service (NHS) and in grants to local authorities, is known as **public expenditure.**

Traditionally, the objective of public-sector organisations was to provide a public service and to break-even financially 'taking one year with another'. A second objective was the equality of the provision of services to rich and poor citizens alike. However, today many public-sector organisations are being charged with being self-financing and making an operating profit or surplus each year. Government funding has been reduced in many cases or made subject to strict controls. National Health Trusts, further education colleges and local authorities, for instance, all have to operate delegated budgets, are charged with meeting government targets, must function according to strict financial guidelines and are subject to financial checks by government appointed auditors. The emphasis now has re-focused on cost management, customers and marketing.

Central government departments

There are a large number of central government departments. These are mainly concerned with the implementation of policy decisions made by government ministers.

Each department has its own budget and submits its spending plans to the Treasury each year. A list of all government departments and their major area of responsibility is given in Figure 1.10. More information on the Budget and its relevance to the economy is given in chapter 2.

Quangos

The name **quango** is short for quasi-autonomous non-governmental agencies! These are regulatory bodies which have been set up by the government to monitor a variety of business activities, from the operation of newly privatised companies to the enforcement of laws and guidelines on health and safety, the environment and employment. Examples include regulatory bodies such as OFWAT (water) as well as the HSE (Health and Safety Executive), the Office of Fair Trading, the Monopolies and Mergers Commission and industrial tribunals.

Department	Responsibilities
HM Treasury	Plans and supervises the spending of all government departments, local authorities and public corporations. Advises the government on economic policy and puts this into effect.
Ministry of Defence (MoD)	Administers the armed forces and implements defence policy.
Department for Education and Employment (DfEE)	Coordinates full-time education for under-16s plus further and higher education. Supervises regional employment policies, Training and Enterprise Councils, employee rights, health and safety (through the Health and Safety Commission), pay and equal opportunities.
Department of the Environment (DoE)	Links with local authorities on local planning and inner cities. Responsible for conservation and environmental protection, including energy efficiency.
Department of Transport (DoT)	Responsible for overseeing airports, coastguards, motorway and trunk road developments, road safety legislation and vehicle licensing.
Department of Trade and Industry (DTI)	Promotes UK exports, gives information and advice to small firms, responsible for company legislation, consumer safety and protection and competition policy. Promotes the use of new technology.
Export Credits Guarantee Department (ECGD)	Assists UK exports by providing export credit insurance to British exporters as well as guaranteeing repayment to British banks which provide finance for exports (see chapter 3).
Foreign and Commonwealth Office	Operates diplomatic missions and embassies worldwide to promote British interests and protect British citizens abroad.
Department of Health (DoH)	Responsible for the operation of the NHS and the supervision of social services.
Department of Social Security (DSS)	Responsible for the operation of the social security and benefits system (eg child benefit, family credit, income support and the social fund).
Home Office	Responsible for the police, probation and prison services and immigration policy.
Ministry of Agriculture, Fisheries and Food (MAFF)	Responsible for agricultural policies (including EU policies), plants, fisheries and forestry as well as food regulations.
HM Customs and Excise	Responsible for the collection and administration of customs and excise duties and VAT.
Board of Inland Revenue	Administers and collects direct taxes, mainly income tax and corporation tax (paid by companies).
Department of National Heritage	Responsible for broadcasting, films, libraries, sport and tourism. Oversees the National Lottery.

Figure 1.10 Government departments and their main areas of responsibility

In effect, they supplement the work done by government departments by monitoring the behaviour of organisations which are subject to government controls. Your school or college will be subject to such controls – either by OFSTED (the Office for Standards in Education) or the FEFC (Further Education Funding Council).

Changes affecting government departments

The major factor which affects government departments is the amount of funding they receive. This is decided by the Treasury and the Chancellor of the Exchequer. Ministers bid for money but their allocation will depend upon many factors including

- conflicting demands from different departments (Social Security versus Health, for instance)

- the political agenda of the government.

If, for instance, the government wants to reduce taxation, then the amount of money raised to pay for services will fall. Some government services may have to be cut or reduced. The current spending plans for each government department are given in chapter 2. Do bear in mind that the money to pay for these must be raised through taxation or government borrowing (see also the Budget on page 74).

Government policies and actions in relation to legislation and regulation (or deregulation), its own spending plans, funding for regional areas and businesses, the economy and new legislation all affect business organisations. These are described in more detail in chapter 2. Trends in the areas of health and defence are given in Figure 1.11.

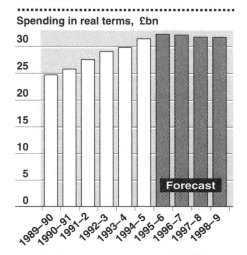

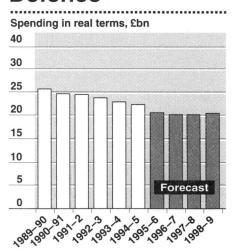

Figure 1.11 Health and defence spending

HM Treasury

Discussion point

1   Examine the trends for spending in defence. How do you think this
     has affected the suppliers of aeroplanes and military supplies (see
     also chapter 2)?

2   The cost of running the National Health Service is extremely difficult
     to control given new technology (the cost of a scanner, for instance)
     and the fact that people are living longer – and old people need
     more medical care. Cuts in the NHS have been greatly criticised in
     the media, yet to finance all the requirements would mean
     increasing taxation considerably.

     If you were the government, what would you do?

Local authorities

Local authorities are responsible for providing a wide range of services on a
local basis. This is because it would be both impossible and impractical for
the government to administer these on a central basis. Areas of the country
vary in what they need – there are many differences between the types of
services required in an inner city and those in the shire counties. Local
delivery means that the money can be targeted more accurately for the
needs of the community.

Local government structure

Since 1986 most of England and Wales has had a two-tier system of local
government consisting of

1   **county councils**

2   **district councils.**

A new type of authority is one which has **unitary** status. Proposals for
unitary authorities were first put forward by the Local Government
Commission in 1993. It suggested that the two-tier system should be
replaced by a smaller number of unitary authorities. The advantages were
argued to be the promotion of local democracy, a reduction in administrative
costs and improved quality of local services. Authorities can bid for unitary
status, the key issue being whether the proposed authority will provide
'effective and convenient' local government and protect 'the identity and
interests of local communities'. So far over 40 unitary areas have been
agreed by the Local Government Commission and the Secretary of State.

Organisation and control

Local people elect their own council representatives (councillors) in council
elections each year. Most councillors represent a political party, so that the

authority may have an overall Labour or Conservative majority. This may not be the same as the political party in power in central government. Indeed, local authority elections are often used to register a 'protest vote' against the government. If there is no overall majority, then there is a 'hung' council – and the balance of power may be held by a minority party, eg the Liberal Democrats. The mayor is a councillor who has had a long service on the council and the major parties usually take it in turns to nominate a mayor.

Local policy is decided during council meetings of various committees, eg Transport, Education, Planning, etc. The day-to-day running of council operations is carried out by paid employees – local government officers. In this way, local provision mirrors central provision – with councillors equating to MPs and local government officers equating to civil servants.

Theoretically, local people have a say in the actions of their council through their vote in the local elections. The government also has a large say in the policy and spending of councils; therefore the administration of local authorities is also controlled by

- Parliament – both by general Acts of Parliament or local legislation

- central government departments – mainly the Department of the Environment

- courts of law which can have a restraining effect on the actions of councils, eg by awarding damages to an individual unfairly treated by a local authority.

Local government finance
Money is raised in a variety of ways.

- The largest contributor is the government through the **Government Revenue Support Grant.** For this reason the Government is particularly interested in controlling the amounts spent by local authorities. The total amount of this grant was estimated at £31 billion for 1996/7.

- **Council tax** levied on each household based on the value of the property relative to others in the area. Discounts are available for some owners, eg if there is only one adult living in the property or if the householder is on a low income or disabled. The amount of council tax is set by the local council and the amount to be paid depends upon the valuation band in which the house is placed. Those in band H pay the full amount, those in band D pay two-thirds and those in band A pay one-third. Changes in house prices will not affect the valuation, but if the condition of the local area changes (eg a motorway is built nearby), then the householder can apply for a revaluation.

- **Business rates** are levied on businesses by the local authority and collected on behalf of the government. The government redistributes the rate monies on the basis of the size of local services and need.

- **Subsidiary income** is raised from
  - loans
  - rents from council houses
  - sale of council services (from swimming-pool or tennis-court charges to concerts or the renting of deckchairs or beach huts!).

Income was also received from the sale of council houses, mainly in the 1980s.

Local authority services and responsibilities

The scope of the services undertaken depends upon whether a council is a county or district council – or whether it is a unitary authority. Generally, services that need either considerable resources or planning and administering over a wide area are provided by county councils, and local or limited services are provided by district councils. A unitary authority is one which will provide all services in a specific area rather than a 'two-tier' system.

At their fullest extent, a council may be responsible for: education, social services, police, highways, fire service, libraries, probation and magistrates' courts, recreation and tourism, environmental health, cleansing and waste disposal, planning, markets, other (eg cemeteries and crematoria, footpath maintenance, etc.).

However, in recent years some traditional functions, such as education, housing and social services, have been transferred to other providers – either in whole or in part. The council can then purchase the services it requires from a range of providers. The aim is to increase competition and thereby reduce costs.

In a further drive to reduce costs, compulsory competitive tendering (CCT) was introduced in 1980. Local authorities were instructed to put out to tender highway repair, building construction and maintenance work. CCT was extended by the Local Government Act 1988 to include other areas such as refuse collection, vehicle maintenance, sport and leisure management, cleaning and catering (eg school meals and meals on wheels). CCT does not mean that a local authority will now not provide the service. It does, however, mean that internal providers must bid against outside contractors – with the contract usually going to the lowest bidder. Again, the argument is that this will promote efficient and low-cost operations.

Change and local authorities

As you have seen, local authorities have been subjected to various major areas of change over the last few years. Below is a summary.

- Reduction in budgets, 'capping' on spending and tighter restrictions and restraints imposed on spending by central government. This has resulted in cuts to local services and agonising over which cuts to make. This is similar to discussion point 2 on page 43 but this time relates to local services.

- The introduction of compulsory competitive tendering in the 1988 Local Government Act which forced local authorities to put many services out to tender or privatise them – from refuse collection to the provision of school meals.

- Deregulation of services traditionally provided by local authorities, eg local transport and housing.

- The redrawing of boundaries or renaming of local authorities.

- The introduction of **unitary authorities** following the 1992 Local Government Act.

- A reduction in the role and power of local authorities through initiatives such as the opting out of schools, the creation of the Training and Enterprise Councils (TECs) and the reformation of police authorities.

Which league is your council in?

All councils publish their budget for the year, together with their Charter document which gives details of the services they offer and their complaints procedure. Anyone can obtain a copy of both documents from their local council.

Council tax payers can compare which council is giving the best service by visiting their library and looking at the league table of services for England and Wales which is published by the Audit Commission. Volume 1 gives information on education, social services, libraries and expenditure; Volume 2 is concerned with council housing, recycling, planning benefits, council tax collection, inspecting food premises, complaints system and expenditure.

Public corporations

The number of public corporations in Britain has declined dramatically over the last 15 years because of the government's privatisation programme.

Public corporations were mainly formed in the immediate post-war years. The state **nationalised** various industries which were in decline, giving a poor service, operating unsafely or requiring massive investment. In many cases these were industries which were considered to be 'in the national interest' – where a decline or shortage would be detrimental for Britain. Examples included coal and steel.

In each case, the state became the owner. However, the industry had a separate identity with day-to-day operations carried out by a chairman and board. An annual report was submitted to Parliament and the accounts were published annually for scrutiny by the Public Accounts Committee.

A government minister was appointed to control policy – usually the relevant Secretary of State. For British Rail, therefore, this would be the Secretary of State for Transport.

Whilst public corporations are financed by the government and may receive subsidies and grants (financed by taxation), they are usually expected to pay their way overall.

The privatisation programme

In the 1980s many public corporations had problems, especially in regard to their returns on capital invested, which were very low when compared to private industry. They were criticised on

- pricing policies, productivity and investment

- overmanning and bureaucracy, resulting in diseconomies of scale

- their protected status as 'public monopolies'

- the burden for taxpayers of supporting unprofitable industries.

In addition, there were ongoing problems in finding the right balance between government control (or interference) and leaving them to manage themselves.

For all these reasons, the Conservative government of the 1980s embarked on a privatisation programme whereby most public corporations would be sold back from the state to shareholders. This has resulted in the privatisation of most former corporations, including British Telecom, British Aerospace, British Airways, British Gas, British Steel, Rolls-Royce, British Coal, the electricity and water companies, Railtrack and British Energy. The money raised from privatisations has meant the government has been able to reduce its own borrowing and raise over £35 billion from the sales.

Golden shares

Although privatisation means that shares are sold to the public, it is not always the case that the government sells *all* its shares. Sometimes it retains shares itself – called 'golden shares'. There are two types of golden shares.

- Those without a time limit. These are retained when the government wishes to retain some control over the organisation, eg to block a takeover which would be unwelcome on the grounds of national security. It was through this means that the proposed takeovers of Midlands Electricity by PowerGen and Southern Electric by National Power could be blocked.

- Those which are only in force for a specified time. These are issued when the government considers the management needs time to adjust to operating in the private sector, free from any worries about a hostile takeover bid.

Companies in which the government holds golden shares include Cable and Wireless, Sealink Stena Line, BT, British Aerospace, British Gas, Rolls-Royce, and several electricity companies.

Advantages of privatisation

- If there is competition within an industry, then industries have to lower their costs so that they can offer their service at a competitive price – which is better for consumers.

- Consumers have wider choice because of increased competition.

- Managers and staff must improve service and increase efficiency as keeping customers is essential to survival.

- The burden on taxpayers and the government is reduced.

- The money raised on the stock market through the sale of shares can be used for investment. The water companies, for instance, have argued that only now can they start to renew old pipes because the money to pay for this was not available to them before.

- Private individuals can buy shares in privatised industries and this will increase private share ownership in Britain.

Disadvantages of privatisation

- If there are no 'real' competitors, then consumers may be worse off – a public monopoly simply becomes a private monopoly.

- Privatised companies will be more interested in keeping shareholders happy than operating in the public interest so will be tempted to pay large dividends rather than to invest to improve services. Many water companies were criticised for this during the 1995 drought.

- Standards do not always improve.

- Increasing competitiveness often means restructuring and redundancies – the result is higher unemployment. BT has axed thousands of jobs since privatisation.

- Unprofitable parts of an industry cannot be subsidised by profitable parts and may be difficult to sell, eg regional rather than Intercity train services and letter delivery services in the Highlands of Scotland rather than in London.

- The financial bonus to the government will only last so long. Soon there will be nothing left to sell.

- Many state assets have been sold cheaply to tempt shareholders to buy shares. This has meant that the nation as a whole has not benefited to the extent it could have done.

It was to counteract some of these charges – particularly in relation to lack of competition, poor services and standards that the government set up several watchdog or regulatory bodies to monitor services, profits, prices and oversee customer complaints. Examples include OFTEL (BT), OFGAS (gas), OFWAT (water) and OFFER (electricity).

Other types of privatisation

Privatisation issues are not just related to public corporations. Other types of privatisation have included the following.

- The introduction of private-sector finance initiatives (PFI) in health and education. In 1996 the first NHS hospital to be built entirely from private funds was announced, in addition to several NHS hospital expansions being financed privately. In addition, the NHS has contracts with private hospitals and in 1995 earned £200 million from private patient work within NHS hospitals.

- The growth in privatised services which were traditionally offered by local authorities, such as home helps, meals on wheels and school meals. In 1992 only 2 per cent of home-help care was provided privately, in 1995 this had risen to 29 per cent.

- The privatisation of government services and administration. The income tax, social security and driving licence computers are now all operated by a US company. There is already one private prison and it is expected that, in the future, the operation of prisons and the administration of the tax system will be future areas for privatisation.

Gas and electric on sale in supermarkets soon?

The government has also been aware of criticisms about lack of competition and is following a policy of deregulation, mainly in gas and electricity, to widen consumer choice. In the south-west of England householders can now select their gas from a variety of other suppliers – even two supermarkets are considering becoming licensed suppliers. The suppliers will buy their gas from a North Sea producer (or extract it themselves) and put it through TransCo – the British Gas pipeline network. No new pipes or meters will be needed, but the meter will be read and the bill will be sent by the new supplier. Householders can shop around for competitive rates.

Over the next few years this type of choice will spread to the rest of Britain. Those in favour of the free market consider this will result in lower prices and improved service. Consumer groups are less optimistic. They are worried that private companies will focus on selling contracts to the most profitable customers, eg industrial users, those in large houses and those who pay on time by direct debit. They fear that poorer customers, such as pensioners and those on benefits – who do not use much gas or have bank accounts – will only be able to buy at higher rates.

Current planned privatisations

In June 1996 these included

- up to 53 research laboratories
- Ministry of Defence Married Quarters Estate – which comprises 60,000 homes on 800 sites in Britain, many around London
- AEA Technology – the science and engineering section of the UK Atomic Energy Authority
- various ports, including Tyne and Ipswich
- the Chessington Computer Centre which is responsible for processing MPs and civil servants' pay
- Her Majesty's Stationery Office which undertakes the production of the government's publishing and stationery
- the Post Office.

The total amount of revenue possible is in the region of £7 billion.

Watchdogs with teeth!

For several years critics have commented that the regulatory bodies or 'watchdogs' whose role it is to monitor the operations of privatised industry are more like pet poodles than bull terriers. However, much to the horror of British Gas, OFGAS, the industry watchdog, gave orders that prices had to be reduced by between 20 per cent and 28 per cent in 1997 and then pegged at 5 per cent below inflation between 1997 and 2001. British Gas immediately gave notice of its intention to appeal to the Monopolies Commission, arguing the average saving for families of £30 a year on its gas bill would result in 10,000 redundancies and threaten savings, as well as reducing dividends to private investors. Given the industry has already cut 23,000 workers between 1993 and 1996 and yet found the money to give its directors a 47 per cent pay rise in March 1996, few commentators had much sympathy with the industry.

A second watchdog proving it intended to bite as well as bark was OFWAT, which produced a scathing report on the water industry's performance in relation to mending leaks. The government responded by promising a law to force water companies to compensate customers if there were any cuts in supply – regardless of heatwaves or low reservoirs. Only three out of nine water companies had actually met their targets in stemming leaks.

Finally, perhaps just to prove it could join the game, OFTEL announced that is was proposing to stop BT increasing telephone charges to residential customers and small businesses. To date large business organisations have benefited most from BT price cuts – simply because the market is more competitive.

Discussion point

1 You were given some shares in British Gas as a present. How do you think the announcement above affected the share price? Give a reason for your answer.

2 Discuss as a group whether you consider the needs of the consumer or the needs of the shareholder should come first
   a from the point of view of the industry
   b from the point of view of the government.

Bear in mind when you do this, that the industry needs shareholders to keep their shares or the price will go down and the government wants to tempt potential private shareholders to invest in new privatisation issues! (Note that you will look at this issue in greater detail in chapter 4, when you study the role of the shareholder.)

Deregulation – another type of change

At the beginning of this section you looked at the government's role as a regulator – from the passing of legislation to the issuing of licences to regulatory bodies.

In contrast, the term **deregulation** relates to the removing of regulations and restrictions. Examples include changing the regulations

- which prevented anyone other than solicitors from undertaking conveyancing work

- which protected public-sector transport services and opened these routes to private operators

- which protected opticians from competition and kept the price of spectacles and contact lenses high

- which prevented stores in England and Wales from opening on a Sunday or pubs from choosing their own opening hours or restaurant licence holders (including pubs) from serving drinks with food all day on a Sunday.

The arguments in favour of deregulation are similar to those in relation to privatisation. Free-market economists believe that businesses work better with minimum interference from the state. Generally, it is believed that private enterprise is more responsive to consumer demand. This is because the owners are motivated to work hard to make a profit and produce what people want, when they want it and at a price they can afford to pay. This interaction of demand by consumers and the supply of goods by producers is known as the **price mechanism.** Goods which are popular are in high demand and this increases profits for producers. If there is a shortage, then prices will rise which will increase profits, tempting other suppliers to enter the market. Those goods which are too expensive or do not meet customer expectations will not be demanded, even at a low price. This will force suppliers out of business – or to move to producing more profitable goods. Any organisation which cannot do this goes out of business.

However, there are problems with depending upon private enterprise, with its desire for profits, and the price mechanism, to meet all the needs and demands of society – which is why no country in the world has a purely 'free-enterprise economy'.

These problems can include the following.

- The needs of the wealthy being satisfied at the expense of the needs of the poor.

- Investors (mainly in large organisations) seeking quick returns on their capital – which can lead to short-term planning and low investment for the future.

- The social consequences of production being ignored. These are called **social costs** and include effects such as the pollution of land, air and water by industrialists and the destruction of natural habitat or wildlife to increase farming output and to build more roads.

- Socially undesirable goods being produced if they will yield a profit, eg drugs and pornographic films and magazines.

- Basic employment rights – such as health and safety, decent working conditions and protection against unfair dismissal – being ignored if they will add to costs.

- Large organisations overpowering smaller competitors and putting them out of business. This can result in one organisation having a monopoly on supply – and dictating the price to consumers.

- Large organisations working together to fix prices and form a **cartel** or 'joint monopoly' which can limit the supply of goods and therefore keep the price high. An example of an alleged cartel is the South African based De Beers Central Selling Organisation (CSO) which controls the supply of diamonds coming on to the market. If all the diamonds were released which were mined, then the price would fall. Therefore the CSO comprises sellers who are interested in keeping prices high. Another example is OPEC – the Organisation of Petroleum Exporting Countries – which limited the supply of oil in the 1970s causing huge price increases.

- Goods which are socially necessary – but unprofitable on a large scale – are not provided. These are often called **merit goods** and include such items as education and health care.

- Goods which can only be sensibly provided for the community as a whole and from which everyone benefits cannot be provided just for a few and individuals charged separately. An obvious example is the defence of the country. These are called **public goods** and other examples include street lighting, the legal system, the police and the prisons.

Some economists consider that it is the role of the state to minimise these problems by putting in place a system of regulations and legislation to control the operation of private enterprise. In addition, there are certain items which the state should provide itself because they are considered socially essential. This, broadly, is the system which today exists in Britain, eg

- Legislation to prevent or control
  - the supply and distribution of socially undesirable substances and materials
  - malpractice by companies, eg Health and Safety at Work Act, Environmental Health Act, consumer protection legislation, employment legislation (eg Sex Discrimination Act, Race Relations Act, Equal Pay Act)

   –   disreputable companies operating against the public interest, eg by
       licensing and regulating operators in certain areas, from public
       houses to loan companies
   –   pollution of the environment and building of industrial units in
       residential areas
   –   the ability of organisations to gain a monopoly position or to operate
       a cartel. Companies which may be likely to become monopolies are
       investigated by the Monopolies and Mergers Commission. Cartels
       are illegal in the UK.

• State provision of public goods and merit goods. Health and education
  are supplied by both the public and the private sectors. The state
  controls the army, navy, airforce, police and prison authorities.

The public sector in the 1990s

Today most political parties agree that the role of the public sector should be
limited in Britain. What they do not agree on is how this should be achieved
– and many political and economic arguments occur over this issue. For
instance, those in favour of regulation argue that technological advances,
financial innovations and global trading mean that the public is more
vulnerable to unscrupulous producers and sales representatives. State
regulations are needed to protect people in areas such as pensions and
insurance advice, food production, additives and health and safety where the
public can easily be misled.

On the other hand, the cost of maintaining the public sector is rising, yet
taxpayers want to pay as little as possible. For instance, education costs
increase as more people wish to stay on in education and health costs are
rising as people are living longer and technological progress means more
advanced (and expensive) equipment is available. Public spending on health
and education is therefore continually increasing and public expectations are
that these areas should be financed by the state. However, this would mean
increasing taxes which people generally do not want to pay!

In addition, the media are quick to seize on issues which affect the public,
such as

• privatised water companies paying large dividends to shareholders and
  failing to mend leaking pipes

• shortages of hospital beds

• redundancies in the teaching profession as cuts are made

• deregulation and lack of controls in the food chain which led to the BSE
  in cattle crisis.

The government is therefore charged with the job of making choices in relation to how much it should interfere with the operation of business and how much it should raise in taxes to provide services itself.

The right choice?

The government was accused of handing over £5.7 billion of public assets to a private **consortium** which was awarded a £3 billion contract to build the Channel Tunnel rail link *and* awarded a £1.4 billion Treasury grant. The deal includes Waterloo International station, 120 acres of land in central London, St Pancras Chambers hotel and Eurostar trains.

A consortium is a group of private companies which forms a temporary alliance to bring together its collective skills and abilities to bid for a contract as a united group when none of the individual members would be able to fulfil the contract alone. This consortium includes Richard Branson's Virgin company, SG Warburg, a banking organisation, National Express and Ove Arup, an international civil engineering company. The government, however, was determined that the link should be built using private-sector money.

The London & Continental consortium has guaranteed to build the high-speed link by 2003, so that trains can travel at up to 160 mph on mainland Britain as well as on the continent. They will operate Eurostar trains and intend to double the traffic in the next two years and then go for a stock market flotation to build the fast-link service. Richard Branson is already campaigning on the group's behalf, challenging the rules banning duty-free sales on cross-Channel trains. He claims this makes competition unfair as airlines are free to sell duty-free alcohol on flights to Brussels and Paris, whereas Eurostar trains are not.

Discussion point

1   How would you answer Richard Branson's argument for duty-free alcohol on trains? Give a reason for your answer.

2   Road-building costs a fortune. One way around this would be to give the job to private companies which then charge tolls for their use. What could be the consequences of this?

3   The government is proposing to reduce the rules and regulations which have limited gambling in Britain as it wants to strengthen London's ability to compete with gambling centres in western Europe and some former communist countries. This will lead to many more casinos and bingo halls being opened. As a group, are you in favour or against the idea – and why?

4   The House of Lords overturned a proposal by the House of Commons to allow BSkyB to pay a large sum of money to show top sporting events *solely* on satellite television. The Commons took the view that if Sky wished to pay for this privilege, it was up to them. The House of Lords, on the other hand, considered that events such as the Olympics, home Test matches, Wimbledon, the Grand National and the FA Cup Final were part of the national heritage and should be available for everyone to view – even if they did not have satellite television. Some chiefs of sporting organisations disagreed – they felt that if the BBC or ITV could not afford to match BSkyB's bid, then to prevent them selling to the highest bidder was both restrictive and unfair.
   a   Which House took the 'free-market' view and which did not?
   b   With whom do you agree – and why?

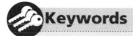

Keywords

The following are the main **keywords** which relate to the private and public sectors. Check that you both know and understand each concept before you continue – if necessary by looking back at the definitions given in the text.

amalgamation	merger
Articles of Association	merit goods
asset-stripping	mixed economy
associate company	monopoly
audit	multinationals
bad debt	nationalisation
capital	oligopoly
cartel	partnership
charitable trust	price mechanism
conglomerate	private companies
consortium	private sector
corporation tax	privatisation
demerger	prospectus
deregulation	public company
diseconomies of scale	public corporation
diversification	public expenditure
downsizing	public goods
economies of scale	public sector
entrepreneur	quango
flotation	sleeping partner
franchise	social costs
globalisation	sole proprietors
holding company	specialisation
horizontal integration	subsidiary company
imperfect competition	takeover
limited liability	turnover
local authorities	unitary authorities
management buy-in	unlimited liability
management buyout	VAT
market share	vertical integration
Memorandum of Association	

Examination practice

Short-answer questions

1 State two legal differences and two financial differences between an ordinary partnership and a private limited company.

2 Give three reasons why the directors of a private limited company may wish to float the company on the Stock Exchange.

3 Give four examples of economies of scale gained as a result of horizontal integration.

4 State three advantages and three disadvantages of privatisation.

5 Identify the similarities and differences between the objectives of private-sector and public-sector companies.

6 Identify three differences between operating as a sole trader and operating as a franchisee.

7 State two constraints on the operation of charitable organisations.

8 Identify two disadvantages for a host country of a large multinational organisation.

9 Identify four sources of income for a local authority.

10 State two benefits and two drawbacks of deregulation.

Definition questions

1 Explain clearly the difference between each of the following terms.
- **a** vertical integration and horizontal integration
- **b** economies of scale and diseconomies of scale
- **c** Memorandum of Association and Articles of Association
- **d** public company and public corporation
- **e** merger and takeover

2 Write clear notes to describe each of the following terms.
- **a** management buyout
- **b** franchise
- **c** unlimited liability
- **d** public expenditure

Essay questions

1 Identify the various ways in which businesses may be integrated. State the reasons for following this course of action.

2 George Evans and his wife jointly own a small hotel. They are considering expanding the hotel and George has suggested that they form a private limited company. Discuss the advantages and disadvantages of taking this course of action.

3 Explain why the government may wish to support a move to encourage the formation of small businesses.

4 Describe the structure and function of local authorities, with specific reference to their role as a service provider.

5 Assess the advantages and disadvantages of the government's privatisation programme.

6 The government has generally followed a policy of deregulation in line with free-market beliefs. Identify the benefits and drawbacks of this approach from the point of view of
   a business organisations
   b consumers.

Case study

Dairy Crest, the nationalised milk company, became a public company in a Stock Exchange flotation in the summer of 1996. The organisation was originally set up by the Milk Marketing Board which is now being wound up. The company has shrunk considerably since 1990 when it had 32 plants and 12,500 employees. Now it operates in 11 locations with 3,500 staff.

a What would be the likely effect on company objectives when the company changed from being a nationalised operation to a private company?

b Identify how the company will be financed once it is privatised.

c The company has reduced in size considerably since 1990. Suggest reasons for this trend.

d Identify the benefits and drawbacks to Dairy Crest from operating in the private sector as opposed to the public sector.

The business environment

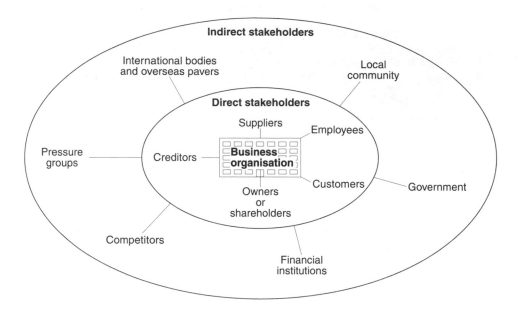

Figure 2.1 The business organisation and its stakeholders

● Introduction

No business organisation operates in isolation. Not only do many events which occur outside the organisation directly affect its activities and profitability, there are also indirect effects on businesses from events occurring in other sectors. You only have to think of the BSE in cattle and human CJD scare to realise that not only were beef and dairy farmers affected – supermarkets, restaurants, food manufacturers and fast-food chains all had to react to this event to keep their customers. As another example, you saw in chapter 1 how the introduction of the National Lottery affected business for football-pool firms and charities. On the positive side, many organisations benefited from England's success in Euro 96 – from sponsors to travel and tourism operators and a variety of businesses making and selling football souvenirs.

This chapter is concerned with the external environment of business. This involves identifying the **stakeholders** (see Figure 2.1) who have an interest in the success of the business and also examining how government actions can affect businesses directly and indirectly – both in relation to their actions in running the economy and changes in legislation.

Finally, this chapter continues our theme on 'change'. As you saw in chapter 1, many external factors cause business organisations to change. In this chapter you are introduced to the way in which the political and economic circumstances which prevail affect business planning. The chapter concludes by giving you a brief introduction to PEST analysis, which is used by businesses to assess the ways in which external forces may affect the way in which they operate. This technique is further developed in chapter 4.

The external environment of business

Many organisations today talk about their stakeholders. These are all the people who have an interest in the business and who are directly or indirectly affected by the actions taken by the business itself. This is a two-way relationship because the business is also affected by actions taken by the stakeholders.

Direct stakeholders

Stakeholders who have a direct link with the organisation include

- the **employees** – who obviously are dependent upon the success of the organisation for their employment

- the **customers** – these may be located in the private or public sector, may be other organisations or private individuals and may be known by a variety of terms, eg customer, client, patient, student, member

- the **owners or shareholders** – who may also be responsible for running the business (in a small private company) or may be large institutional investors or disparate private individuals (in a large public company)

- **creditors** – who may be suppliers (see below) who have sold goods to the company on credit or large financial institutions which have made loans to the company

- **suppliers** – who may supply several organisations or be dependent upon tailoring most of their output to the requirements of one 'giant' customer. Suppliers may provide goods or services – therefore the latter category covers many external agencies such as solicitors, consultants and even catering services that provide lunchtime sandwiches!

Indirect stakeholders

These include other groups which interact on a more indirect basis with the organisation.

- The **local community** – the organisation will provide employment for local people and will have expectations of services from the local authority – from road and waste disposal to street lighting and policing.

- The **government** – which can affect the organisation through its political or legislative actions and economic policy. Changes in income tax rates, for instance, will affect the buying behaviour of customers. Increases and decreases in corporation tax will affect the amount of

On your Marks!

Marks & Spencer is renowned for having strong relationships with its suppliers. The supplier receives a detailed specification of the product it has to make and supply and the management works with Marks & Spencer's managers to ensure that the output will be of the desired quality and delivered on time. The danger for some small suppliers who gear all their manufacturing output to the needs of Marks & Spencer is their high dependence on future orders. If they lose the contract, the firm is in grave danger of going out of business. However, **diversifying** production may be difficult if there is heavy investment in equipment required to produce Marks & Spencer's goods which may

not be suitable for other types of output.

profits which a company can retain for investment or for distribution to shareholders as dividends.

- **Financial institutions** – these include banks, insurance companies, the Stock Exchange and finance houses.

- **Competitors** – these may be found in the same country or abroad. If a competitor offers a more technologically advanced product or sells its goods more cheaply, then this may prove a serious threat to the organisation. Equally, as you saw in chapter 1, the operation of the price mechanism attracts more suppliers to an industry if potential profits are high. This obviously increases competition.

- **Pressure groups** – these range from 'interest groups' (eg Friends of the Earth) to trade unions and also include the media. The aim of a pressure group is to promote change and to bring its activities to the attention of the public.

- **International bodies and overseas powers,** notably the EU. The action taken by the EU to ban British beef following the BSE scare severely exacerbated the problem facing the British government and beef producers. EU directives override national law in member countries.

Shell not going well

The multinational oil company Shell has had more than one disastrous brush with stakeholders in recent years. Five years ago it was fined £1 million after 150 tonnes of oil leaked into the river Mersey. Then it failed to take sufficient notice of rising public concern for green issues and the environment when it announced it intended to sink the Brent Spar Oil Platform in an Atlantic trench – and was rewarded by a consumer boycott which cost the company dearly.

In 1995 it hit the headlines again after the execution in Nigeria of the activist and writer Ken Saro-Wiwa when it was accused of ignoring political pressures to withdraw operations in Nigeria and was then alleged to have breached international standards and caused extensive pollution in Nigeria. Full-page adverts against Shell were funded by the Body Shop International, Friends of the Earth, Greenpeace and Chaos Communication Ltd. Shell responded by taking out full-page adverts to argue its own position. Shell shareholders were advised to vote against the report and accounts at the 1996 Annual General Meeting, in protest at its environmental record in the country.

Basically, on these occasions Shell had ignored the power of the stakeholder. In the case of Brent Spar, experts said Shell spent too much time trying to convince the government of its case and too little consulting stakeholder groups, including staff, customers, suppliers and consumer groups. The irony of the case is that Greenpeace later apologised for misinterpreting the statistics relating to the environmental damage which could be caused by Brent Spar! The main lesson to learn is that the power of pressure groups to influence consumers and businesses directly is growing – and it is a foolhardy management which does not take account of this when deciding company policies.

🗨 Discussion point

In one Gallup survey, 33 per cent of 30,000 consumers interviewed stated that they had boycotted stores or products because they were concerned about ethical standards. Sixty per cent said they would be prepared to do so in the future and 57 per cent said they were more concerned about **ethical issues** than they were five years before. These are the moral and social issues which may influence the behaviour of a business organisation.

1   How did the power of the consumer and other groups influence government and food manufacturers' policies during the beef crisis of 1996?

2   Have you or any members of your group felt strongly about an environmental issue or boycotted particular goods or stores because of their actions? If so, to what degree are these feelings shared by the rest of the group? What do you think such feelings imply for the future management of organisations?

3   For each stakeholder group identified on pages 61–2, try to think of one action they could take (other than the examples given in the text) which could affect or change the behaviour of an organisation.

● The economic environment

The aim of every British government – no matter which political party is in power – is for a sound economy. Ideally, it would want

* **economic growth**

* sustained low **inflation**

* **full employment**

* a healthy **balance of payments**

* a **strong currency.**

The government will therefore implement policies to try to correct any economic problems – and these can have both positive and negative effects on business organisations. Unfortunately, there is no single 'package' of measures that will solve every problem. If there was, then there would be no discussion about the best way to run the economy – a conundrum which regularly causes disagreement amongst economists and politicians alike. The problem is that policies to solve one problem often create or exacerbate another – for instance, the measures required to achieve low inflation are considered by many economists to contribute to rising unemployment. Many of the actions taken by government affect businesses in one way or another.

Economic growth

If the economy is growing, then this is because the nation as a whole is earning more money each year. This is measured by comparing **National Income** on an annual basis. Basically, National Income is the amount of money earned by the country. It is derived from the monetary value which is placed upon the country's production, known as **Gross Domestic Product (GDP).**

In 1994 the figures for Britain were

	£ billion
Gross Domestic Product	579.1
plus net property income from abroad	10.6
Gross National Product	589.7
less capital consumption	68.2
Net National Product (National Income)	521.5

You may like to note the following.

- UK residents may own 'property' abroad (eg shares in a foreign company) and non-UK residents may own 'property' here. The income earned abroad less the income payable abroad results in the net property income from abroad.

- Capital consumption is similar to depreciation, ie the monetary cost of using an item which results in its reduced value, eg a secondhand car. In this case, however, it concerns the monetary cost of the 'capital items' (equipment, buildings, roads, etc.) which have been used up in earning the income and therefore need replacing.

There are three methods of calculating GDP.

1 **Expenditure method** – involves calculating the amount of national expenditure each year.

2 **Output method** – involves calculating the value of goods and services produced each year.

3 **Income method** – involves calculating the income of all UK residents in a year.

Technically, all these methods should result in the same figure. Why? Think of it this way: Fred is a jewellery maker who has no other source of income and doesn't believe in saving. If he sells 200 items of jewellery at £300 each, his income is £60,000. His output is valued at £60,000 and his expenditure will also equal £60,000 in the year. This may seem very simple, but is the basis on which GDP and National Income are calculated.

You may like to note that the Inland Revenue would be very interested if Fred spent £70,000 in one year – as this is evidence that Fred has been operating in the **black economy,** eg by selling some of his jewellery for cash 'off the books'. The black economy is the name given to all the activities which are not recorded to evade tax – and the size of Britain's black economy can be estimated at the difference between the income and expenditure of British residents each year.

Measuring the black economy

Economists disagree about the size of the UK's black economy. Professor Kent Matthews of the University of Cardiff estimates it at about 12 per cent of GDP (approximately £85 billion). This would mean each household earns about £2,000 a year on the black economy. Andrew Dilnot, Director of the Institute for Fiscal Studies, considers it is nearer 3 per cent. In April 1996, the Office for National Statistics (ONS) started an enquiry to find out more precisely the size of the black economy.

Calculating National Income

In reality, despite various adjustments, the figures produced by the three measures do not agree – so an average measure is also calculated. Adjustments also need to be made because the real world is more complicated than Fred's world. For instance, consider the following.

- The government pays people money they have not earned, eg pensions, income support and various benefits. Equally, people may win money or receive money as a gift or inheritance. These are called **transfer payments** and are deducted from the calculations. If Fred won £10,000 on the National Lottery and his wife collects her family allowance from the post office each week, neither of these payments can be counted as they are not connected to Fred's output.

- The government would have taxed Fred for earning his money, therefore he would not have had the full amount to spend. Equally, Fred may have saved some of his money or invested in new buildings or equipment.

- Fred may buy some of his metal or precious stones from abroad or sell some of his finished pieces to foreign buyers. Imports and exports mean that some of Britain's output is purchased overseas and some of the expenditure of Britain's residents is spent on imported goods.

- Some money is spent each year on investments. These are not 'consumed' in the current year but benefit society for years to come, eg schools and hospitals (or Fred's investment in his own business). However, capital investments depreciate each year and become worth less. Eventually, they need replacing.

GDP calculations

The components of the three measurements are shown in Figure 2.2.

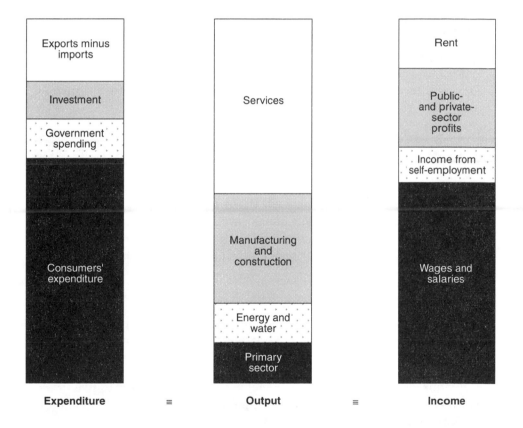

Figure 2.2 Gross Domestic Product: basic components

National Income and the standard of living

Basically, if National Income is rising, then the country is getting richer and people have more money to spend. Therefore, the **standard of living** is rising. However, care must be used. You cannot just assume that because National Income is rising that living standards must also be rising, or rising by the same amount. For instance, consider the following.

- A rising population will mean that the increased earnings are being shared by more people.

- Inflation (ie increasing prices) can mean people feel no benefit as it takes more money for each person to buy the same amount of goods and services.

- The standard of living may not rise immediately if the growth in income is being spent on investment – or to cope with an emergency such as war.

- Many people provide their services without any form of payment – a typical example could be Fred's wife, who may work hard all week looking after their elderly parents or children for no monetary return at all.

- Economic growth means more economic activity. This has both benefits and drawbacks. In chapter 1 you saw that the negative effects are called **social costs** and can include damage to the environment through pollution. Other costs include depletion of natural resources such as oil and gas, damage to society through stress caused by people working longer hours and the resultant family problems. Even increased unemployment can coincide with economic growth if the latter has been partly created through replacement of human labour with technology.

- If incomes are not shared proportionately, then the rich may benefit and the poor may not.

- A country may have high growth but still have a relatively low National Income – this is the case if it is starting from a low base line (such as applies in the case of third world countries).

- Economic growth does not always mean a country is better to live in. Mortality rates, levels of health care, political and religious freedom are all factors which are not measured by National Income – but are important to the inhabitants of a country.

Sea Empress: good or bad?

When the *Sea Empress*, an oil tanker, foundered off the coast of South Wales in 1996, most people considered this to be a disaster. Oil spillage at sea has disastrous effects on the environment and wildlife and can cost millions of pounds to clean up. Yet such an event can *improve* National Income – as more people are employed to clean up the mess, salvage the ship and write reports on what went wrong. In contrast, damage to the environment does not. Some economists are suggesting that negative aspects should also be included in GDP calculations to give a measure that is more closely related to actual standards of living.

Discussion point

1 Individually, identify 10 features which you consider positively contribute to your own standard of living. Then compare your list with those of other members of your group. Finally, identify how many of these are directly related to financial aspects of your life and how many are not.

2 Figure 2.3 shows the league table for GDP per person in 1979 and 1994. What do think this indicates about life in Britain in relation to the other countries mentioned?

	1979	1994
1	USA	Luxembourg
2	Switzerland	USA
3	Luxembourg	Switzerland
4	Canada	Japan
5	France	Belgium
6	Sweden	Norway
7	Iceland	Denmark
8	Netherlands	Canada
9	Denmark	Iceland
10	Austria	Austria
11	Australia	France
12	Belgium	Germany
13	**UK**	Italy
14	Germany	Netherlands
15	Italy	Australia
16	Norway	Hong Kong
17	Japan	Singapore
18	New Zealand	**UK**

Figure 2.3 GDP per person league table, 1979 and 1994

Britain's economy in a nutshell

Government policies from 1946 up to the early 1970s were mainly concerned with stimulating economic growth and reducing unemployment by increasing **aggregate demand** in the economy. Aggregate demand is the total amount of goods and services demanded by individual consumers, businesses and the government. If expenditure increases (because demand has increased), then output must also increase – so National Income increases and so do employment levels (see Figure 2.4).

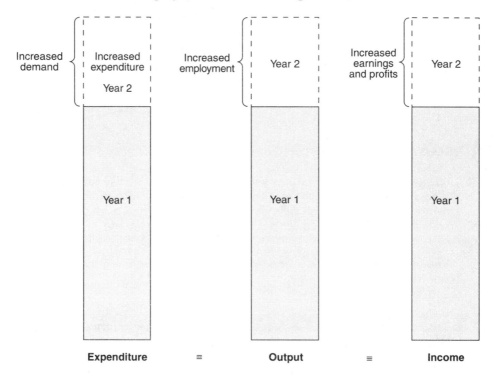

Figure 2.4 The effect of an increase in expenditure on GDP and National Income

A famous economist, John Maynard Keynes, influenced government policies in the post-war years. **Keynesian economists** believe that it is the job of the government to manage demand so that

- there is minimum unemployment

- people have more money to spend, which will then result in higher demand for goods and services.

Keynes argued that the two would reinforce each other as companies would take on additional labour to meet rising demand. This is because there is a **circular flow of income between firms and households** (see Figure 2.5 and also page 78).

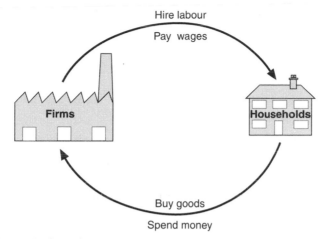

Figure 2.5 The circular flow of income

In Keynes's view it was therefore the job of the government to

- encourage consumers to spend by setting low tax rates and paying state benefits to those below a certain minimum income level

- encourage businesses to increase **investment** in new machinery, equipment and staff by keeping **interest rates** low and promoting **business confidence** – this is the degree to which businesses believe levels of future demand will be sustained or increased

- encourage exports of goods and discourage imports

- increase government spending on new projects for the future – from road-building projects to new hospitals and schools.

The concept of investment and the importance of investment is often difficult for students to understand. Basically, investment means using profits or borrowing money to buy increased assets, eg machinery, capital equipment or buildings. Companies which invest stay up to date with their production methods and may take on additional staff if production levels increase. This is obviously good for the economy.

Changing tax rates and the level of government spending is known as **fiscal policy.** At the time Keynes's predictions appeared very effective and Britain benefited from consistent economic growth between 1951 and 1970 of about 2.8 per cent per year with consistently full employment. This means that there is generally a situation when all the people who want a job can find one.

Inflation and stagflation

Changes in the economy then occurred which meant people started questioning Keynes's theories. In the 1970s the British economy became subject to a combination of rising **unemployment** coupled with rising inflation. Unemployment occurs for several reasons (see page 77). In the 1970s there was insufficient demand for goods in the economy and the government followed the Keynesian route of lowering taxes to encourage people to spend more. However, many industries were changing their methods of operation from labour-intensive methods (ie people) to capital-intensive methods (ie machines). Therefore, even when demand increased the high levels of unemployment continued.

Inflation occurs when the general level of prices is rising. In this case the **cost of living** is increasing. The measure to assess the cost of living is the **Retail Prices Index (RPI)** which is calculated by working out the cost of a representative 'basket of goods'. The difference in price for the same basket, from one year to the next, gives the rate of inflation (see Figure 2.6).

Once inflation is higher than about 5 per cent or 6 per cent a year, problems occur for both businesses and individuals. People on fixed incomes (eg pensioners) find they cannot keep pace with the increasing cost of living. Savings rapidly lose their value and buy less and less each year.

Businesses also have problems with rising costs – both of raw materials and of labour as people demand wage rises to help them cope. This triggers even more price rises as firms seek to retain profit levels. British goods then become more expensive and less competitive than those made by other countries and demand for exports falls. British people are more likely to buy cheaper imports than home produced goods which affects the balance of payments (see page 80). Demand for goods falls and businesses lay off workers.

The only people who benefit from inflation are borrowers (as it becomes cheaper to pay the money back) and those people with jobs where they can

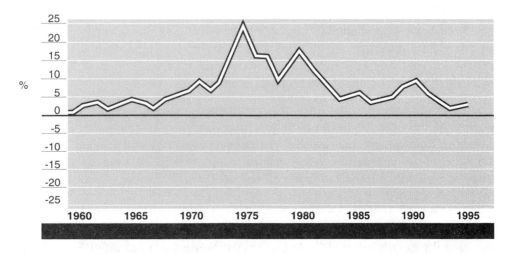

Figure 2.6 UK inflation levels, 1960–95

be certain of an annual pay rise which will keep pace with the rate of inflation.

The combination of a stagnant economy (ie zero economic growth) and rising inflation (see Figure 2.6) resulted in **stagflation** – a situation which was unique in that the normal relationships between economic factors no longer seemed to apply. A new way of economic thinking was required – this time with the focus of government policies on reducing inflation – and people started turning to **monetarist economics.**

No more fish suppers!

In 1996 the Government's Central Statistical Office, now the Office for National Statistics, updated the 'basket of goods' used to measure retail prices. It argued that spending habits had changed since the basket was last formulated and people's lifestyles have changed. All the new ingredients were reflective of the new trends. Out of the basket went fish suppers, certain brands of chocolates, sweets and cigarettes and some types of alcohol, such as mild beer. Into the basket have come green peppers, private school fees, car steering locks and aerobics classes!

Not everyone agreed with the changes however. Clare Short, the Labour MP for Birmingham Ladywood, commented that for her constituents the old basket was still more representative than the new. If you live in Birmingham, perhaps you would like to add your views as to who is right and who is wrong!

Controlling inflation

Monetarist economists believe that inflation is caused by too much money chasing too few goods. This is called **demand pull inflation.** In addition, these economists considered that in the 1970s inflation was made worse by the power of workers demanding pay rises in times of full employment. If the firm did not agree, it had few options – as there were very few people left looking for jobs. Once a firm had agreed to a pay rise, it then had to increase the prices of the goods it sold to retain its profit levels. This is termed **cost push inflation.**

If there is too much money in the economy – and not enough goods to satisfy consumer demand, then prices rise. An easy way to think of this is to consider what would happen if you went with some friends to an auction. Imagine you all want the same antique ring and you have £100 each to spend. The ring would therefore be bought for £100. This is because there is only one ring and its price is limited by the amount each person could spend.

If each person took £1,000 to the auction, the ring would be sold for ten times as much – because people have more to spend but there is still only one ring. This is broadly the belief of monetarists.

The amount of goods demanded by consumers in an economy in a period of full employment must therefore be matched by availability of goods. In addition, if the goods cannot be produced quickly in this country, people will spend their money on imports instead – and this will create further economic problems with more money flowing out of the country to pay for the imports than is earned by British exports.

Monetarists believed there are three ways in which inflation can be reduced.

- Control the **supply of money** so that people have a limited amount to spend.

- Increase the **supply of goods.**

- Make adjustments to the **supply of labour** (so that wages fall).

It is therefore not surprising that monetarist economics became known as **supply-side economics.**

Government policies to increase supply
In the 1980s and 1990s these have included

- adjusting interest rates to either deter or encourage spending by consumers and businesses and to keep a check on the amount of money in circulation – adjusting interest rates to influence the economy is known as **monetary policy**

- reducing regulations which restrict business activities to increase competition (competition generally lowers prices), eg Sunday trading and privatisation policies

- reducing or removing **subsidies** to inefficient industries – this reduces government spending and also makes the industry more competitive

- making labour cheaper so that more staff are taken on (eg by abolishing any Minimum Wage Rates)

- removing the power of labour to 'bid up' wages (trade union power was progressively reduced during the 1980s)

- restricting benefits so that people have more incentive to work than to be on benefit.

In addition, the government was determined to reduce its own spending.

Government finances and the Budget
The government receives its money from two sources – taxation and borrowing. The total amount of money borrowed is known as the **PSBR** – or

public sector borrowing requirement. If all the PSBRs are added together, this equals the National Debt – the total amount owed by the government.

Each November the government announces the Budget and gives its spending plans for the year (see Figure 2.7). Before the Budget it has to decide

- how much it will spend

- how much it will raise in taxes

- how much it will borrow.

If it aims to pay for all its spending by money raised as tax, then it is aiming for a **balanced budget.** If it aims to have some money left over, it is aiming for a **budget surplus.** If it will have to borrow money to cope, then it is predicting a **budget deficit.**

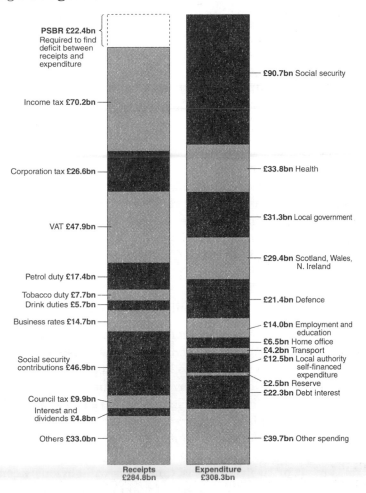

PSBR £22.4bn
Required to find deficit between receipts and expenditure

Income tax £70.2bn

Corporation tax £26.6bn

VAT £47.9bn

Petrol duty £17.4bn

Tobacco duty £7.7bn
Drink duties £5.7bn

Business rates £14.7bn

Social security contributions £46.9bn

Council tax £9.9bn

Interest and dividends £4.8bn

Others £33.0bn

£90.7bn Social security

£33.8bn Health

£31.3bn Local government

£29.4bn Scotland, Wales, N. Ireland

£21.4bn Defence

£14.0bn Employment and education
£6.5bn Home office
£4.2bn Transport
£12.5bn Local authority self-financed expenditure
£2.5bn Reserve
£22.3bn Debt interest

£39.7bn Other spending

Receipts
£284.8bn

Expenditure
£308.3bn

Figure 2.7 Government spending plans, 1996/7

The government can, of course, choose whether to raise or lower **direct taxes,** such as income tax or corporation tax, or **indirect taxes,** such as VAT. In the case of direct taxation the burden of paying the tax is levied directly on the person or organisation which must pay it (eg income tax). Indirect taxes are paid through a third person, eg VAT, which you pay to the seller who then pays the government.

Direct taxes are considered fairer because they are **progressive** – the more you have the more you pay. However, increases directly reduce the amount people have left to spend (which lowers demand in the economy) and people dislike paying more – so they are politically unpopular. Indirect tax is not felt so keenly (do you ever think about how much VAT you are spending?) but they increase the prices of the goods on which they are levied, so they are inflationary. In addition, they are **regressive.** This means that they are a greater burden for the poor than the rich.

The danger with operating a budget surplus is that people have much less to spend – as income tax is likely to be high. To operate a surplus the government also has to reduce its own spending because it is having to manage on much less money. Therefore the level of demand in the economy falls because both consumers and the government are demanding fewer goods. Businesses start to pile up unsold stock and lay off workers. This exacerbates the problem still further – and eventually there is an economic **recession.**

A budget deficit has the opposite effect – income tax is lowered to encourage people to spend and the government may combine this with low interest rates to try to encourage organisations to borrow money for future investment. The government is likely to follow these policies if there is a recession – to try to get the economy moving again. There are two dangers with this. The first is that, in a recession, there is high unemployment. Therefore the government may receive less in tax than it anticipated and pay out more on benefits to the unemployed. It will then have to borrow more than it expected. The second danger is that demand will suddenly spin out of control and create a **boom** where demand is too high for supply – and the result will be high inflation.

It is for this reason that the economy is often considered to be **cyclical** because it operates in cycles of booms and **slumps** (see Figure 2.8) with the government introducing policies to try to keep the economy on a more even keel. During the 1960s this led to the term **stop-go policies** when the government constantly changed its policies – first to reflate the economy and then to check its growth. This type of change is particularly problematic for business organisations as managers cannot predict with any certainty what will be government policy on issues such as taxation, government spending or interest rates in six or twelve months' time. This will obviously contribute to a lack of business confidence and a fear of making any important decisions which could be affected by policy changes.

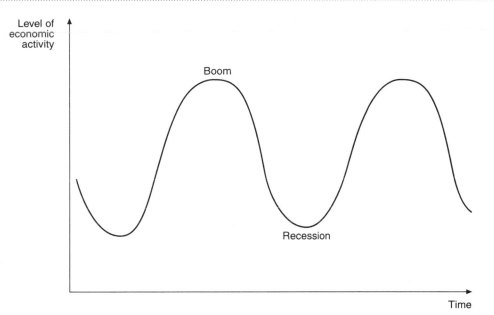

Figure 2.8 Booms and slumps in the economy

 Discussion point

Some economists argue that changing indirect tax rates (eg VAT) has a more direct effect on spending and is fairer because no one is exempt from paying it. In addition, the fact that 'essentials' (eg food) are either zero-rated or exempt mean that the poor are not affected as much as some people imply.

A contrary argument disputes this idea. Some social scientists have identified a typical lifestyle for the poor which includes spending habits that will increase the burden of VAT – take-away fast food, drinks in the pub, cigarettes, football matches, etc.

As a group, what is your view? If you were a politician and had to increase tax, which would you be most likely to choose and why?

The rise of unemployment

The result of government policies aimed at reducing inflation have been successful in that inflation levels are now far lower than they were in the 1970s. At that time, they had been as high as 25 per cent in a year. Today they are nearer 3 per cent.

However, the problem was that demand fell when the government operated a budget surplus to reduce spending. This, coupled with increased competition from overseas and a low level of exports, meant that the market for British-made goods was considerably reduced. Firms stopped investing and started laying off workers – the result was rising unemployment. Partially unemployment was caused by a downturn in the economy, ie a recession. This is known as **cyclical unemployment.** However, another type of unemployment worsened the situation – **structural unemployment.** This occurs when whole industries fail, often through cheap imports. In Britain this has occurred in cotton, shipbuilding and coal. Too many people lose their jobs too quickly for the economy to cope.

The difficulty today is in the government trying to reflate the economy to lower unemployment levels without inflation returning as well.

The net effect of government economic policies on business

As you saw on page 71, Keynes argued that there is usually a **circular flow of income** between firms and households. Firms hire workers and pay them a wage, which the workers then spend on buying goods from the firm. (In effect, the firm then gets its money back.) Anything which causes a **leakage** from this flow will reduce the amount of money received by firms. Keynes identified three leakages: **savings, taxation** and **consumer spending on imports.** However, he also argued that injections would increase the amount of money received by firms – **government spending, investment** and **selling to the export market** (see Figure 2.9).

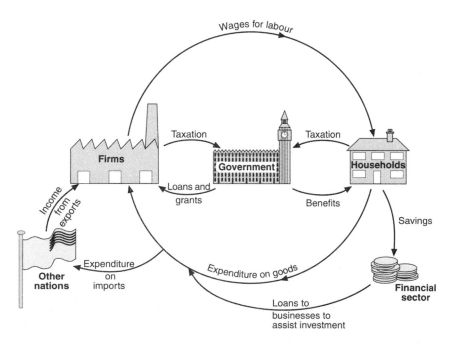

Figure 2.9 The circular flow of income with leakages and injections

He also argued that the effect of any of these is greater than may be originally thought because of the **multiplier effect.** This means that actions taken affect a variety of individuals and organisations. In other words, there is a 'spin-off' effect throughout the economy – rather like throwing a stone in a lake and seeing the ripples.

Let us take an example. Suppose a firm decides to invest £2 million in new machinery. It places an order with its suppliers which take on additional staff to produce the items required. The staff now receive wages (assume they were unemployed before) which increases their own spending potential. This benefits local shops who may also take on more staff – and so on.

The multiplier can, of course, operate in reverse. Suppose a large shipyard closes and all the workers are laid off. All now have reduced incomes and can spend less. Local shops and cinemas close and are boarded up because no one has any money to spend. The whole area goes into decline.

Therefore a wide variety of businesses can be affected by different actions taken by the government.

 Discussion point

1   A business is considering borrowing £250,000 and investing in new machinery. This will increase output and enable the company to employ additional staff. The organisation had undertaken calculations which show it can afford to take on the loan if interest rates remain at about 5 per cent and demand for its goods continues to increase. As a group, discuss the effect a change of government policies may have on this decision.

2   As a group, examine the injections and leakages identified by Keynes carefully and try to work out the 'spin-off' effects which would be caused by a change to each one. How many effects on business can you identify?

International trade and the exchange rate

One important aspect of the economy is the amount of money earned by British exports. This has to be balanced against the amount of money spent on imports and the difference is calculated every month and detailed in the balance of payments. The balance of payments records

- **visible trade** – ie goods and commodities exported and imported

- **invisible trade** – ie services exported and imported

The balance of trade

This is the calculation on the receipts and expenditure on **goods** – called **visibles.** Today most items exported by Britain are high-quality manufactured articles, chemicals, machinery and transport equipment – and, of course, North Sea oil. Almost one-half of our imports are food, fuel and raw materials with manufactured goods mainly making up the balance.

Traditionally, Britain has a deficit on the balance of trade. This means that more goods (visibles) are imported than are exported. Such a deficit is often called the **trade gap.**

The balance of payments on current account

In this calculation *both* goods and services are included. Services are known as **invisibles** and include such items as government spending, tourism, financial services, sea and air transport. Therefore, if a British insurance company insured a flock of Australian sheep, this would be classified as an invisible export (because Britain would earn money from the transaction). Similarly, when you go abroad on holiday you are an invisible import (because you take money earned in Britain and spend it abroad). Britain often achieves a surplus on invisibles.

The balance of payments on capital account

This is the final calculation which includes capital and investment flows, eg in the banking sector. Therefore, if an Arabian oil sheik invested money in London, this would count as an export because money has flowed into Britain.

When the calculations have been completed a 'balancing item' is introduced – so that the balance of payments actually balances (see Figure 2.10).

		£bn	
Balance of trade {	Visible exports (goods)	+134.5	
	Visible imports (goods)	−142.1	
		−8.4	Balance of payments on current account
	Invisible exports (services)	+32.4	
	Invisible imports (services)	−26.8	
		+5.6	
Balance of payments on capital account {	Capital inflows	19.0	
	Capital outflows	22.0	
		−3.0	
Bear in mind it must balance! {	Overall balance of payments	−5.8	
	Balancing item	+5.8	
		—	

Figure 2.10 The UK balance of payments

Earning royal favour

Each year a number of companies are rewarded for their export efforts by receiving the Queen's Award for Export. A winning company can celebrate the achievement by flying a flag with the award's logo, incorporating the logo on their letterheads, in advertising campaigns and on special cufflinks and lapel badges.

In 1996 winners included Reynard Racing Cars, a small company in Oxford which designs and builds cars for American, European and Japanese championships, and Storehouse (which owns Mothercare and BHS) for exporting a variety of goods from clothing to lighting.

However, an unusual winner was Reilor, a Preston-based company which specialises in producing many thousands of cat and dog flaps a year at prices ranging from £6.99 to £70. Brian Kerr, the managing director, considers its success has been due to considering the different cultures of foreign countries and acknowledging the different perceptions of his various buyers. Americans, for instance, will spend heavily on electronic models which will also keep out wild animals and spend far more on dog flaps than Europeans. Even the packaging has been redesigned to incorporate different languages and live animal photographs – which customers in all countries appear to prefer.

Government policies and the balance of payments
The government has tried to increase the level of exports.

- By giving help, advice, assistance and support to exporters, eg through the Department of Trade and Industry (DTI) Enterprise Initiative in the early 1990s and through diplomatic initiatives.

- By encouraging financial institutions to make money available for loans for exporters at competitive rates and by keeping interest rates low. However, there is a contradiction with interest rates as *high* interest rates encourage foreign investors to invest on the London financial markets – thereby improving the balance on capital account.

- By offering insurance against exporting risks through the **ECGD – Export Credit Guarantee Department** which will insure against risks such as political coups and war. The ECGD is a financially independent government department which covers 'special risks' related to the export trade.

- By providing funds for inward investment through the Invest in Britain Bureau. This department has a £10.5 million budget to give financial incentives to foreign companies that want to set up in Britain. In 1994/5, 453 projects were handled amounting to £8.3 billion.

- By membership of the EU – which has increased the potential market for British businesses.

Various measures can be used to reduce the level of imports. Britain still uses these but to a lesser degree than in the past.

- Imposing **import tariffs** which make the price of imports more expensive. However, this is not possible for goods imported from the EU as a key agreement is that there will be no import restrictions between member countries.

- Imposing **import quotas** which restrict the quantity of imports allowed into the country. This is mainly done for goods which must be restricted for the public good, eg drugs (for medical use) and armaments.

- Imposing an **embargo.** This is a political ban on trading, eg as with Argentina during the Falklands crisis and Iraq since the Gulf War.

Today, however, most countries subscribe to the view that increased international trade is beneficial to all countries. Developing nations need to increase exports to improve their standards of living. Western nations can specialise in high-technology or specialist products. Exchanging goods is considered both cost-effective and beneficial for international relations.

The World Trade Organisation

The World Trade Organisation (WTO), (formerly known as GATT, the General Agreement on Tariffs and Trade) has its headquarters in Switzerland. Its objectives are to reduce tariffs and other barriers to trade in order to produce a worldwide free-trade area. This means the end of any subsidies, tariffs, quotas and bureaucratic rules and procedures. It is argued this would be beneficial to all nations. Over 100 countries – including Britain – are members. Past efforts have been relatively successful – tariffs had fallen overall to about 5 per cent by 1990. The WTO also bans dumping – a practice of exporting surplus products at very cheap prices to get rid of them (which can virtually wipe out a home market).

Discussion point

The problem for WTO members is to commit themselves to free trade whilst their main concern is often employment levels in their own country. Cheap imports can signal the end of a home industry (such as British cotton products), whilst protectionism leads to higher prices for consumers.

As a group, discuss the pros and cons of world free trade and decide how you would vote if you were Britain's WTO representative.

Exports, imports and company profitability

Business organisations can, of course, be adversely affected if they are caught in the middle of a political storm with another country. Companies involved in exporting to Iraq when the Gulf War broke out obviously suffered losses. However, opportunities can be gained from rebuilding and re-equipping countries – such as Kuwait – in the aftermath of such a crisis.

Generally, companies will not be concerned with major international events unless they are heavily involved in trade to the country involved in the crisis. They are more likely to be concerned about the **exchange rate** as this can make a major difference between trading at a loss or a profit.

The value of sterling

The value of sterling is its value against other world currencies. If you were going to the USA on holiday, you would be concerned about how many US dollars each pound would buy. If sterling is **strong,** then you will get more dollars in exchange for your pound than if sterling is **weak,** eg if you had saved £500 then you can easily calculate the difference this would make.

£1 = US\$3 (sterling strong) = US\$1,500

£1 = US\$1.5 (sterling weak) = US\$750

You would obviously have a much better holiday if you had \$1,500 dollars to spend than if you had \$750!

Discussion point

1   Imagine you were an American who had been saving to come to Britain. Would you want sterling to be strong or weak? Give a reason for your answer.

2   As a group, how many business organisations can you identify that would benefit from an influx of American tourists? Try to think as widely as you can!

Changes in value

What causes changes in the value of sterling and, more importantly, how does this affect businesses?

Britain has a **floating** pound. This means that its value is affected by demand and supply. If foreigners are constantly demanding pounds to buy British goods (or to visit Britain on holiday), then the price of pounds **rises** (just like most other commodities when demand is greater than supply). Conversely, if no one wants pounds, but everyone is demanding dollars, then the value of sterling against the dollar will **fall.** You can see how the rates fluctuate, virtually on a daily basis, by looking in a newspaper.

The government can influence the demand for pounds through interest rates (or by getting the Bank of England to buy or sell pounds – see page 101). High interest rates will encourage foreigners to invest in Britain – and they will have to exchange their savings for pounds before they can invest them with a British financial institution. Therefore, high interest rates and a strong pound often go together.

British businesses are affected by the exchange rate, either because

- they buy raw materials from abroad

- they sell their goods overseas

or both!

A *strong pound* – in this case, imports will be cheap. If you were going on holiday, you would find this out first hand, as the goods you bought abroad would seem cheap to you because you had received a considerable amount of currency in exchange for your sterling. However, British goods would be expensive abroad and this could lead to lower demand.

A *weak pound* – in this case, British goods are very attractive to foreigners as they seem cheap, but imports are more expensive. This may be good for the balance of payments but not so good for a company which buys most of its raw materials abroad.

The major problem for businesses is that the rate fluctuates. Therefore, projected profits on an international transaction may all disappear if the exchange rate moves against them between the time the deal is agreed and payment is finally made. Indeed, in the early 1980s the combination of high interest rates and a strong pound was blamed for the failure of many companies.

Banks and other institutions can offer financial advice and services which can help to minimise the problems relating to **currency fluctuations** (see page 103).

EuroDisney 0, Britain 1

Eurodisney profits suffered a downturn when the price of the French franc rose against other currencies. Many Europeans decided that it was too expensive to visit France and changed their holiday plans. The result was fewer visitors than projected and much lower profits at the end of the year than Disney had originally forecast.

However, the falling pound made Britain far more attractive as a weekend retreat – particularly after the opening of the Channel Tunnel. The number of French, German and Dutch visitors coming to Britain for short holidays has increased by almost 40 per cent over the last few years.

Discussion point

Marks & Spencer is setting up a chain of stores in France, based on the popularity of its Paris stores. If the pound is weak, then the company may sell more goods – unless the cheaper prices make the goods less desirable to French shoppers (because, for example, they become associated with inferior quality). The problem is that when the company converts its earnings in francs into sterling (to bring the money back into Britain), it will receive less than it anticipated on a particular volume of goods.

If the pound is strong, the goods will become more expensive. If the goods still sell, then this will be beneficial for Marks & Spencer, however, if they become too dear in relation to the competition, then sales may fall.

1   A Marks & Spencer's tie costs £5 in England. How much will it cost to a French buyer if
    a   the exchange rate is 10fr/£
    b   the exchange rate is 8fr/£
    c   the exchange rate is 12fr/£?

2   Which scenario do you consider is best for Marks & Spencer – and why?

The millennium and a common currency?

You may have heard or read in the press about the idea of a single European currency from 1999. There have been many debates in Parliament about whether Britain should join or remain outside this – and hold on to sterling. Those who believe we should not join (or not have anything to do with the EU) are often called **Euro-sceptics** by the media.

Many business people would like the advantages of dealing in a single currency. They would not need to pay bank charges on exchanging currencies (known as transaction costs) nor to worry about currency fluctuations – within Europe at least. Consumers would be able to calculate prices more easily and many economists argue that the move would result in lower interest rates and a more stable economic environment within which firms could plan more easily.

Other economists argue that Britain could operate more effectively outside the Euro currency and that fulfilling the economic conditions for entry would be very difficult both for Britain and several other European countries. In addition, there is the argument that Britain would no longer be in control of its own currency – much of its economic power would be transferred to a European body.

In a *Guardian*/ICM poll published in 1996, 64 per cent of voters did not like the idea of sterling being replaced by a Euro currency – although among young voters aged 18–24, the majority were in favour of the idea.

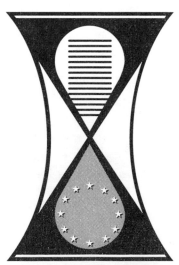

Figure 2.11 The new logo for European Monetary Union

Discussion point

1   Take a poll around your group. How many people
  a   are in favour of a Euro currency
  b   are against the idea
  c   feel they don't understand enough about the issue to give an informed opinion?

2   If the government held a **referendum** on the subject, it would ask voters to give their opinion on a single issue. The last referendum was on whether or not Britain should confirm its membership of the European Community. What is your opinion on the wisdom of holding a referendum and why?

3   Consider the implications if all currency was converted to Euro currency overnight. As a group, how many alterations do you think would have to be made to the standard ways in which we live and work? As a start you could consider the cost of changing all vending machines and cash machines!

The economy and business organisations

As you have seen, businesses may be affected directly or indirectly by government economic policies and the decisions it makes.

In a recession

The government will be worried about increasing levels of cyclical unemployment. It will want to encourage businesses to invest and take on more employees. Interest rates are likely to be low and the pound may therefore be weak against many currencies. Raw material imports may be expensive. Businesses will be concerned about the future – unless they truly believe there will be increased demand for their goods, and have evidence through increasing orders, they are unlikely to have confidence to expand.

Income tax rates may be reduced to increase disposable income and encourage people to spend. Low interest rates will deter people from saving. Corporation tax rates may be reduced to leave organisations more money for investment.

The government may try to reduce unemployment by encouraging new business start-ups, introducing government-sponsored training courses, reducing regulations which hamper small business and increasing grants and financial awards for companies involved in urban regeneration and development schemes. Regional assistance can be targeted to help those areas with the highest unemployment. Policies to reduce unemployment may include lower benefits and training schemes which will help companies to reduce their wage rates.

In a boom

The government will be worried that increased spending will lead to rising inflation. It is likely to increase interest rates and increase taxation to reduce the amount of money borrowed and the amount of money being spent. Companies will be urged to keep wage and price increases down. However, increased demand for workers may mean that wages increase in shortage or specialist areas. The government may consider increasing VAT – which will make goods more expensive and may lower demand, but which could also result in increased inflation.

The government is likely to be concerned about the amount of money being spent on imports and, where possible, may introduce restrictions. High interest rates may result in a strong pound and British exports may become uncompetitive – though raw materials will be cheap. People will be encouraged to save money because the return on their investments will be high. The government may introduce other schemes to encourage people to save rather than spend, such as tax free investments, eg TESSAs.

Government spending policies

Government spending can have a direct effect on many organisations. For example, building contractors find that much of their work disappears if the government stops building roads, hospitals and schools – especially if the housing market is also depressed. Many organisations are directly involved in supplying public-sector organisations, such as local authorities, the NHS and educational establishments and any government cuts also affect them.

Lobbying from on high

Many of the large industries dependent on government spending for their livelihood work hard at lobbying politicians to support their interests. A typical example is British Aerospace, which wants to win all the government defence contracts and argues military requirements for Britain should be made by British companies, not by overseas firms (see government spending on defence on page 42).

 Discussion point

You work for a toy manufacturer with a large export market. Most raw materials are bought in England. Explain which will please your employer the most – a strong pound or a weak pound. Give reasons for your answer.

The British economy – spring 1996

- **Economic growth** fell in 1995 from an annual rate of nearly 4 per cent in the first quarter to 2 per cent in the final quarter. However, it is now expected to have stopped falling. The average growth of GDP is 2.5 per cent and is predicted by the government to rise to 3 per cent later in 1996.
- **Standards of living** have risen. A person earning £18,000 will be £4,500 better off in 1996 than in 1979 when tax and inflation have been taken into account. However, families are typically paying at least £600 more in taxes than in 1992 and the UK has fallen from 13th to 18th in the world prosperity league. In addition, the gap between rich and poor has been widening.
- **Inflation** has averaged about 2.8 per cent during 1996 – and is still forecast to remain steady at about 2.5 per cent for the rest of the year. This has kept wage claims down – average earnings rose by 3.25 per cent during 1995.
- **Consumer demand** is expected to rise during the year, mainly because of tax cuts in the November budget which took effect in April 1996 and 'one-off' factors – such as maturing TESSAs and payouts from building society mergers and conversions. This is likely to boost spending.
  Against this must be set the lack of a 'feel-good' factor because of relatively static house prices and job insecurity. This is likely to tempt people to save any additional income rather than spend it – despite low interest rates. This has resulted in a disappointing growth in retail sales – annually the rate is about 2 per cent but only rose by 0.5 per cent during the last three months of 1995. It is predicted to rise to about 4 per cent in 1997.
- **Investment** has fallen because firms are not certain about the future. They are therefore unlikely to be tempted to invest or expand. Firms overanticipated demand in 1995 and overstocked. They have therefore sold from stocks for much of the autumn and winter, rather than expanding output. The result was a fall in investment spending to 0.7 per cent and very low manufacturing output – only 0.5 per cent during the whole of 1995.
- **Unemployment** has fallen by 750,000 over the past 29 months. It stood at a total of 2.2 million at the end of 1995. The national jobless rate is 7.9 per cent. This is still more than double the 1979 level and is a million higher than in November 1990 when John Major became Prime Minister.
- **Interest rates** are around 6 per cent and unlikely to fall further because of fears this may trigger inflation through increased spending.
- **The government's target of a PSBR** of £22.5 billion for 1996/7 is likely to be overshot – and will end at about £30 billion. This is a fall from the 1994/5 PSBR of £35.9 billion and the 1995/6 PSBR of £32 billion, but only just – and will narrow the government's options of tax reductions before a general election.
- The **balance of payments** was affected by a fall in demand in export markets – mainly the US and Europe. This undermined the growth in manufacturing output growth and worsened the trade balance on the balance of payments. This increased the deficit from £2.1 billion in 1994 to £2.9 billion in 1995. In the first quarter of 1996 the current account deficit was estimated at about £1.1 billion. There was a deficit in traded goods and a surplus in services – but slightly lower than during the last quarter of 1995. However, this was offset by a lower level of UK capital transfers.
- The **value of the pound** is strengthening against the dollar (now £1.52) and against the German mark (DM2.35). This means the Chancellor could cut interest rates again if he wishes. However, imports are becoming dearer and there is a worry that people may ask for wage increases which could trigger inflation.

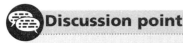

Discussion point

As a group, go through the economic information on the previous page and discuss anything you do not understand with your tutor. Try to obtain updates on each of the measures given. Your tutor will guide you as to where you can find this information. Then assess whether, in your view, the economic situation has improved or worsened since this book was written!

The political and legislative environment

In addition to the economy, the government is also involved in taking other actions which are related to its political agenda. Examples have already been given, such as privatisation and deregulation, where government action was taken which promoted certain industries and resulted in problems for others. Other actions can include entering into trade agreements with specific countries which encourage exports or introducing an embargo which forbids trade with a particular country.

A political decision to eliminate subsidies to non-performing industries, where they had been given to protect jobs, created difficulties for many organisations including paper and car producers, steel plants and shipbuilders. Government spending plans can encourage investment in new businesses and new areas or reduce incentives in these areas. These may be for economic or political purposes. For that reason the political environment is often said to be cyclical – with governments spending more near a general election to influence voters than mid-term.

As you saw in chapter 1, the government also has a regulatory role. Parliament is the main legislative body in the United Kingdom although international laws and European directives also affect the operations of business as they have the force of law throughout the EU and have precedence over national legislation.

Every business has a legal relationship with its stakeholders. Important areas of law for businesses include

- **company law** – which you already met briefly in chapter 1 – regulates the activities of a business mainly in relation to its directors and shareholders

- **consumer law** which regulates the relationship between an organisation and its customers and includes the sale of goods and services, credit transactions, etc.

- **the law of contract** which affects dealings relating to purchases, sales, leases and employment (contracts of employment are covered in chapter 7).

- **employment protection legislation** which regulates the working environment for employees (see chapter 7)

- **health and safety laws** which provide protection for employees, customers and other visitors to an organisation (see chapter 7)

- **data protection legislation** which relates to the type of information that can legally be held on computer (see also chapter 7)

- **banking and financial services Acts** which control the operation of banks, building societies and those offering investment services and advice

- **environmental law** which restricts the way in which organisations dispose of waste products and toxic substances and limits or forbids the development of business organisations in residential areas

- **other laws** – from those which control advertising or the selling of restricted goods (eg tobacco and alcohol) to those which relate to monopolies, cartels and other restrictions to competition.

Quite obviously, all organisations will keep a watch on any legislative changes which may directly or indirectly affect their business operations. In a public company, this is likely to be one of the duties of the **company secretary** who must be a member of a recognised professional body and preferably also be qualified as a barrister, solicitor or legal advocate. His or her role includes

- making certain that the company complies with the law

- maintaining shareholder registers and ensuring that shareholders receive appropriate notification of dividend payments, AGMs, etc.

- calling the meetings of the board of directors and taking minutes (see chapter 4)

- administrating the company pension scheme and giving information to employees

- arranging insurance, contracts, royalty payments, patent registrations and licensing.

In a small private organisation this work is usually carried out by the company accountant.

Assessing the effect of external events

You may think, after reading this chapter, that the task of assessing the extent to which external changes can affect a business would be a nightmare activity. This is not so – mainly because of a useful technique called **PEST analysis.** PEST analysis provides a structure whereby relevant external events which may affect a business can be grouped under four different headings: **political, economic, social** and **technological.** In this chapter you have been concentrating mainly on the political and economic aspects which might affect companies.

A more detailed explanation of PEST analysis, together with a practical example, is given in chapter 4.

Keywords

The most important keywords which you need to know from this chapter are listed below. Check that you are clear on each concept and discuss with your tutor any which you do not understand.

aggregate demand	indirect taxation
balance of payments	inflation
balance of trade	interest rates
black economy	investment
business confidence	invisibles
cost of living	monetary policy
cyclical unemployment	National Income
direct taxation	PSBR
dumping	referendum
economic growth	social costs
embargo	stakeholders
exchange rate	standard of living
fiscal policy	structural unemployment
Keynesian policy	trade gap
import tariffs	visibles
import quotas	

Examination practice

Short-answer questions

1   Briefly describe why a government policy of increasing interest rates might create problems for a business organisation.

2   Identify two initiatives the government might introduce to reduce unemployment.

3   Identify the primary stakeholders in a business organisation.

4   Give three reasons why inflation is dreaded by many pensioners.

5   Identify three areas of legislation with which companies are concerned.

6   State two reasons why the government may increase interest rates.

7   Identify two effects of high unemployment levels on business organisations.

8   Briefly describe the role of the company secretary in a public limited company.

9   State three effects of a high exchange rate on business organisations.

Definition questions

1   Explain clearly the difference between each of the following terms.
    a   fiscal policy and monetary policy
    b   interest rates and exchange rates
    c   cyclical unemployment and structural unemployment
    d   balance of trade and balance of payments

2   Write clear notes to explain each of the following terms.
    a   national income
    b   trade gap
    c   embargo
    d   referendum

Essay questions

1   a   Explain clearly the difference between the balance of trade and the balance of payments.

    b   Describe how fluctuations in the exchange rate might affect the balance of payments.

2   Describe how the levels of investment made by a business organisation can affect economic growth. Explain how investment may be affected by the current rate of interest.

3   'Economic growth results in improved standards of living.' Critically analyse this statement.

4   Your boss is extremely annoyed that the latest government budget includes an increase in VAT, income tax and fuel tax. Explain her reaction from the point of view of her position as manager of a large distribution company.

5   a   Explain how the government may wish to increase the size of the national income.
     b   Why might the government think such actions are desirable?

6   a   What measures could the government take to encourage businesses to export?
     b   Why might the government prefer to increase exports rather than impose restrictions on imports?

Case study

Fortune Wines is a private limited company which produces a popular local beer: 60 per cent is sold in direct-sale outlets and the remainder in pubs. The directors are considering expanding the company in response to increased demand.

a   Analyse how the current economic and political climate might influence this decision, particularly in relation to interest rates, unemployment levels and government policy on taxation.

b   How might the government's exchange rate policy influence the directors' decision to move into the export market by selling in Europe?

c   What would be the major differences to the way in which the company operates if Fortune Wines became a public limited company?

External agencies and business

Introduction

In the last chapter you saw how decisions made by the government in relation to its political agenda and the economic environment can affect businesses. You also learned about stakeholders who have an interest in business organisations.

Many business organisations are suppliers or advisers to *other* businesses. They may be in business to provide goods, services or to help businesses by providing expertise which may not be available 'in-house' (see Figure 3.1).

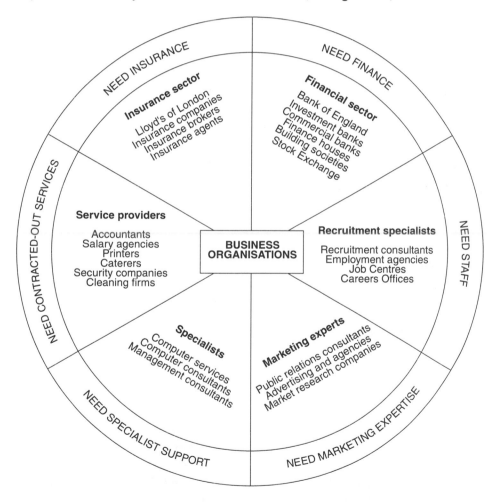

Figure 3.1 Service providers

The most obvious source of assistance, of course, is those organisations which can help with finance. This chapter looks at the different banks which operate in the UK and the role of the Stock Exchange, which is integral to the operations of public limited companies. It also examines other organisations which provide business services – from insurance companies to advertising agencies and management consultants.

Finally, this chapter examines the concept of **contracting out** – an option which is being chosen more and more by companies because of its effect of lowering costs and reducing the number of staff required.

Organisational finance

All organisations need **capital.** They may require **fixed capital** on a temporary or permanent basis, to fund capital investment projects (such as land, new buildings or expensive equipment) or to supplement their **working capital** at a time when there are cash shortages. One method of obtaining additional funds is to approach a financial institution – such as a bank or finance house.

To understand organisational finance, you first need to know the *type* of finance businesses may need and then the institutions which provide it.

Finance for business

Businesses raise money from a variety of sources and for a variety of reasons. The decision about which type of institution to approach will depend upon

- whether the business is a small, medium or large-scale enterprise

- whether the business is just starting up or expanding

- whether finance is required on a short-, medium- or long-term basis – or even permanently

- whether it wants to increase their working capital or fixed capital. Working capital is used to finance everyday transactions – buying stock, paying wages and other expenses, selling goods on credit. Fixed capital is required for building, equipment or expansion projects, eg to take over another business.

Small business start-ups

Small businesses usually find it the most difficult to borrow money from financial institutions – although many banks will give assistance and advice. If the business plan is sound, then an initial loan of up to about £15,000 may be available, depending upon existing assets and the collateral which can be offered. This is the security offered to guarantee the loan will be repaid, eg the owner's private residential property.

Other sources of assistance include local authorities (which keep information on regeneration schemes and European funds for development areas), local Training and Enterprise Councils (TECs) – which, among other things, manage the Enterprise Allowance scheme for the unemployed to start up in business – and the Prince's Youth Business Trust, which is particularly keen to help young people.

Increasing working capital

Sometimes a business may already have enough capital but much of it may be tied up in stock or in debts owed to the company. **Cashflow** is used to describe the net amount of money flowing in/out of the business. A minimum amount must always be available to pay current debts.

Cashflow problems (ie lack of cash to pay for current expenses) are the single most common reason for the failure of small businesses. Frequently, a small organisation may have to wait months for payment from a large customer, but during this time it still has its own bills to settle.

Ways of increasing working capital include the following.

- Obtaining extended credit from suppliers

- Leasing vehicles or equipment rather than buying them outright.

- **Factoring** debts. This means that all the invoices are handed over to a factoring organisation which pays a percentage of the total amount due immediately, collects the money owing and deducts a percentage charge from the total amount. The disadvantage is the fee which has to be paid. The advantage is that the money is available for use immediately.

- Obtaining a bank **overdraft.** This is usually a temporary arrangement but can actually be cheaper than obtaining a bank loan as interest is only paid on each day the overdraft is used. An arranged overdraft is always much cheaper than one which has not been agreed beforehand. Indeed, the latter is a very risky proposition, as the bank can demand the money outstanding at any time!

Obtaining medium- and long-term loans

All financial institutions offer **loans.** The amount of security and terms of the loan will vary depending upon the assessed risk of lending to that particular organisation. Some loans have fixed interest rates, others have variable rates. Fixed rates enable businesses to plan with more accuracy as the payments are a known factor. Variable rates have the advantage that payments will fall if interest rates go down, but the disadvantage that a rise in interest rates will mean higher payments. Commercial banks offer repayment periods from one to 20 years and the amount on offer can be up to about £250,000. All recommend that the repayments are protected by insurance cover in case of an illness or accident.

Larger amounts of money can be borrowed from investment banks and specialist finance houses by **blue chip** companies which have an established trading record. The term blue chip is given to high ranking industrial shares with a good track record. Another alternative is **venture capital** where money is invested in return for a share in the equity. The term **equity** is often used to describe ordinary shares (see below) because these divide the share capital into 'equal portions' (eg 50,000 £1 shares) – hence the name equity.

The Loan Guarantee Scheme

This government scheme was introduced in 1981 to provide development capital to small firms. The scheme is administered by the Department of Trade and Industry. Loans are granted for a minimum of two years and the government provides two levels of debt guarantee. Established businesses which have been trading for two years or more can obtain a loan of up to £250,000 with 85 per cent guaranteed by the government. Other businesses can only borrow up to £100,000 with a guarantee of 70 per cent.

The guarantees are given to persuade banks to lend to small businesses even if they cannot offer sufficient security.

The government also offers grants to businesses through the Single Regeneration Budget (to assist areas of unemployment) and through Training and Enterprise Council schemes and projects.

Obtaining semi-permanent or permanent capital

Traditionally, the only way in which a small business could expand was for the owner to continually plough back all the profits, year after year. An alternative was to take a partner or become a private limited company and issue shares to a selected number of shareholders (often the original owner's family) to gain increased permanent capital.

A medium-sized businesses may seriously consider floating the company on the Stock Exchange – thereby becoming a public limited company. Because shares can now be sold to the public the capital can be vastly increased. The company has a choice between issuing ordinary or preference shares.

- **Ordinary shares** are the most common type of share. **Dividends** are paid on these only after other classes of shareholders have been paid. The dividend will vary – if profits are good, then the dividend may be generous, conversely no dividend may be paid at all in a poor year.

  All ordinary shareholders have one vote per share, except those holding a special class of ordinary share called 'A' shares who have no vote. 'A' shares are slowly being phased out.

- **Preference shares** have a higher claim in relation to the payment of dividends. The rate of dividend is usually fixed. Dividends can be deferred if the company has a poor year, but most preference shares these days are **cumulative** which means the holders have a later claim to unpaid dividends when the company is more successful. **Participating** preference shares enable holders to obtain additional dividends in a very good year. If the company goes into liquidation, preferential shareholders will receive repayment before ordinary shareholders.

An existing public limited company can raise additional capital by

- a **rights issue** – when additional shares are offered to existing shareholders at a discount – usually in proportion to their existing share holding

- issuing preference shares – which increases capital without giving shareholders any voting rights

- calling up **uncalled capital** from a previous share issue. Often shareholders pay in tranches, or instalments, eg 20p on application, 30p on allotment of the shares, 25p first call and 25p second call

- issuing **debentures** – these are *not* shares but long-term loans to a company. Debenture holders receive a fixed rate of **interest,** *not* a dividend. Interest is paid to debenture holders before dividends are calculated on shares. Usually the risk factor is very low as most debentures are secured against company assets. In addition, in the case of the company failing, the debenture holders will have a higher claim on any remaining assets than shareholders.

Spurred on to a rights issue

Raising capital through rights issues is not just restricted to ordinary business organisations. Tottenham Hotspur was one of the few football clubs to have a Stock Exchange quotation – and then raised £11 million through a rights issue to build a new North Stand at White Hart Lane. The money was also being used to reduce the club's £5.8 million debts although the Chairman, Alan Sugar, stated publicly that no cash would be used to buy players. The rights issue was a one-for-four issue and was priced at 270p per share. At the time of writing the shares are trading at about 325p.

Discussion point

Read the article on the Spurs rights issue carefully. As a group, can you answer the questions that follow?

1 What does the phrase 'one-for-four issue' mean?

2 How much discount are existing shareholders being allowed?

3 What will happen to the **gearing** (see below) of Tottenham Hotspur after the issue?

4 Is the rights issue being used to increase working capital or fixed capital? Give a reason for your answer.

● The ability to borrow

Whilst nearly all business organisations need to borrow money from time to time to increase capital, financial institutions normally prefer to lend money to large, profitable companies with a good track record because the risk of not being repaid is low. For this reason, small organisations, such as sole traders and partnerships, may find it both difficult and expensive to borrow any money they need. Public limited companies have the most choice of all – as they can increase *either* their **share capital** (by issuing more shares) or their **loan capital** (by borrowing).

The ratio between share capital and loan capital is known as **gearing.** A company which is highly geared is one which has a greater proportion of loan capital than share capital. Usually high gearing is viewed with suspicion in the UK as there are fears the organisation may be over-stretching itself and be very vulnerable to interest rates increases. Interestingly, the opposite often applies in the United States!

Financial institutions

In the UK the main financial institutions which provide finance for businesses are

- **commercial** (or high street) **banks**

- **investment banks** (previously known as merchant banks)

- **finance houses** – specialist institutions, lending money to individuals and businesses. Their services usually include hire purchase, leasing, factoring and other loans.

Other organisations which are classed as being part of the financial sector, but which are not directly involved in making loans to businesses include the Bank of England (the central bank), the **Stock Exchange** and building societies. Insurance companies, pension fund managers, unit and investment trusts all invest in business organisations, mainly by buying shares on the Stock Exchange. You may remember you met these in chapter 1, under the term **institutional investors.**

The Old Lady of Threadneedle Street

This is the nickname given to the Bank of England – the **central bank.** All countries have a central bank which usually monitors government economic and monetary policy as well as acting as a bank to the government. This means that all tax revenues find their way to the Bank of England and all government payments are made from the same source – from state pensions to the salaries of civil servants.

The Bank of England also maintains the accounts of all the British high street banks and adjusts their balances after all the daily transactions between them have been completed. The Bank is responsible for issuing bank notes and distributing new notes and coins to the high street banks.

It manages the country's reserves of gold and foreign exchange and may help to support the exchange rate by itself buying and selling sterling. Finally, it also helps the government to raise money by borrowing, both on a short-term basis from financial institutions and on a long-term basis by issuing **gilt-edged shares** (see below) on the Stock Exchange.

Commercial banks

You probably know commercial or retail banks better by their everyday name of 'high street banks'. The main four banks are Barclays, Lloyds, Midland and NatWest but there are others too – including the Royal Bank of Scotland, Co-operative Bank and Yorkshire Bank – together with several building societies which have recently become banks – such as the Abbey National.

You are probably well aware of the services retail banks give to private customers. However the services they offer to businesses include facilities not usually required by individuals. Figure 3.2 gives details of these

---

The holding of money and valuables
- Current accounts and investment (interest-bearing) accounts
- Safe-deposit boxes

The transferring of money – at home
- Cheque, debit card and credit card
- Direct debit, standing order and credit transfer
- The issue of bankers' drafts
- Automated teller machines (ATMs) and cash points

The transferring of money overseas
- Foreign exchange dealings for importers and exporters
- Payment services for importers and exporters

Business services
- Credit rating and credit worthiness
- Economic information – at home and abroad
- Guides to importing and exporting
- Advice to small businesses
- Insurance services
- Leasing and contract-hire finance
- Factoring services

Investment and other services
- Advice on acquisitions, mergers and takeovers
- Investment management advice on surplus funds and cashflow
- Buying and selling stocks and shares

Credit services
- Business start-up and development loans
- Overdraft facilities
- Finance packages for international transactions

Figure 3.2 Retail bank services

services. By now, you should understand most of the terms used, though one or two others need a word of explanation.

Bankers' drafts

These are cheques made out on the bank itself and are used for large payments when the credit worthiness of the buyer is not known. The bank issues its own cheque to an account holder and then transfers the money out of the holder's account and into the bank's own account. This guarantees payment to the seller.

Import and export finance and assistance

There are more risks in dealing with overseas buyers and sellers than those in this country.

Exporting risks include the danger of not getting paid by the buyer, the problem of the exchange rate moving against the seller, the difficulties of providing credit to overseas purchasers and of financing the production of large items until a later date when payment is received.

Banks will undertake credit terms, advise on payment terms, offer credit to exporters in addition to ordinary loans, organise payment documentation (such as Letters of Credit or Bills of Exchange) and help firms to manage foreign exchange rate risks. One method of doing this is to arrange a **forward exchange rate** for future currency exchange where the price for the exchange is agreed at a fixed rate for a particular date in the future.

Importing risks and problems include the danger of dealing with unknown suppliers, organising import licences and checking any quota restrictions, paying import VAT or arranging concessions, arranging freight and insurance for the goods and paying the supplier.

Banks can organise a range of methods to guarantee payment to the foreign seller which may mean that discounts are available for the buyer. The bank can also help with shipping and import documentation.

 Check it yourself

All the major banks give assistance and advice to importers and exporters. Both Barclays and NatWest issue a *Guide to Importing and Exporting* which is worth obtaining for further information.

Investment banks

Until quite recently these banks were known as merchant banks. However, during the last few years most large commercial banks have undertaken investment activities and the distinction between the two types of banks is now less distinct.

Traditionally, investment banks were involved in higher levels of corporate (ie business) finance such as new share issues, acquisitions, takeovers and mergers. The investment bank will help a company which wishes to take over another to assess its value and make an offer. Equally, it will help a company to defend itself from a hostile takeover bid by another organisation.

Investment banks will give advice on new issues of shares or rights issues and may underwrite or guarantee the issue by agreeing to buy up any unsold shares itself. They will advise on the pricing of shares. A public company which requires additional finance would approach an investment bank for advice on whether to increase loan or share capital – and the best way to do this.

Finally, investment banks give advice on managing any surplus funds – for instance the very large funds amassed in company pension funds, taking into account tax implications. They can offer investment advice which covers most worldwide financial markets.

The changing role of building societies

Building societies are traditionally **friendly societies** – mutually owned by savers and borrowers. Their main function has been to make loans to members for house purchases. The Building Societies Act of 1986 gave societies the opportunity to convert into public limited companies and into banks if they so wished. The Abbey National took this route in 1989 and the Halifax intends to become a plc in 1997 – with the aim of becoming Britain's third largest high street bank. In 1996 two other societies gave notice of their intention to convert to a plc –

the Woolwich and the Alliance and Leicester. Becoming a bank removes restrictions in raising capital from the stock market and allows the societies, so they claim, to become increasingly competitive by extending their range of products and services. However, the Consumers Association disputes this claim and says that banks traditionally give poorer returns to investors than building societies because the latter do not have to pay dividends to shareholders – which reduces the amount available to pay interest to account holders.

Discussion point

As a group, discuss the differences between the needs of individuals and the needs of business organisations in relation to financial services.

Which type of financial institution do you think is most beneficial to each type of customer – and why?

The London Stock Exchange

Although the Stock Exchange does not itself provide finance for businesses, its role in the business economy of the country is too important to be ignored. The Stock Exchange is simply a market where stocks and shares are traded. Its existence enables the conflicting objectives of business organisations and investors to be reconciled. Organisations want permanent, reliable capital which they can use to finance the businesses. However, investors wish to lend money on a temporary basis, so that they can recall their funds if necessary. The Stock Exchange enables shares to change hands from one investor to another without the organisation ever becoming involved.

The main categories of stocks and shares include

* **ordinary** and **preference shares**

* **gilt-edged shares** (more often known as 'gilts'). These are loans to the UK government which carry a fixed rate of interest and are usually repaid on a specific date. The reason for their name is simply because, in times of old, the name of the shares was recorded in a book edged with gilt!

Today all share dealings take place by computer using an electronic dealing system called SEAQ (Stock Exchange Automated Quotations). This has enabled individuals to buy shares from share shops and banks as easily as they would buy anything else. This system is to be replaced by SEQUENCE – a technologically more advanced system.

Stock exchange prices for the largest companies are printed every day in several newspapers. The entries are easy to follow and give up-to-date information on whether individual shares are rising or falling (see Figure 3.3). An overall measure is given by the *Financial Times* Stock Exchange (FT-SE) 100 index which gives the daily rate based on the performance of the 100 leading companies in Britain.

Variations in share price

Shares rise and fall depending on demand and supply. If more shares are being sold than bought, then the price will fall. Conversely, if there is strong

Share price information appears on the financial pages of several daily newspapers. It is grouped under headings such as Building and Construction, Household Goods, Insurance, Media, Pharmaceuticals, etc. This helps you to find company shares more easily and to compare the performance of companies operating in the same sector.

Below is shown the entry for Lloyds TSB shares for 16 August 1996 with explanations for the different headings.

52 week			Price		Yield	
High	Low	Company	(p)	+/−	(%)	P/E
365	$294\frac{1}{2}$	Lloyds TSB	$359\frac{1}{2}$xd	$+5\frac{1}{2}$	4.2%	15.2

High   365p is the highest price the share has reached over the past 52 weeks

Low $294\frac{1}{2}$p is the lowest price the share has reached over the past 52 weeks

Company The name of the quoted organisation

Price   The average or mid-price of the shares yesterday. The letters 'xd' stand for 'ex dividend'. They tell potential buyers that the next dividend is due to be paid and, for administration purposes, will be paid to existing holders of the shares not new buyers, who will have to wait until the next dividend payment.

+/−   The increase or decrease on share value from the previous day. Lloyds TSB shares increased by $5\frac{1}{2}$p yesterday.

Yield   This is the **true** rate of return for investors – calculated by expressing the latest dividend price as a percentage of the current market price. Investors can see from this that the current return on Lloyds TSB shares is 4.2 per cent and can compare this with current bank or building society rates. The dividend alone does *not* give this type of indication. Dividends are quoted in pence per share based on the nominal (issued) price of the shares, eg 6.5p. Quite obviously, this return would be excellent if the shares had only cost you 50p, but very poor if the shares had cost you £3 each. This is why the yield is so important.

P/E   This is the price/earnings ratio and indicates whether a share is expensive or not. It does this by comparing the price of the shares with the company gross profit. By this means an investor can see that Lloyds TSB is a better buy than Barclays, whose P/E on the same day was 9.9. You can really only compare companies in the same line of business as the ratios may be very different in another sector.

Figure 3.3 Share price information

demand for a share, its price will rise. If the overall price of shares is rising then this is known as a **bull market.** If the price of shares is falling generally, then this is called a **bear market.**

Individual shares may increase in value if investors believe a company is doing well and will pay a good dividend – as this will increase the demand for shares. The value will also increase if the company has published good annual results or if it is subject to a takeover bid. Other factors can also influence trading in shares particularly if an event occurs which could affect their profit figures. In a severe winter, for instance, the shares of insurance companies may be marked down as it is likely that paying out increased claims will adversely affect their profits.

Laura Ashley goes for growth

The Laura Ashley chain of women's clothing and home furnishings stores had a disastrous year in 1994/5 with a loss of £31 million. However, new chief executive Ann Iverson turned this into a profit of £10.3 million after only seven months with the company. Not content with this success she and her finance director, James Walsh, intend to restructure the company by reducing the number of lines held by the stores, expand store sizes and open more stores in the United States. Goods would be sold through wholesaling, franchising, licensing and mail order.

Her plans for expansion will cost the group £9.2 million and to meet the demand for new capital the group has obtained a loan of up to £50 million to meet both capital expenditure and working capital needs.

This did not depress shares, however. With sales up to £336.6 million last year, shareholders were rewarded by a dividend of 0.5p and shares closed at 177p yesterday – their highest level for the past nine years.

Finance and computers – a look to the future

Most people have heard of telephone banking. However, banks predict that the system of the future will be **virtual banking** where all transactions are carried out by computers linked to the information highway.

In the Stock Exchange electronic trading has been a feature for several years. However, in early 1997 a new computer share settlement system called CREST will come into operation – with traditional paper share certificates replaced by entries on computer disks.

AIMing to please

AIM is a new Stock Exchange market, set up in June 1995, for the shares of very small companies. Businesses with a quotation on the **Alternative Investment Market** range from the Trocadero (the leisure and entertainment business) to Pet City (a range of pet superstores) and Celtic Football Club! La Senza, a lingerie and underwear retailer, used AIM to finance the opening of more than 100 new shops across Britain. In 11 months over 140 firms had joined AIM.

The idea is that small companies are not limited to raising capital through bank loans, overdrafts and venture capital. There is the minimum of regulations to encourage companies to join. Their accounts must conform to UK or US standards and each company must retain an adviser nominated by AIM. But no minimum size or trading record is required and neither does the company have to sell a set percentage of shares to the public – therefore the owners can retain overall control if they wish.

For investors, AIM shares are more of a gamble than other shares and values can change considerably. AIM shares may also be harder to sell – however, any investor brave enough to have put money into the first 10 companies to join would have made a profit of over 100 per cent in 12 months!

Discussion point

As a group, select about 10 or 12 shares to follow. Choose your own companies – but try to include one or two of your larger local organisations. Then subscribe to a newspaper either every day for a week, or on selected days over a month and chart the progress of your shares. Try to see which reported events are affecting their value. You could even find out which of you would make the most money as an investor!

• Insurance companies

Everyone has heard of insurance companies – you may have taken out an insurance policy yourself to cover a holiday, perhaps. If you are a driver, then you need insurance by law. Other types of insurance policies cover buildings and contents. Many people also have life assurance policies such as an endowment policy which is paid out at the end of a fixed term or on the event of death, if this takes place within the term.

Insurance is usually sold by **insurance brokers,** who will 'shop around' for their clients, advise on the best policy to buy and make any claims on their behalf. Brokers receive a commission from the insurance companies for each policy they sell or renew. Today some insurance companies will only sell their services direct to the public as they say this makes them more competitive (eg Direct Line).

However, many individuals find themselves buying insurance through **agents.** These are organisations which sell insurance as one of their services – travel agents sell travel insurance, estate agents offer buildings insurance and life policies, car distributors sell motor insurance and so on. Again the sellers receive a commission for their services which in some cases (such as estate agents) may be quite substantial.

Business organisations need a wide variety of insurance without which they could not afford to operate. Some are legal requirements (such as motor insurance), in other cases businesses simply could not afford to run the risks of trading without some form of protection.

The idea of insurance is similar to the National Lottery – except in the case of insurance, it is the losers who benefit and not the winners! Quite simply, the insurance premiums are used to compensate those who suffer a financial loss from the risk against which they insured. Risks are calculated, using statistical information, by an **actuary.** Anything where the risk can be calculated can be insured – from injury to a tennis star's legs to the chances of it raining and ruining a garden fete!

Businesses are likely to cover their buildings and contents against disasters – as well as any vehicles they own. They will also cover any of their employees who travel abroad on business. Other types of insurance taken out by businesses include the following.

- **Employers' liability insurance** is the most important type as it is compulsory by law. All employees must be protected against injury or disease – for instance, a machine operator being injured because a machine has not been maintained.

- **Public liability insurance** covers risk of injury to people or damage to property because of negligence or carelessness by the organisation or its employees. The event can be as simple as a company driver backing into someone's garden wall and as wide-ranging as an explosion at a chemical factory which destroys nearby property.

- **Fire insurance.** In most cases this covers 'special perils' such as damage by water or flood, malicious damage, etc. It is usually linked to business interruption insurance to cover the loss of earnings which occur when the company is re-organising its offices and production facilities after a disaster.

- **Theft.** This relates only to theft where there has been forcible entry. Shop-lifting *cannot* be covered by an insurance policy. Theft policies can be extended to include collusion by employees and **fidelity guarantee** – a special policy to cover employees who handle large amounts of money. The employee must be prosecuted for a claim to be made – otherwise, of course, the owner could be in collusion over the theft.

- **Engineering insurance** is a specialised class which relates to large machines and equipment such as engines, lifts and cranes. A policy would generally cover the cost of replacement. Damage and injury caused to others is more likely to be covered under employee liability or public liability insurance.

- **Goods and cash in transit.** Both can be covered by insurance. Goods in transit only relates to the transportation of goods within Britain. Cash in transit insurance is not required if a security company such as Securicor is hired, as the service usually includes such cover.

- **Credit insurance** may be taken out on financial transactions if there is a risk that the company will not receive payment.

- **Specialised insurance.** Special classes include those of aviation and marine insurance. The first is only used by those who own an airplane or work in the aviation business; the second is used to cover exports by sea in case the goods are lost in transit and more extensively by shipping owners to cover other risks, such as damage to the ship or other hazards. Ironically, goods carried by air are still usually covered by marine insurance, rather than aviation insurance!

When a loss is suffered, the policy holder completes a claim form which describes the loss and usually receives compensation from the insurance company. In the case of large claims an assessor is appointed to judge whether the value of the claim is accurate.

Discussion point

You are an actuary working out whether an 18-year-old male student, with a powerful car, who lives in a city and keeps his car on the road has a greater chance of making an insurance claim than a 48-year-old teacher who runs a small car, lives in a rural area and locks up his car in a garage every night.

Now state who you think should pay the lower premium.

No prizes for the correct answer!

Petted as an insurer

The idea of insuring domestic pets against vet bills was thought laughable by large insurance companies in 1976. So Patsy Bloom set up her own business with a partner David Simpson. Both put up £250 and formed Pet Plan Insurance. She started by insuring the pets of friends but the business soon grew to the point where 400,000 policy holders were on its books, paying a total of £40 million a year in premiums. In 1995 the company had expanded to the point where major resourcing was required and Patsy Bloom had the option of floating the company on the stock market or selling out. She chose the latter – selling the company to Cornhill Insurance for £32.5 million. However, both Patsy Bloom and David Simpson

will stay with the company working as key members of the management team.

Patsy Bloom was named as Business Woman of the Year in 1993 for her success. However, she considers that many people do not realise how hard she had to work for her achievements and cautions anyone wanting to follow in her footsteps that setting up in business with £250 of borrowed money would be virtually impossible today.

The principles of insurance

Anyone taking out insurance is well advised to be aware of the six principles of insurance as these determine the situations which must prevail for payments to be made.

1 Insurable interest

I cannot insure your car and you cannot insure mine! Why? Because neither of us will suffer financial loss if anything happened to the other's property or possessions. It would obviously be against the public interest for this to be allowed (as I could damage your car in order to benefit). You can therefore only insure an item if you have insurable interest in it, ie you will personally suffer financial loss if the event occurs.

Insurable interest in relation to *people* is more complicated. You only have an insurable interest in someone if you will suffer a financial loss if they die. Usually insurance companies restrict this to married couples, partners who live together (but not always) and business partners. Parents cannot normally take out cover to be paid to *them* if anything happens to their children. They would obviously suffer a huge emotional loss if anything happened to their offspring but whether they would suffer a financial loss is much more debatable. The problem of 'against the public interest' would also apply.

2 Utmost good faith

The premiums for an insurance policy are calculated from the details given on the proposal form. It is therefore vital that these details are accurate in every respect. It is also held to be vital that all information relating to claims is completely accurate. The insurance company also has a similar obligation in relation to its clients.

These two principles apply to *all* insurance policies – including life policies.

3 Indemnity

If you were out for an evening with friends and a stranger nudged your arm, causing you to spill your drink on the floor, you might well expect that social courtesy demands the stranger buys you another drink. An insurance company, however, would assess how much you had in your glass at the time the accident occurred and simply refill it to that level! This is the principle of **indemnity** – the aim of insurance is to restore you to the position you were in before the event occurred – not to make you better off!

The principle of indemnity can obviously not apply to life policies – you can hardly be 'restored to your previous position'! For that reason, because life and death are certainties, rather than risks, policies for life cover are called **assurance** rather than insurance.

4 Contribution

You may find that inadvertently one item is covered on more than one insurance policy. In the home, for instance, freezers may be bought with a breakdown policy which includes damage to food if it defrosts. However, such an item may also form part of a house contents policy. In this case, the companies would both contribute towards the claim – in the ratio which relates to the cover and premiums on each.

5 Subrogation

A little-known principle is the fact that once you have received payment from an insurance company, the item which has been paid for then belongs to them. If a child lost her bike, her parents claimed for it and after receiving the cheque the bike was found by the police, technically the bike now belongs to the company. Insurance companies are not particularly interested in having old bikes returned to them! However, in the case of large claims, their attitude would be different!

6 Proximate cause

This is the substance of most exclusion clauses to be found in the small print of insurance policies! The principle states that payment will be made only if the most immediate (or proximate) cause of the disaster was the one covered by the policy. To give an example, a householder covers his house against storm damage. During a storm, lightning strikes a nearby tree which then falls on the house. An insurance company may refuse to pay out on the basis that the immediate cause of the damage was the tree, not the storm. Whether or not the householder is covered for damage caused by falling trees would now be the main issue.

The Names at Lloyd's of London

Lloyd's of London is one of the most famous insurance organisations in the world. It is unique in that it operates in a different way from standard insurance companies and will also take on expensive risks, such as giving cover to shipping tankers and jumbo jets.

In reality there is no such company as 'Lloyd's'. The corporation provides the facilities for Lloyd's members to transact insurance business on behalf of their own **syndicates.** A syndicate is a group of members with similar interests who specialise in the same type of insurance business. The members of the syndicates are called

Names – who personally underwrite (or guarantee) policies between them. Neither the syndicates, nor the Names, deal directly with the public who must take out a policy with Lloyd's through a Lloyd's broker.

Names have **unlimited liability** for their debts – and this has caused severe problems at Lloyd's in the last few years. A rush of expensive claims – totalling £8 billion – meant that several Names were left in the situation where they could not afford to pay their debts so were virtually bankrupt. To cope with the problem, it is likely that Lloyd's will undergo considerable reorganisation by the end of 1996.

Discussion point

The government has stated that the insurance industry could do more to prevent industrial pollution by increasing premiums for those companies which ignore environmental risks. Fifty of the world's leading insurance companies have already signed a statement pledging their commitment to this idea. They are concerned, in particular, about climatic changes caused by pollution. Between 1987 and 1993 over US$1 billion was paid out because of environmental catastrophes – mainly connected to windstorms.

1   Traditionally, businesses have never taken into account social costs when costing their products. What are social costs? (If you need help, look back to page 53.)

2   State three products where the price would increase if social costs were taken into consideration.

3   As a group, think of at least three actions a company could take which would lead to it being classed as environmentally friendly.

4   Debate whether or not you agree that the environmental behaviour of firms should be left to the control of insurance companies or be under direct government control. Try to think about the advantages and disadvantages in each case.

5   Think of one disaster which could occur to either a business organisation or a private individual which would be classed as an environment-related catastrophe. Then work through the principles of insurance, seeing how each would apply in this particular case.

External agencies and consultancies

There is a range of agencies and businesses in existence with the sole aim of providing services to other business organisations. These include

- employment and recruitment agencies

- public relations, advertising and market research companies

- computer services and consultants

- management consultants

- other service providers – from security firms to catering organisations.

Employment and recruitment agencies

These may be used for recruitment for different types of vacancy within the organisation. Agencies fall into three main categories.

1   Those that specialise in executive and management recruitment (often known as **recruitment consultants**).

2   **Employment agencies** specialise in a variety of fields from engineering to accounting and insurance. Most frequently, agencies deal with office and administrative vacancies.

3   Government agencies including the **Job Centre** (for adults) and the **Careers Office** (for young people).

Recruitment consultants

You can read advertisements placed by this type of consultants in newspapers such as *The Sunday Times* every week. They are often identified by the phrase 'our client' at the start of the advertisement.

Such consultants are often used to recruit high flyers or top-level executives. If no one suitable is on their books, then they may **'head hunt'** a suitable candidate to find out if he or she is interested in changing job. This means trying to tempt a particular person to take a job, even though he or she may not have made a formal application.

Such consultants are not cheap, but reduce the costs of advertising and wasting time sifting through unsuitable applications. They can be extremely useful when a key top appointment is being made as the agency can advise on suitable personnel on its books – and some others who are not!

Employment agencies

These are the standard agencies found in every town and city. They usually advertise vacancies in their windows and in the press and will handle both temporary and permanent vacancies. Some specialise in providing certain types of staff, eg accounting staff, administrative and clerical staff or manual staff. Others are more general and will handle a wide range of vacancies.

'**Temps**' are contracted by the agency and paid by them at a lower rate than that charged to the client. The difference is the agency profit. It does mean, however, that the contract of employment is between the temp and the agency and this saves the company from any legal complications relating to employment rights when taking on and laying off temporary staff.

Permanent staff can also be hired through an agency. The agency will advertise the vacancy, **short-list** suitable applicants and liaise with the company about interview arrangements. The fee charged to the company is usually a percentage of the annual starting salary.

All reputable agencies set aptitude and/or skill tests for both temporary and permanent staff on their books and check the validity of their qualifications.

The advantages of using an agency are the time and money saved in advertising and short-listing. However, fees are quite high and unless an excellent reputable agency is on a company's doorstep it might be more cost effective to use them for temporary office staff rather than for permanent staff.

Job Centres and Careers Offices

Job Centres handle a variety of vacancies, though these are apt to be mainly for semi-skilled and manual workers. These are advertised on cards in the Job Centre window and in the centre itself. The Job Centre will also handle the distribution and receipt of large-scale applications for organisations, for instance an organisation requiring a large number of seasonal workers or a company relocating to a new area.

The Careers Office also advertises vacancies on its premises, usually only for 16–19-year-olds. The Careers Office will also give advice and information to employers on any training schemes in operation, such as the Youth Training Scheme or Modern Apprenticeship Scheme and help to recruit suitable candidates for places.

Surf the Net for a job!

Online recruitment is the buzz-word for the 1990s! If you have access to the Internet, then you could use cyberspace to become employed! Job-seekers register by submitting their CV to Worknet – which also receives employer vacancies and matches the two. A human resource manager can be looking over CVs within a day of advertising the vacancy. Traditional employment agencies aim to follow suit – Reed Accountancy is one, with its secretarial division, Reed Employment, about to follow.

Public relations, advertising and market research companies

These agencies are concerned with providing a specialist service to augment the basic marketing skills possessed by company employees. It is one thing to ask marketing staff to draft a small advertisement for the local paper, but quite another to ask them to orchestrate a multi-million-pound advertising campaign which includes TV and press adverts with an accompanying promotional campaign!

Public relations

The latest term to describe public relations (PR) people – particularly in politics – is **spin doctors.** Their job is to convert any problem into an opportunity by selling the right angles and the benefits to the public. Therefore, if a party wins an election campaign, its spin doctor will give all the arguments why it won so easily, how this is a sign of the times, etc. If it loses, then the spin doctor will say that this is a mere blip, that it is not indicative of future events, etc!

In relation to a business organisation, PR people are involved to obtain free publicity in the media by capitalising on anything that is newsworthy and putting this over to the outside world in the best way possible for the company. They will also arrange press conferences, brief the media, prepare press releases, organise photo sessions and ensure that the company is kept permanently to the fore in the minds of all its stakeholders.

They are involved in company **image** – both its creation and maintenance. In the case of a company disaster they are absolutely essential. **Crisis management** can be a key area for business organisations and the role of a good spin doctor can mean the difference between a permanently tarnished image and a minor problem that the public quickly forgets!

Perrier 2, Hoover 0

A massive disaster shook Perrier, the bottled mineral water company, to the roots when a faulty machine contaminated thousands of bottles of water with benzene in 1990. Only after the bottles were on sale was the problem discovered. Perrier risked losing everything – its sales in the short term and, more importantly in the long term, its reputation for high standards and reliability as a top brand.

Perrier acted fast. All its bottles were recalled despite the cost, customer hotlines were set up and spin doctors were employed to give daily bulletins to the media. Today the incident has largely been forgotten and Perrier sales are threatened more by increasing competition than memory of the disaster.

In contrast, Hoover ran into serious trouble when it advertised free flights to the USA with sales of many of its products. The demand for flights completely outstripped forecasts so that Hoover simply could not cope. Many customers were turned down or 'fobbed off' with a myriad of qualifying difficulties. When the story hit the media Hoover was still in disarray and kept denying there was any problem at all. Matters went from bad to worse until its American parent company stepped in to sort out the mess – and has since 'sold off' Hoover to another organisation. Many people remember the Hoover problem and would be loathe to trust the company if ever it launched another 'special offer' on to the market.

Discussion point

1 In what way do you think Hoover's image has been affected by the debacle over the free flights?

2 Whose sales do you think will be affected most in the long term – Perrier's or Hoover's – and why?

3 Hoover made a classic mistake when it 'denied there was a crisis'. According to most PR gurus, all disasters should be acknowledged immediately with an apology and a clear statement of the action to be taken. If you had been the company's PR consultant on the first day, what would you have done and why? Discuss your answers with your tutor.

4 Some writers consider that PR people in general and spin doctors in particular are overpaid professionals simply employed to deceive the public. To what extent do you agree with this view and why?

Advertising agencies

There are many famous advertising agencies employed by well-known companies such as Levi, Coca-Cola, Heinz and Heineken to conceive and co-ordinate their advertising campaigns. In advertising jargon the client is known as an **account** and an account manager is the executive who supervises the operation of the account. He or she acts as liaison between the agency and client and organises his or her creative team to produce the materials required.

The 'materials' can be anything from a basic advertisement to a full-blown media campaign to promote a new company. The agency will plan and buy the space required – whether booking slots for TV advertisements or space for press adverts, produce storyboards which convey the theme of any filmed adverts to the customers, organise the production of the advertising copy or film and then monitor the results of the campaign on product sales.

The agency earns its money both by charging its clients a fee for its services and by obtaining commission from the media owners for the 'space' it books – whether on TV, radio or in the press.

Clients' accounts are worth a lot of money. When British Airways abandoned its 12-year association with Saatchi and Saatchi (now called Codiant) and moved its account to 'New Saatchi' – the agency created by Maurice Saatchi – Codiant lost revenue estimated at approximately £7 million. The Mars account, also originally at Codiant, was valued at about £30 million and that has also been moved. No wonder Codiant's shares fell during 1995.

To sell or not to sell?

Each year the world's leading advertising agencies compete for their own top awards. The irony is that the advertisements which win the industry's own awards often appear to result in lower sales of the products!

Guinness, Mazda and Mercury were all examples of campaigns which apparently failed to work on the customer – Guinness lost 25 per cent of its market share to rivals, Mazda sales fell by 15 per cent and Mercury profits slumped in 1995 – despite all their campaigns winning awards for the advertisement or the company responsible.

Brand managers argued that many agencies were more concerned with clever campaigns to win awards than selling the product. Not surprisingly the leading agencies did not agree. John Bartle, of Bartle Bogle Hegarty, gave examples of a variety of successful campaigns which had won awards, including Levi's jeans, British Airways and Haagen-Dazs, all of which resulted in increased sales.

Market research companies

Market research companies are in the business of assisting organisations to find out more precisely

- the profile of their key customers
- what the key customers think of their product (or service)
- what the key customers want in future products
- details of the total market for their product
- consumer views on competitors' products
- the results of advertising campaigns.

The industry has its own professional association, known as the Market Research Society.

Independent market research organisations exist because it is usually uneconomic for even a large organisation to undertake its own market research – and impossible for a small or medium-sized business. Market research is not usually a constant requirement of a company. It may be required because sales of one product are falling or because the company is reviewing its product range. Not only are a large amount of up-to-date data and statistics required but also the compilation of questionnaires and undertaking of client surveys demands specialist skills. In addition, there is the added problem of deciding upon which sector of the public to interview to obtain a **representative sample** of views and making contact with enough people to obtain a valid sample. Too few people in total, or too few people of one age or income group can skew the **survey** and give an inaccurate result. Many major agencies have large computer databases of volunteer respondents and will also use the latest technology to help them to analyse the large number of replies quickly and accurately.

Many advertising agencies and management consultancies (see page 122) have market research experts. Other specialist companies concentrate on either particular types of research, such as telephone surveys, or large-scale mail shots with incentives for respondents. Virtually everyone has heard of MORI which specialises in opinion polls. BARB and JICTAR are concerned with audience research for the media and Neilson concentrates on the food and pharmaceuticals industries. Other famous names include Verdict Research, Mintel and ICM.

Check it yourself

The DTI and the Association of British Market Research Companies have produced a free introductory guide to market research. Called *The Information You Need to Win,* you can obtain a copy by ringing (0171) 510 0144 quoting reference 96/529. This will tell you all about market research!

£66,000 to keep YOU each year!

Recent research by ASDA, the supermarket chain, revealed that parents spend, on average, £24,461 on each child aged between 16 and 21. At the top of the scale a teenager can cost up to £66,190. The 'lowest cost' teenagers who leave school at 16, get a job and contribute to their own upkeep still cost £7,659. But this figure does not apply to anyone still in full-time education.

Where does the money go? On supporting students at college and university, paying for driving lessons, an extensive social life and . . . clothes!

Teenagers spend twice the national average on clothes – and boys spend more than girls. Most cannot pay for everything themselves so ask their parents for more.

So why did ASDA do this research? Because it knows that it is still profitable to appeal to teenagers to spend money. With each person spending an average of £5,463 on food, £570 on toiletries, £1,815 on clothes and £850 on birthday gifts each year, that's a fair-sized market in anybody's book!

Computer services and computer consultants

Computer services may be provided by an in-house department or hired externally. A medium- or large-size company is more likely to have its own computer services department whereas this would obviously not be cost effective for a small firm. However, in the case of a specialist installation or upgrading – or the solving of a particular problem – even a large organisation may call in the expert skills of a specialist consultant.

The aim of any computer services organisation – whether internal or external – is to provide expert advice and technical skills in relation to

- the purchase and installation of a new computer system

- the expansion or upgrading of an existing computer system

- advice on software – or tailor-made programs written for the business itself

- support and maintenance of the system – both hardware and software

- training for staff

- problem-solving.

Specialist consultancies exist to deal with problems occurring on large-scale **networks** or in relation to virus detection. Many businesses would literally cease to function if their computer systems were off-line for any length of time, so the cost of paying an outside specialist to solve the problem quickly is normally considered excellent value for money.

On a more routine basis, computer services will be involved in the purchase and maintenance of equipment – both the hardware and software. Many organisations today link their personal computers (PCs) by means of a network. Setting up the network, installing the software and providing

When the chips are down

Some computer services organisations specialise in disaster recovery – from data stored on disks which have corrupted (when nobody bothered to take a back-up copy!) to those ruined by a virus program or by a faulty hard drive. In one famous example an author had virtually finished a book when his hard drive crashed. No hard copies were available nor back-up copies of his work. In panic he sent his disks to a specialist company. They managed to retrieve 85 per cent of his work.

guidance for users is the obvious first stage, but ongoing maintenance work is essential for it to continue to operate effectively. As the needs of the users change or increase then it will be up to computer services to analyse how best their needs can be met by the system and the ways in which the network will need adapting.

Management consultants

Management consultancies are specialist organisations which employ highly qualified managers or accountants who are both professionally qualified and have several years' experience in industry. Any organisation that is experiencing a problem or difficulty outside its own area of expertise can then hire the services of the consultants to analyse the problem in detail and produce a report which recommends the best course of action to take.

A benefit of employing outsiders is that they are less personally involved and may find problems easier to identify – a case of 'the onlooker seeing most of the game'. If the report is adopted by the company, then the consultants may 'move in' to implement their own recommendations.

Some management consultants are 'multi-purpose' and can undertake a variety of work. Others are more specialist and are concerned mainly with marketing or financial aspects of business. Overall consultants cover virtually every business area including

- **management** – corporate strategy and objectives, writing a mission statement, planning and forecasting, organisation structures and restructuring, mergers and demergers, takeovers and acquisitions

- **marketing** – market research, advertising and promotion policies, pricing, product evaluation and exporting strategies

- **finance** – advice on financial structure and investment policy, acquiring capital, controlling cashflow, costing systems, budgets and budgetary control

- **human resources** – personnel policies, recruitment and promotion policies, health and safety procedures, job evaluation systems, reward schemes, management development and training schemes, manpower planning, industrial relations

- **production** – factory layout and machine utilisation, production planning and control, quality systems, purchasing systems and stock control, productivity schemes

- **administration** – introduction and development of systems and procedures, monitoring and control, information flows, customer service

- **information technology** systems and systems developments; telecommunications and data flows; program design and development

- **advising on regulation and privatisation issues.** This is a new area for management consultants, but a very profitable one. Many consultants such as Coopers & Lybrand have contracts with regulatory bodies, eg OFGAS, OFFER and OFWAT, all of which are expected to spend over £2 million each on consultancy fees during 1996/7.

Management consultants are not a cheap option. The cost of the average consultant is at least £500 a day with top experts commanding more than that each hour! However, their input can be invaluable as they are more likely to view the organisation dispassionately and be less concerned with office politics or the feelings of individual managers or executives. The main challenge for the company, however, is to sustain the changes introduced by the consultants after they have left.

Calling Miss Selfridge

McKinseys, the strategy management consultancy, was hired to help improve the Miss Selfridge chain. The problem was that the chain was viewed as the most fashionable retailer on the high street and to keep up that image the buyers at Miss Selfridge had to be at the forefront of fashion design. However, buying what is the most recent line in fashion does not always mean buying the most profitable line to sell. Too often too many of the latest fashions were left unsold on the rails – so that profits were adversely affected. Managers were worried that if buyers acted more conservatively, Miss Selfridge would lose its image.

McKinseys started by drawing up a lifestyle portrait of the typical Miss Selfridge customer. After considerable market research they drew a portrait of 'Emma', an 18–year-old media studies student in her first year at college. Emma likes to spend most of her time in jeans but dresses up at weekends. They also analysed how much Emma spends on each item of her clothes. All buyers have to consider Emma when they are buying her clothes. The system seems to have worked – sales increased substantially soon after the system was introduced. Although options were reduced by 30 per cent there were few, if any, complaints. So if you know Emma, you might like to tell her!

Other services providers/contracting out

Many services can be provided for an organisation by outside suppliers – from window-cleaning to painting and decorating. In all areas where the need for a specific skill is temporary, companies have customarily called in outside experts or workpeople. Today, however, contracting out has become more popular, and many of the services traditionally provided within the organisation are now offered by outside specialists. The decision for the organisation is then whether to provide the service itself in-house, or whether to contract it out to an external organisation.

Examples of contracted-out services in the private sector include

* accounting

* wages and salaries (calculations and payments)

* printing and reprographics

* catering

* security

* cleaning.

Public-sector organisations, particularly local authorities, have been involved in compulsory competitive tendering (CCT) for some years – as you saw in chapter 1. This means that they must invite private organisations to **tender** (or bid) to undertake a service – this can range from providing school meals to repairing roads. Unless the local authority can prove that it can provide the service itself more cheaply, it is forced to contract it out to an external supplier.

The advantages of contracting out are usually that

* a wider range of skills can be purchased

* skills which are required on a temporary basis do not need to be hired permanently

* the organisation only has to pay for output produced

* the organisation does not have to worry about any personnel aspects related to contracted-out services – any personnel are the responsibility of the contractor, not the organisation

* in many cases a more comprehensive service can be offered. In the area of catering, for example, vending machines can be installed and maintained by the supplier for people wanting drinks and snacks out of standard canteen hours, a wider range of sandwiches and other foods may be available if they are bought from a supplier than made in-house.

The problem for the organisation is to ensure that an external contractor is offering a competitive service by reviewing its terms and conditions at regular intervals. Another key aspect is quality. This is not as easy to monitor when the service is being provided externally – yet poor quality supplies can obviously be detrimental to the organisation itself, its customers or the morale of its workforce. Usually, therefore, the terms and conditions of the contract specifically cover the quality standards which must be upheld by the supplier.

Outsourcing – internationally

Another term for contracting out is outsourcing. Some companies have virtually divested themselves of everything that is not their 'core business' in order to focus on their own key activities. Other firms profit from these decisions. All BP accounting is now contracted out to Arthur Andersen. All accounting staff, still sitting at their old desks, are now employees of Arthur Andersen! In a recent survey, accountants said that they made more money through contracting-out services than through undertaking their traditional accounting role.

Bob Dickhaus is someone else who has benefited from this trend. He heads an

American company, Johnson Management, which provides services worldwide for multinational companies. Currently the company holds commercial and government service contracts worth over £650 million – and he sees the future of outsourcing worth ten times as much in the next ten years.

Johnson Management is a cross-breed between a management consultancy and a support service provider. The company can advise on change and restructuring, instigate employee training and free managers to concentrate on the jobs they are paid to do.

Discussion point

You work for an organisation which has recently decided to open a creche. The aim is to provide a suitable facility for employees' children aged between 2 and 5. At a future date it may be possible to extend this to cover very young children but your boss is aware that the regulations governing their care are very strict and a far higher ratio of trained nursery nurses per child is required for this age group.

At present he is undecided whether to employ the staff himself and operate the creche as part of the company provision, or contract it out to a private provider.

As a group, discuss the pros and cons of each of these alternatives.

Keywords

The keywords you should know and understand from this chapter are given below. Check to make certain that you clearly understand the concept behind each one.

actuary	gilt-edged shares
assessor	head hunt
blue chip	indemnity
cashflow	insurance agent
central bank	insurance broker
commercial bank	investment bank
consultants	loan capital
contracting out	ordinary shares
debenture	preference shares
dividend	share capital
equity	Stock Exchange
factoring	syndicate
finance house	underwriter
fixed capital	venture capital
forward exchange rate	working capital
gearing	yield

Examination practice

Short-answer questions

1 State three business services which may be provided by a commercial bank.

2 Rosemary Parsons is a small grocer who owns her own premises and has two employees. Which types of insurance cover
   a must she have by law
   b would she also be advised to have?

3 State why a company may consider it is advisable to contract out some of the functions currently provided in-house.

4 The directors at Dovetail Electronics plc are dismayed to see the company's share price fall. Give three reasons why this might have occurred.

5 State two benefits and two drawbacks of recruiting a permanent member of staff through an employment agency.

6 Identify three services which may be provided by a computer services organisation.

7 Your major competitor has employed a PR specialist to manage its affairs. Briefly outline how this may affect *your own* organisation.

8 Identify two benefits of using a management consultancy to solve a problem.

9 Your boss has decided to contract out some of the functions carried out by your organisation. Identify four functions which might be suitable.

10 Explain why an organisation might use a market research company.

Definition questions

1 Explain clearly the difference between each of the following terms.
   a public relations consultants and management consultants
   b ordinary shares and preference shares
   c dividend and yield

2 Write clear notes to explain each of the following terms.
   a central bank
   b debentures
   c insurance brokers
   d factoring

Essay questions

1 Explain the main differences between a commercial bank and an investment or merchant bank.

2 **a** Identify the main types of insurance which might be taken out by a business organisation.
b Describe the principles of insurance which must be considered by both the insured and the insurer.

3 Explain how
a management consultants
b advertising agencies
assist the business community.

4 Explain how the services offered by commercial banks and insurance companies benefit business organisations.

5 Describe the short-, medium- and long-term sources of finance that a private-sector organisation might try to obtain.

6 Explain the contribution made by the central bank and the Stock Exchange to the British economy.

Case study

Mademoiselle is a popular magazine for readers in the 16–25 age group. However, the management has recently been concerned about escalating costs and falling sales. They have decided to reduce these as far as possible and to employ the services of several specialists to assist them.

a What advantages would the magazine gain from employing

i an advertising agency
ii a market research agency
iii a PR consultancy

to promote the magazine?

b If the managers approached their bank for some short-term finance, what options are they likely to be given?

c Identify two services which could be contracted out to save money, and explain how quality could still be ensured.

Help me to become the kind of leader my management would like to have me be. Give me the mysterious something which will enable me at all times satisfactorily to explain policies, rules, regulations and procedures to my workers even when they have never been explained to me.

Help me to teach and to train the uninterested and dim-witted without ever losing my patience or my temper.

Teach me to smile if it kills me.

Give me that love for my colleagues which passeth all understanding so that I may lead the recalcitrant, obstinate, no-good worker into the paths of righteousness by my own example, and by soft persuading remonstrance, instead of yelling and screaming.

Make me a better leader by helping develop larger and greater qualities of understanding, tolerance, sympathy, wisdom, perspective, equanimity, mind-reading and second sight.

● Introduction

So far you have been concerned with the types of business organisations and their external environment. It is now time to move inside an organisation to examine the way in which it operates, the role of the different executives and managers who work in the organisation and why they choose to run the organisation in a particular way.

A sensible starting point is examining the role and responsibilities of different levels of management. At the top of the organisation the senior managers are responsible for making the long-term or **strategic** decisions. These affect everything within the organisation – from the way it is organised and controlled to its business plans and the systems and methods it uses to put these into operation and measure the results.

From the role and responsibilities of senior, middle and supervisory management, this chapter then concentrates on a rather more in-depth view of the relationship between management and shareholders of public limited companies and the benefits and flaws of this association. It also covers the issue of mission statements, strategic and operational planning and the factors which must be taken into account when plans and decisions are made.

This leads into the two most common forms of analysis which inform strategic planning – PEST analysis and SWOT analysis. You were briefly introduced to PEST analysis at the end of chapter 2, and may remember that this is a useful structure for identifying external changes which may affect the business. SWOT analysis, on the other hand, examines both internal and external conditions which affect planning.

Finally, you will look at quality issues, charters and the types of awards and kitemarks which can be earned by business organisations.

The role and responsibilities of management

There are probably more definitions and descriptions on the role and responsibilities of management than there are books in a library! A whole wealth of management literature is devoted to the subject with one writer (Robert Heller) going so far as to say that any attempt to define management is doomed to failure, mainly because it is so diverse and is continually changing!

In many large organisations there are three levels of management

- **senior management**
- **middle management**
- **supervisory (or first-line) management.**

Some aspects of the management role are common to *all* these types of managers. However, there are other aspects of the job which change as a person is promoted through each level.

A word of warning – do not be misled by job titles! In some organisations the word 'manager' seems to be allocated very freely, perhaps even simply to increase the morale or status of a particular member of staff. In other cases, people may clearly be undertaking a management role and yet not carry that particular title. At the end of this section, you should be able to identify those people who really are managers – regardless of their formal title – and those who are not!

Common aspects of management

The following is a checklist of the basic responsibilities which differentiate a management role from a non-management role.

- A manager's job has two aspects.
  - Deciding what to do. This involves planning, setting objectives and making decisions.
  - Deciding the best way of doing it. This involves setting up a system, communicating with staff, controlling and monitoring the results, organising staff training and acting as the coordinator or link between those involved.

- A key aspect of a manager's role is getting things done through other people. He or she is no longer personally responsible for all the output produced but must work with others – making sure they have the information to do the task and complete it properly

- Managers have **responsibility** for the actions of their subordinates. They have **accountability** to their own boss for the success or failure of their own section and are personally judged on these results – if a serious mistake is made by a member of his or her staff, then the manager is held to blame by his or her boss (see also chapters 7 and 8).

- Managers must prioritise tasks and assign work to an appropriate member of staff. This may mean balancing the conflicting needs of the organisation and the staff for whom they are responsible. For instance, if there is urgent work to complete and a member of staff wants a day off, the manager has to make the decision whether to risk the work not being completed by pleasing the member of staff or to insist that he or she defers the day off.

- Managers are problem-solvers and must be prepared to make difficult decisions when necessary – even if this will affect their personal popularity. It is important for managers to be able to analyse a problem from a variety of different aspects and to consider the future implications of taking different forms of action.

- Managers must be able to build up a relationship not just with their own staff but also with others across the organisation. This may mean building alliances for support. They must also be able to mediate between any warring factions so that disputes are settled quickly before they get out of hand.

- Managers must be able to act as official representatives of the organisation both inside and outside the company.

One of the first management writers, Henri Fayol, identified five key elements of management as being

- **planning** – being able to look ahead and decide what needs to be achieved to make provision for the future

- **organising** – providing the resources required for the business to operate, eg equipment, materials, finance and people, and organising a structure so that the activities can be carried out

- **directing** – making decisions and giving orders and instructions to those carrying out the activities

- **coordinating** – uniting and linking all the parts of the work to assist a successful outcome

- **control** – checking that everything is going according to plan. This also relates to making sure that work is being completed within its allocated budget.

The Noddy Club

The Noddy Club is a playgroup which operates in Claygate, Surrey. It was bought by Debra Hunt in 1992 for £6,400 and operates five mornings and three afternoons a week in a local youth club.

Debra's main aim is to provide high-quality care for children aged between $2\frac{1}{2}$ and 5 years – but such care doesn't come cheap. Regulations insist on a minimum ratio of one adult to eight children and Debra Hunt's staffing bill for morning sessions alone last year amounted to £14,000. On top of staffing and rent there are also the costs of extra helpers, insurance and consumables – from photocopying paper to paints and glue.

Three other playgroups in the area mean that she has to work hard to make sure she has the edge over her competitors. Without sufficient children she would not earn the income required for the playgroup to keep going.

She considers the job is far from simple. She says that complying with the requirements of the Children Act and all the other regulations, dealing with new entrants and watching the finance is a full-time occupation – and that does not include time for playing with the children!

Discussion point

1 'Debra Hunt is just as much a manager as Richard Branson.' Explain how this statement could be justified.

2 As a group, decide which of the following would be classed as 'managers' and give a reason for your answer in each case.

Prime Minister	Film director
Priest	Lorry driver
Head teacher	Plumber
Actor	Farmer
Chief constable	Local butcher

● Levels of management

Although there are many common aspects to management, it is fairly obvious that the tasks assigned to managers will vary depending upon the level at which they work.

Senior management

Senior managers in a large organisation comprise

- the **chairman**
- the **managing director**
- **executive directors.**

Together with any **non-executive directors,** they comprise the **board of directors** of a company. With the exception of the chairman, the titles of the managing director and directors may change depending upon the type of organisation. In the public sector, for instance, a local authority or hospital trust has a **chief executive** and a university has a vice-chancellor instead of a managing director. Similarly, executive directors may be known as operational directors or deans.

A key function of senior management is to look forwards and decide what the company should be doing in the future and what resources it will require to achieve its goals. There are obviously severe penalties attached to making wrong decisions in these areas – which is why the role of senior management is so important.

Senior managers are responsible for the total enterprise. Their major role is in relation to deciding the long-term direction of the organisation and defining its strategic objectives. This vision is then translated into a plan for achieving the stated objectives. In simple terms this means deciding

- where the organisation is going
- how it should get there
- what measures will be used to check if it has arrived!

Other responsibilities attached to senior managers include

- representing the organisation to the outside world – from giving statements to the media to **networking** with other top managers
- deciding on organisation policies – this includes deciding on the **values and ethics** of the organisation in relation to such aspects as the environment, staffing and customer care. Values and ethics relate to the standards which the company holds, eg regarding its stakeholders and the permitted behaviour of staff.

The individual responsibilities of different members of the senior management team are discussed below.

The chairman

The chairman takes his or her title from the role of chairing the board of directors. Key attributes are a knowledge and experience of the industry, a proven track-record of success and a good public image. He or she is not only expected to lead the top management team and act as adviser to the managing director but also to be the 'public face' of the company. For that reason, if an event occurs which results in national publicity for the organisation, it is usually the chairman who is chosen for interview by the media and his or her words which are quoted. All chairmen therefore need to have one eye on their public relations role at all times.

Profile of a chairman

Sir Bob Reid was born in 1934 in Cupar, Fife. He achieved a degree in political economy and modern history at St Andrew's University and in 1956 started his career with Shell International. He worked there for 34 years. His last five years there were spent at the helm of Shell UK as Chairman and Chief Executive. In 1990 he moved to British Rail as Chairman where he spent five years and took up a new job in 1995 as Chairman of Sears. Sears is foremost a retailing giant, which owns Selfridges department stores, Freemans mail order and various shops including Richards, Adams, Dolcis, Wallis and Shoe City.

He has not had an easy ride at Sears so far. Sales have been poor for the last few years and 1996 saw him reporting on a pre-tax loss of £120 million and at the Annual General Meeting he was faced by angry shareholders.

Bob Reid is well known for his support for his staff – both at British Rail and at Sears. Staff consider him a motivational chairman, always trying to get the best out of people. His key ally at Sears is Liam Strong, the Chief Executive, who moved from British Airways to Sears in 1992. However, Liam Strong is not proving popular with the company's institutional investors given current performance – and may need all the support he can get from his Chairman.

Sir Bob Reid has also been a non-executive director of the Bank of Scotland since 1987 (see page 138).

Another vital PR role is networking with other top people in the same industry or representing other stakeholder groups – from government ministers to consumer groups. He or she will obviously need a basic appreciation of the legal requirements relating to the company in general and to the board of directors in particular – and will be advised on specific aspects by the company secretary (see also chapter 2).

On a more practical level the chairman's primary function is to regulate the proceedings at board meetings and at the Annual General Meeting (AGM). This is the meeting to which shareholders are invited each year and is a legal requirement of all public limited companies. The chairman's words will be quoted in the press release which follows and will be scrutinised carefully by stakeholders and the financial markets.

In some organisations the role of chairman and managing director is a joint position. This is usually inadvisable as the role of the chairman and managing director should be complementary. Each can counsel and guide the other on key strategic issues and policy decisions – and give frank advice and support when necessary. Being at the top can be a lonely position but being in the position of a virtual dictator can also be very dangerous.

The chief executive/managing director

The title 'managing director' (MD) comes from his or her joint role in both managing the company and being a member of the board of directors. As a director he or she is responsible for deciding policy; as a manager he or she is responsible for making sure that this policy is implemented across the whole of the organisation. For that reason, the MD must take a global view of the organisation – in contrast with the executive directors who will each be in charge of a specific section or department and will therefore be keen to promote their own individual areas. Promotion to MD therefore means moving from a specialist job to a more generalist role – running the executive side of the business in addition to carrying the burden of everyday high-level administration.

The job entails being the link between the governing body and the rest of the organisation – which implies excellent communication and negotiation skills. He or she is appointed by the board, reports to it and (theoretically, at least) takes instructions from it. If the board is to be effective, the MD must be frank in his or her reporting of events and able to tolerate the opinions of his or her juniors who attend the meetings.

Key responsibilities
* Ensuring that strategic objectives are defined with company interests to the fore.
* Ensuring that strategic objectives are continually kept in mind by the whole organisation.
* Acting as a link between the board and the organisation.
* Supervising changes over long-range planning and strategy.
* Monitoring the financial contribution of all departments, divisions or branches.

- Maintaining an effective organisation structure and implementing restructure plans as and when required.

- Networking with MDs and senior managers in related organisations. The term networking is used to describe informal links made between people with the same interests.

- Ensuring that control systems are in force to ensure that strategic plans take effect.

- Motivating all staff to do their best (see chapter 7).

Qualities

The qualities of a good MD include drive, initiative, vision and the ability to plan ahead. However, he or she also needs excellent personal leadership skills and the confidence to steer the business positively, especially when times are difficult.

Profile of a chief executive

Dr Brian Davis's early leanings gave no indication of his job today. He was involved in academic research in rocket fuel technology and then joined Esso as a researcher. He later became involved in a management development programme, gained expertise in computers and then moved to Nationwide Building Society to work as General Manager, Technology. After two promotions he was awarded the top job when Tim Melville-Ross, the previous Chief Executive, left to become the head of the Institute of Directors.

As Chief Executive of Nationwide,

Brian Davis will be in charge of the largest mutual building society in the UK once the Halifax has joined the stock market in 1997. Although Nationwide is very successful – its profits were £345 million before tax in 1994 – the society has had its problems with complaints about poor service and ineffective though expensive TV advertisements. On paper Brian Davis is still backing the benefits of remaining a mutual society as this means he has no shareholders to please. However, other critics consider this may change in the future. Only time will tell which way Brian Davis really wants Nationwide to go.

Boards of directors

Most large organisations have some form of **governing body** – usually as a legal requirement, eg

- boards of directors (public limited companies)

- council members (local authorities)
- boards of governors (schools and colleges).

Most governing bodies are selected democratically (at least in theory). Directors of plcs are elected by shareholders at the AGM. School governing bodies have parent representatives.

Senior executives from the organisation are usually represented on the governing body. For example, in a public limited company, the managing director, marketing director, finance director and others could be on the board.

The title 'director' usually differentiates a senior manager with a seat on the board (who is known as a director) and a middle manager who has not (who is known as a manager).

Power and authority (the theory)

The board of directors (or governing body) will have several duties or responsibilities. It should

- formulate and endorse policies and long-term strategies
- agree other major actions (eg the acquisition of another company or the restructure of the company)
- appoint or dismiss senior executives
- authorise major items of expenditure
- ensure there is an availability of adequate capital to link with the strategic plan
- publish financial and other information to stakeholders
- have overall responsibility for the actions of all employees
- evaluate results and maintain control by adjusting priorities where necessary
- comply with legal requirements which regulate the operation of the organisation
- give professional advice to executives.

Power and authority (the reality)

In reality not all of these duties are always discharged by governing bodies for a variety of reasons.

- Meetings of the governing body may be infrequent and some items may be glossed over or omitted.
- Senior management may engage in manipulative strategies to have their proposals accepted, such as fixing the agenda or lobbying for support before the meeting.

- Executives spend their working hours involved in company affairs so know what is happening and what are the key issues. They may control the information (both type and quantity) which is given to the board.

- Some issues may be too complicated for members to understand. A famous management writer, C Northcote Parkinson, gave the example of a bike shed which is a little out of date but serves its purpose. He said that a board would spend hours arguing about the cost of a new bike shed which amounted to a few pounds but would quickly agree a major item of expenditure of millions of pounds because nobody could understand all the details and the implications! He concluded that the amount of time involved in discussing financial matters was inversely proportionate to their financial value.

- Meetings can be notoriously unreliable or erratic in relation to the quality of decisions which are made.

Executive and non-executive directors

Most public limited companies have both executive and non-executive directors – the latter recruited from outside the company. The aim is to provide additional experience and expertise as well as acting as a check on the executive members. For instance, a politician, leading business person, solicitor or bank manager may be invited to have a place on the board because he or she could give members valuable and objective information and advice. Major shareholders (such as banks and pension funds) may also nominate a non-executive director to monitor performance and keep a check on their investment.

Cadbury and non-executives

The Cadbury Report, published in 1992, reported on the responsibilities of boards and the role of executive and non-executive directors. It concluded that non-executive directors should be of a high enough calibre and appointed in sufficient numbers for their views to carry some weight. The majority should be free of any financial or business connection with the company to ensure their views are independent.

The report was criticised that its ideals for non-executives were too demanding

and the pool of available non-executive talent was too small to provide suitable high-quality directors for all UK companies. Two ideas for easing this shortage were for companies to allow more of their senior executives to be available to act as non-executives in other companies and that the pay should increase. At the time the report was written the remuneration for non-executives was between £5,000 and £15,000 a year.

The disadvantage is that a non-executive director is not dependent upon the organisation for employment and this lack of personal involvement may mean a lack of interest and commitment in the future prospects of the company. A major institutional investor is more involved but has the option of selling its shareholding (or threatening to do so) if it is dissatisfied with current returns.

However, it is generally true that an effective board should have a mixture of executive and non-executive members.

The pay row – directors versus Greenbury

A major row broke out when Cedric Brown, then Chief Executive of British Gas received a 75 per cent pay rise. This was fuelled even more by the fact that the announcement was made at a time of major redundancies in gas showrooms.

The issue of top executives' pay has been an issue for the past few years. One argument is that key directors play such an important role that the company should be free to set its own pay and award any bonuses it likes linked to performance (such as allowing share options, which means that as the shares increase in value the executives can personally benefit). Only in this way will organisations be able to attract the top people.

Those disagreeing with this argument say that over-large payments to directors are not matched by increases to the rest of the workforce, that penalties for poor performance are very small and that there should be some controls to prevent boards of directors simply awarding themselves all the benefits of an increase in profits every year. Theoretically, this could be

vetoed by the shareholders at the AGM but it is very difficult for individual shareholders to link together to form a united group (see page 144).

In 1995 the Greenbury Report was published following an investigation into this issue. The report rejected formal regulation of executive pay but recommended a change in the law to provide for fuller disclosure. It also recommended that directors' increases should not exceed the average rise received by staff, long-term bonus schemes should replace share options and details of all directors' remuneration should be included in the company annual report.

However, all the recommendations were for voluntary action and a survey by the consultancy Hewitt Associates in 1996 found that 44 per cent of companies did not intend to adopt Greenbury's recommendations.

For the record, Sir Richard Greenbury, author of the report is Chairman of Marks & Spencer on a salary of approximately £807,000 per annum.

The effectiveness of the board

To be effective

- all meetings should have a well-structured and comprehensive agenda

- members should study the related paperwork beforehand

- the directors should be prepared on issues such as policy formulation

- the key emphasis for the board should be visionary and concerned with the way ahead

- time should be allocated effectively for discussion

- discussions should be translated into action

- meetings should be free from self-interest and company politics.

Discussion point

The salaries of top business people have long been a topic of debate and argument. In 1992 the average pay of the directors of the top 100 (FT-SE) companies was reported as being £535,000 – more than £10,000 a week. Today it is obviously higher.

Critics allege that top business people in the UK and USA simply look after their own interests – and often make workers redundant to increase profits so that they can personally benefit. This is different from the European or Japanese perspective – because companies in Germany, France and Japan do not usually follow this route. However, in contrast with the USA, British business salaries are low. Americans believe that top performers are well worth the money they are paid, that if they do not receive enough they will go elsewhere and both businesses and the economy will suffer.

As a group, debate this issue. In particular, contrast the salaries of top business people with those who are high earners in the entertainment or sports worlds – such as Anthea Turner or Eric Cantona. As a small point, George Michael is expected to earn £10 million just from his 'Older' album! Who do you believe gives best value for money?

Middle management

In many organisations the number of middle managers has been considerably reduced over the past few years as part of a **delayering** process to make the organisation less **hierarchical** (see chapter 5).

Their traditional role is in supporting top managers by translating strategic plans and objectives into operational functions which can be undertaken by their staff. Their role is mainly administrative in terms of getting the job done and producing the required results for their own unit, division or department. They are therefore the link between those at the top and the supervisors for whom they are responsible. Middle managers spend a considerable amount of time liaising with their own manager and the staff who report to them. Key aspects of the role therefore include coordination and communication – however, they will be expected to have enough technical expertise to understand the problems being encountered by their own staff – and be able to contribute to an effective solution.

Their expertise as the link between the top manager and the supervisors means that they may often be able to counsel and guide their own boss on aspects of the organisation and future developments which can usefully be used by top management to inform **strategic planning.**

First-line management

This level of management usually comprises supervisors who have direct contact with staff on a daily basis. They are therefore the 'first-line' of management. They will need technical expertise to be able to solve problems

Climbing the ladder

Anna, Susie and Keith left school at the same time, but all pursued different careers. Anna had always wanted to enter nursing but decided to do a degree first so that she could rise to ward manager quickly. Her mother had a friend who was a nurse manager and also knew the director of nursing and quality at a large private hospital. Anna felt she knew exactly where her future lay.

Susie, on the other hand, had always longed for a career in publishing. She started as a desk editor but looked at the commissioning editor with longing. Occasionally, she had tried to watch the editorial director when he was in negotiation over a new development or difficult problem. She knew that the MD relied upon her senior staff to keep as many problems as possible away from her desk!

Keith had taken a different route. His interest had always been in computers. He had started out in programming and soon been promoted to head programmer, responsible for three junior members of staff. A year ago he was promoted to Technical Manager, directly reporting to the Development Director of the organisation.

quickly but will also need good 'people' skills to be able to coordinate the work required and motivate their own staff to be able to carry it out. First-line managers usually have a considerable amount of administrative responsibility and may also represent the organisation externally if there are special events which cover their own area of technical expertise.

Discussion point

1   From the previous article, give the titles of the first-line managers, middle managers and senior managers in
   a nursing
   b publishing
   c computing.

2   Find similar examples for each of the following areas.
   a education (your own college, perhaps?)
   b local government
   c the media (film or television)

3   Discuss, as a group, how you think the jobs of Anna, Susie and Keith will change as they move up the ladder.

Changing skills and abilities

A considerable amount of research has been undertaken on the way in which managerial roles change at different levels.

Robert Katz, an educator and business executive, identifies three skills which he considers are needed by all managers.

- **Technical skill.** This relates to the mechanics of the job – understanding the procedures or techniques used in a particular field. Quite obviously, a nurse will need a different type of skill to a desk editor and this is different again for a computer programmer.

- **Human or 'people' skill.** This is the ability to get the best out of other people – either as individual workers or as members of a team or group. It means being able to work with, understand and motivate other people.

- **Conceptual skill.** This is the skill of being able to understand the organisation, how its various parts fit together and to take into account how a change in one area would affect others. Good managers should be able to make decisions which are in the best interests of the organisation as a whole because they can consider all the possible implications and results of their actions.

However, the degree to which each of these skills is required varies considerably between first-line and top management, as Figure 4.1 shows.

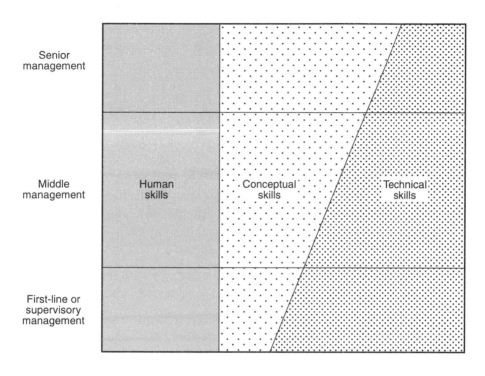

Figure 4.1 Levels of skill required by managers

A good person can manage anything – true or false?

Can a good person manage anything? Certainly the government seem to think that this is the case. Cabinet ministers, for instance, are regularly moved around in a reshuffle. Kenneth Clarke is one example – having undertaken various key posts at Education, Health, the Home Office and as Chancellor of the Exchequer. Yet some would consider that moving people around like this is unproductive – how can Kenneth Clarke be expected to be a specialist in all of these areas? Surely, it will take him several months after each move to 'get his feet under the desk' and really appreciate what is going on. In the meantime, taxpayers' money is being wasted while he gets to grips with the job.

Discussion point

1　As a group, discuss the pros and cons of the argument that a good person can manage anything. (You may also like to look back at the profile on Sir Bob Reid on page 134 before you answer this question.)

2　Do you think that the level of job held makes any difference to the answer?

Management and shareholders

This relationship is often criticised in the media. Firstly, because of the pressures upon management to please shareholders and secondly, because of the inability of shareholders to influence management! It is fairly easy to identify the problem if you remember two points.

- Shareholders usually buy shares because they want them to increase in price and to earn a good dividend.

- Each shareholder has one vote per share. This is quite substantial if you are a large institutional shareholder with 250,000 shares but rather inconsequential if you only own 200 shares.

The problems for management

At the end of the year let us assume a company has earned a reasonable net profit. Out of this profit it then pays tax. The remainder can either be invested in the business or paid out as dividend to shareholders. The problem for directors is how much to invest and how much to pay out.

If a large amount is invested, then dividends will be low, shareholders may sell their shares and this will cause the price to fall.

If dividends are large, then shareholders will be pleased, more people may want to buy shares – so the shares will increase in value – but the company will have very little money left to invest.

Remember that investment is vital for long-term growth and prosperity. Therefore directors who concentrate on pleasing shareholders are often accused of **short-termism.**

The problems for shareholders

Problems for shareholders can arise if they are unhappy with the way the organisation is being managed. Traditionally, the opportunity for individual shareholders to form a united group to force change (by voting against the current management) has been very small. This problem is often caused by the **divorce between ownership and control** which is a feature of all public limited companies. The shareholders own the company (technically) but struggle to make themselves heard to those who control the company – ie the directors. (In a private limited company there is **unity** between ownership and control as shareholders and directors are usually the same people.)

However, shareholder activism is increasing in an effort to protect shareholdings. Two individual shareholder action groups have been formed – the UK Shareholders Association was set up in 1992 and has about 450 members; the Guild of Shareholders is run by a former MP and has about 3,000 members. These action groups are welcomed by institutional investors who are also taking more of an interest in the companies in which they invest.

The government has also promised to investigate the problems encountered by private shareholders and Ian Lang, the Trade and Industry Secretary has pledged to make it easier for them to criticise a board of directors. This may lead to changes to the Companies Act.

Buy Argos not Eurotunnel!

Argos management pleased shareholders when they handed back half the £200 million profits to shareholders in a 42p a share special dividend. The Chief Executive, Mike Smith, said that this would not reduce the company's ability to make new acquisitions.

In contrast, furious Eurotunnel shareholders in France have threatened legal action against the company's bankers at the same time as they appointed an agent to act for them at the company's Paris AGM in a battle to oust the board. The shareholders are desperate to unite following two years in which they have seen the value of their shares fall by two-thirds at the same time as annual losses on the tunnel have doubled to almost £1 billion. The total debt mountain is now almost £9 billion with an interest bill estimated at £2 million a day! Meanwhile, Eurotunnel directors have been trying to negotiate a finance package to get the company out of trouble at the same time as they lowered prices to tempt more people away from the ferries.

Determining corporate objectives

Corporate planning

Corporate planning relates to the long-term goals and objectives of the whole enterprise. A time period of about five years or even longer may be covered. From the corporate plan it is possible to decide on the courses of action to take and the resources which are required for the goals to be achieved.

Many organisations start by deciding upon their **mission** – or their major aim – and publish this in their **mission statement.** Ackoff, one management writer, argued that mission statements should not focus on what 'an organisation should do to survive, but what it has chosen to do in order to thrive'. To be worthwhile, they should be positive, visionary and motivating.

These are the key requirements of a good mission statement.

- It should give an insight into the organisation and differentiate it from its competitors.

- It should define the business that the company wants to be in, which is not necessarily that in which it is currently involved.

- It should state the strategy or broad purposes of the organisation – and preferably include objectives so that progress towards these can be measured.

- It should promote a feeling of pride in the organisation, and inspire and excite those who read it.

- It should give identifiable guidance for behaviour by individual managers.

- It should contain information in relation to the customer needs it intends to satisfy, the market in which it operates and the way in which it intends to meet these needs.

- It should be relevant to and state its intentions towards all the stakeholders in the organisation, not just shareholders and managers.

The role of the mission statement should be to

- act as the main 'steer' for the organisation

- help set objectives

- define management decisions

- improve communication within the organisation.

One management writer, Pearce, argued that 'a mission statement should contain the same fundamental elements that exist in the mind of the founder of the business at its outset. The company mission describes the firm's product, market and its technology in a way that reflects the values and priorities of the strategic decision makers'.

An example of a company mission statement and goals – that of British Airways for 1990 – is shown in Figure 4.2. Their mission statement is currently under review because the company wants it to be shorter and snappier.

MISSION AND GOALS

MISSION
- To be the best and most successful company in the airline industry.

GOALS

Safe and secure
- To be a safe and secure airline.

Financially strong
- To deliver a strong and consistent financial performance.

Global leader
- To secure a leading share of air travel business worldwide with a significant presence in all major geographical markets.

Service and value
- To provide overall superior service and good value for money in every market segment in which we compete.

Customer driven
- To excel in anticipating and quickly responding to customer needs and competitor activity.

Good employer
- To sustain a working environment that attracts, retains and develops committed employees who share in the success of the company.

Good neighbour
- To be a good neighbour, concerned for the community and the environment.

To achieve these goals, we must:
- Deliver friendly, professional service consistently through well-trained and motivated employees.

- Search continuously for improvement through innovation and the use of technology.

- Employ planning and decision-making processes that provide clear direction and sense of purpose.

- Foster a leadership style throughout the organization which encourages respect for individuals, teamwork and close identification with customers.

- Strive constantly to achieve agreed standards of quality at competitive cost levels.

Figure 4.2 BA's 1990 mission statement

BA's mission to the world

Colin Marshal, Deputy Chairman and Chief Executive, British Airways, is on record as saying 'A corporate mission is much more than good intentions and fine ideas. It represents the framework for the entire business, the values which drive the company and the belief that the company has in itself and what it can achieve'.

Discussion point

1   As a group, do you consider that BA's mission statement lives up to the aims of its Chairman?

2   Below are mission statements from three major companies. In each case identify how much you consider they meet the criteria for a good mission statement.

   - **BT:** 'British Telecom's mission is to provide world class telecommunications and information products and services and to develop and exploit our networks at home and abroad.'
   - **Kentucky Fried Chicken:** its aim is 'to provide families with affordable, delicious chicken-dominant meals'.
   - **McDonalds:** 'McDonalds will provide great-tasting food backed up by excellent operations and friendly service in a relaxed, safe and consistent restaurant environment.'

3   As a group approach four different organisations for a copy of their mission statement. Try to obtain examples from the public sector (eg your local authority or NHS hospital trust), a charity and a commercial organisation in your area.
   a   Analyse the way in which public-sector mission statements differ from private sector statements.
   b   In which ways do you consider the mission statements reflect the different types of objectives of private- and public-sector organisations?

4   Obtain a copy of the mission statement for your own college. As a consumer at your college, to what extent do you think the college lives up to its stated aims?

Strategic planning

Strategic planning is related to making long-term plans in relation to the whole enterprise. It is concerned with where the enterprise wants to be – rather than where it is at the moment. Its major aim is **effectiveness** – making sure that the organisation is *doing the right thing*. It is undertaken by senior managers who will decide

- the strategic goals of the company
- the resources which are required
- the outcomes by which success will be measured.

Strategic planning really means planning for the future, ie moving the 'mission' one stage on and identifying the planned route over about five years. Deciding future plans involves consideration of the views of stakeholders and changes relating to the external environment. It is likely that the executives will undertake a PEST analysis (see below) to assess these changes and the impact they may have on the organisation. This can then lead to a reevaluation of the type of markets in which the business operates.

Finally, the executives will look at the impact of any changes on the internal operations of the organisation. This may involve reconsidering the current organisation structure, reappraising the organisational culture, and considering the staffing provision and training required to enable the plans to be fulfilled. All these aspects are covered in later chapters.

Tactical planning

Tactical planning is concerned with devising the activities (or tactics) by which the strategic plan will be put into effect. Usually tactical planning concentrates on a two-year period and is the responsibility of middle managers.

Middle managers are normally responsible for one specific area within the strategic plan. It is their job to examine the plan, consider objectives for their own area and then suggest ways of meeting these.

Operational planning

Operational planning has a much shorter time scale – usually a matter of months – or a year at most. It involves making plans to ensure that activities are undertaken successfully so that objectives are met. Operational planning is concerned with **efficiency** – making sure that the organisation is *doing things right*.

This type of planning covers the systems, procedures and controls which are required to make sure that tasks are carried out correctly and that quality is assured. When these have been agreed and determined, they form the basis of the **operating statement** which identifies the way that the company will operate (ie the route it will take) during the coming year. First-line managers, or supervisors, are responsible for meeting the objectives within the period specified in the operating statement.

Setting objectives

The only way in which it is possible to assess whether plans have been successfully achieved is to set **objectives** so that progress can be measured. An objective can be defined as a stated and *measurable* level of achievement. For instance, if you are always late in the morning, your strategic objective might be to improve your time-keeping, but your operational objective could be to get up 15 minutes earlier each day. You could easily measure whether you achieved this or not.

Here are some basic rules about objectives (before you start setting any yourself!).

- They should link to the strategic plan.

- They should be a realistic challenge for those involved.

- Their achievement should be measurable in relation to time, quantity, quality, cost or other relevant criteria.

- They should be set by agreement with those involved.

- They should be capable of being adapted if circumstances change.

In the example above, therefore, if you started in a job which meant you had to be at work at 8 am, you would have to revise your objective quite considerably! In addition, if someone else set the objective for you, then it is less likely you would be agreeable to trying to achieve it. For that reason, it is always better for staff to be consulted before objectives are set that relate to their future performance.

All managers are usually given **targets** which enable them to see if they are meeting their objectives. A sales manager, for instance, might have the objective of increasing sales by 5 per cent, whereas a production manager might have the objective of reducing rejects, or substandard articles, by 4 per cent. It is usually more satisfactory to set numeric objectives as these are easy to measure. An objective of 'improving customer service' would be difficult to assess unless it was accompanied by a specific requirement, eg 'and reduce complaints by 10 per cent over the next 12 months'.

Areas of overlap

It is important to realise that senior managers and middle managers do not work in isolation – merrily setting objectives and deciding strategies apart from one another! Indeed, in some organisations strategic planning is undertaken using a 'bottom-up' approach, where all staff are asked for their views. These are given to first-line managers to add their own comments and pass these upwards again and so on.

There are several overlapping areas which all managers must constantly consider. These are shown in Figure 4.3.

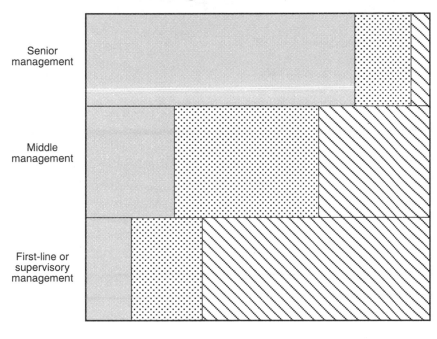

Strategic planning – broad focus
Long term (5 years)

Tactical planning – focus on area
Medium term (1–2 years)

Operational planning – focus on technical operation
Short term (under a year)

Figure 4.3 Corporate planning: areas of overlap

Manchester United – an objective not a goal!

Many large organisations today have changed their objectives so that they focus on their 'core business' and divest themselves of anything else. They can do this by selling subsidiary companies not in their main line of business or by contracting out services which are not part of their main area (as you saw in chapter 3).

Manchester United took a different approach. A public limited company since 1991, the football club has followed a deliberate strategy of supplementing its **core business** through merchandising and other business. Note that core business relates to the main business of an organisation, from which most of its profits are usually made. Last year, a third of Manchester United's income came from gate receipts and programme sales. This amounted to £19.6 million.

A further £23 million was earned by merchandising and £18 million through television rights, sponsorship deals, conferences and corporate hospitality. To add to its diverse interests, Manchester United has since launched its own Nintendo Game Boy, a premium whisky and its own brand of wine – red, naturally!

The club employs 299 staff with an extra 750 on matchdays. Last year its pre-tax profits amounted to £16.28 million. A big business as well as a football club, less famous names than Alex Ferguson or Eric Cantona include Martin Edwards, the Chief Executive and Robin Launders, the Finance Director and Company Secretary. Their alleged salaries for last year were £153,000 and £94,000 respectively, but shareholders and fans may both be united in agreeing they deserved them!

🗨 Discussion point

1 What would you consider is Manchester United's core business?

2 As a group, imagine you are setting objectives for both the 'core business' employees and the other employees at Manchester United. Write some objectives which match the criteria on page 150 and check these with your tutor. Remember they must be realistic and measurable!

3 Below are five objectives. Which one do you think applies to
  a a hospital
  b a local authority
  c a charity
  d a car manufacturer
  e a school?

   i Increase proportion of money raised from direct-mail appeals from 20 per cent to 25 per cent over the next 12 months.

   ii Reduce admission waiting lists from an average of 14 weeks to 10 weeks.

   iii Increase the output of the new model by 35 per cent by next June.

   iv Improve examination pass rate from 82 per cent to 86 per cent by next August.

   v Reduce response to waste collection requests from 3 days to 2 days within the next 12 months.

4 Write down your own strategic plan which encompasses your personal aim on this course. Now write two objectives that will help you to assess whether you are progressing 'according to plan'. Compare your answers with those of other members of your group.

The practicalities of planning

It can be one thing to make plans but quite another to see them through! You probably know this from your own personal experiences. Overly ambitious plans are usually doomed to failure from the outset. So are plans where there is much talk but little action – or where no one knows what anyone else is supposed to be doing. For that reason, an organisation takes a more methodical approach. Before it starts its strategic planning process it will begin by identifying the factors that will help or hinder the achievement of any goals.

PEST analysis

PEST analysis relates to considering the external events which may affect the business.

Relevant events are given under four headings – **political, economic, social** and **technological.** You have already learned about political and economic factors in chapter 2. Social changes relate to the different ways in which people live their lives and their changing needs and wants.

Technological change is fairly obvious. You are familiar with computers, probably use a digital telephone system, might own a CD player and take advantage of a bank's computerised system every time you withdraw money from a cash machine. When you go to a supermarket you no longer find people putting price tickets on items because of bar coding – and everyone is used to bar-code scanners and electronic tills. All these changes affect the way in which business organisations operate.

For instance, the Noddy Club mentioned earlier in this chapter (page 132) may identify the following aspects relevant to its own undertaking.

- **Political** – changes to regulations governing creches and nursery schools, the effect of the Children Act.

- **Economic** – current interest rates, levels of unemployment in the area, competition in the area.

- **Social** – people working longer hours, more mothers working, couples having fewer children, the increase in single parents.

- **Technological** – the administrative functions which could be carried out on a personal computer.

All these factors will influence the strategic decisions which would be made by the owner. A fall in interest rates coupled with social trends which show an increase in demand for places could lead to a strategic plan that concentrates on expansion of the club.

Further examples of the areas which might be identified under each heading are given in Figure 4.4.

Political	Government regulations
	International relations
	Legislation (eg health and safety, employment, consumer and company law)
	Pressure groups (eg Greenpeace or the AA)
	Political stance
	Current national issues
	Government action which threatens industry or increases costs (eg increasing regulations or tax)
	Government action to promote/support industry or reduce costs (eg export drives, deregulation, lowering tax)
	Tax incentives and grants
Economic	Government economic policy
	Interest rates
	Tax rates (including VAT)
	Strength of sterling
	Fuel/utility policy/costs
	Employment measures and benefit rates
	Investment incentives
	Level of consumer spending
	Level of government spending
	Budget plans
	Competition/competition policy
Technological	Technological developments – computers, robotics, telecommunications, lasers, etc.
	Changes in production methods
	Development of synthetics
	Research and development innovations
	Changes in crafts/skills
	Training requirements
	Expert requirements
	Action of competitors
	Product life-cycle may shorten
Social	Increase in nuclear families/lone parents/working women (greater dependency on creche/flexible hours at workplace)
	Higher marriage age
	Smaller families, birthrate falling
	Increasing ethnic mix
	Increased leisure time
	Greater car ownership
	Increased standards of living
	Increased expectations of workforce for consultation
	Changing patterns of work (more part-time, weekend, home, flexi- and unsocial hours working)
	Changing skills
	High rate of unemployment

Figure 4.4 PEST analysis

Discussion point

Divide into groups of four and identify the current factors which would apply to your PEST analysis if you were the managers of one of the following organisations. Some of your earlier reading and studies should help you here!

- A taxi firm.
- An accountancy firm.
- A brewery.
- A company making expensive sports cars.
- A supermarket.
- A private hospital.

Discuss your ideas with your tutor.

SWOT analysis

A second technique, which identifies both external *and* internal factors is **SWOT analysis.** SWOT stands for strengths, weaknesses, opportunities and threats. The Noddy Club, for instance, might carry out this type of analysis and come up with the type of conclusions illustrated in Figure 4.5.

This will obviously inform the planning and decision-making process. If there is very little money available for investment, then it is no use having

INTERNAL FACTORS	
Strengths	**Weaknesses**
Young, dynamic workforce	No administrative staff
Well-qualified assistants	Limited range of play equipment
Trained nurse	Leased premises
Modern premises	No expansion possible on existing premises
Range of toys	
Good reputation	
EXTERNAL FACTORS	
Opportunities	**Threats**
New estate being built nearby	Additional regulations likely
Closure of one competitor	Opening of new competitor in March
following Children Act	Unemployment rising
Growth of single parent families	Increased number of young mothers working at home

Figure 4.5 SWOT analysis for the Noddy Club

ambitious plans for new machines and equipment. Equally, if a major problem is lack of qualified staff, then an obvious part of the strategic plan should look at overcoming this weakness. Quite obviously, any internal constraints – such as lack of resources or fundamental organisational weaknesses – will affect the ability of the organisation to meet its objectives (see also chapters 5 and 8).

Meeting quality standards

It is, of course, absolutely hopeless meeting targets in relation to increased production, increased sales, reduced waiting times, etc. if the quality of the product or service deteriorates.

It is very difficult to define quality because it means different things to different people. The easiest way to consider it is in terms of value for money. Therefore you would have different expectations if you bought a Metro rather than a Porsche. Similarly, if you went into hospital on the NHS you would have different expectations than if you were paying privately.

For most people, quality involves the following factors:

- courteous treatment by staff

- availability of product or service

- a product or service which conforms to the description given and which does the job intended

- prompt and efficient delivery

A mission for quality

W H Smith is just one organisation which built quality into its mission statement. In 1993 the company announced: 'We are in business to delight our customers. We will do this by offering them memorable products, good value for money and legendary service.'

Smiths is not the only one that talks about delighting its customers – Kwik-Fit, the care servicing chain also proclaims 'the most important person is the customer and it must be our aim to delight 100 per cent of our customers 100 per cent of the time. Our success depends on the loyalty of our customers'. Kwik-Fit emphasises its promises with a nine-fold code of practice which hangs on the wall of each centre, making a promise to customers about the technical skill and dedication of its staff. Dissatisfied customers can speak to the manager or ring the free helpline any time, day or night.

- reliability and durability

- reasonably priced

- good after-sales service

- overall value for money.

Quality awards and certification

Product quality, customer service and commitment to staff training and development are frequently included in mission statements, strategic plans and corporate objectives. Yet how can progress be measured and, even more importantly, how can organisations be encouraged to improve in these areas?

One method is through giving awards and certification to those companies that achieve specified standards. The companies can then obtain publicity and advertise the appropriate logo or award badge on company stationery, thereby informing all stakeholders and potential customers of the standards they uphold.

ISO 9000

ISO 9000 is a **quality standard** which has been earned by over 44,000 British companies. It is awarded to companies which can demonstrate that they have consistent quality procedures at all stages of production – not just as a 'check' at the end. It therefore links with **total quality management** schemes which were introduced in the 1980s as an improvement on the previous idea of quality control which mainly linked to checking the product before despatch.

To gain ISO 9000, a company must have quality procedures in force in relation to

- purchasing raw materials

- storage of raw materials

- design and development

- manufacture and assembly

- installation

- inspection and testing

- packing and distribution.

Even **subcontractors** retained by the firm may only be hired if they have the same quality standard to ensure that they also follow the set procedures.

ISO 9000 is an international standard which is recognised throughout Europe. It replaced the old British standard BS 5750. However, many small firms have been critical of IS0 9000 arguing that it is more suitable for large organisations – and they are backed in their views by the Forum of Private Business which represents 23,000 small businesses. Its Chief Executive, Stan Mendham, argues that the procedures which must be introduced are too formal for small, personally managed firms.

This scepticism does not appear to be echoed north of the border. A 1995 survey carried out by Price Waterhouse and *The Sunday Times* (Scotland), showed that the majority of private companies in Scotland had either attained ISO 9000 or BS 5750 or intended to do so.

Fit for an award

Kwik-Fit (see page 157) has won no fewer than 30 awards for customer service excellence since 1983. Other customer service award winners in 1995 included:

- Air Miles (run by British Airways), which reduced complaint response times from 10 days to 2 days
- Principal Hotels which not only assures customers of exceptional service but also operates a computer-based guest database which records details of guests' pet likes and dislikes
- Allied Carpets which has specially

trained staff to assist customers and has installed PCs which can show a computerised image of the customer's own room complete with different carpets.

A variety of awards are on offer through the media, consumer associations and other agencies. In some cases customers are asked to nominate suitable companies; in other cases the companies can make their own nominations. The aim is to award those companies which can clearly demonstrate that they consistently put the customer first.

Charters and the Charter Mark

In the public sector, following John Major's Citizens Charter initiative, a variety of charters have been produced by organisations ranging from the Inland Revenue to HM Customs and Excise. All are available to members of the public and all detail the service customers have a right to receive.

The Taxpayers Charter, for instance, is a list of 'promises' from the Inland Revenue on how it will handle your affairs; the Travellers Charter details how customs will treat you when you re-enter the country; the Job-seekers Charter gives the standards to be achieved by the employment service and so on. About 40 are in existence issued by organisations ranging from BR and the Post Office to schools, hospitals and utility companies.

In 1992 the government extended this initiative by introducing a **Charter Mark Award** for top public-sector companies. A Charter Mark is given to public-sector organisations and private utility companies which can prove with clear evidence that they have achieved specified standards of public service and can impress the judges with the quality of their performance. The award is given for three years and holders can then apply to be reassessed. Unless holders can prove that they have made further progress, the award is withdrawn.

There are nine criteria relating to the award (see Figure 4.6). A detailed application must be submitted to the judging panel together with background information. The awards are usually announced each December.

1   **Standards** – the setting, monitoring and publication of explicit standards for the services that individual users can actually expect

2   **Information and openness** – full, accurate information readily available in plain language about how public services are run, what they cost and how well they perform and who is in charge

3   **Consultation and choice** – regular and systematic consultation with those who use the services

4   **Courtesy and helpfulness** – courteous and helpful service from public servants who normally wear name badges

5   **Putting things right** – well-publicised and easy-to-use complaints procedure

6   **Value for money** – efficient and economical delivery of service within resources

7   **User satisfaction** – users satisfied with quality of service

8   **Improvements** – measurable and demonstrable improvements over the last two or more years

9   **Innovation** – innovative enhancement without extra cost to taxpayer or user

Figure 4.6 Charter Mark criteria

Is your school or college a winner?

If you attend Winstanley Sixth Form College near Wigan, Dixons City Technology College in Bradford or Thomas Telford School in Shropshire, then you should be able to ask your tutor for details of the Charter Mark. All these institutions won awards in 1995.

Other winners included Greenwich Leisure Services, the Preston Disablement Services, Swale Borough Council Cleansing Services Unit, the Walsal Arboretum and Southwark Library Service. As an example of the type of service expected from a winner, Southwark won its award for renting out personal computers at £1 and providing computer facilities, including Internet, for £3 an hour. Southwark has also developed new technology for children and is establishing a collection of material on CD-Rom, including GCSE collections. Homework centres, open after school and on Saturdays, were introduced in 1996.

It is interesting to note that in 1995 British Gas withdrew from the scheme before the awards were announced and none of the Charter Marks previously awarded to water companies was renewed. After the problems encountered with water leaks and shortages during 1995, this might not be surprising!

Discussion point

1   Look at the Job-seekers Charter, reproduced in Figure 4.7. As a person who is likely to be seeking a job in the near future, assess how helpful you think it will be to you as a future consumer.

2   As a group, obtain examples of at least three other charters. You can do this by visiting or contacting any of the organisations which issue a charter – from your town hall to the nearest post office. In particular, obtain a copy of the Students Charter which concerns you *now* and find out if your school or college has adapted this to publish its own charter.

National targets for the delivery of services must be published each year.

Local targets must be displayed in each local office on

a   waiting time (up to a national limit of 10 minutes)
b   time to answer telephone calls
c   promptness and accuracy of benefit payments
d   numbers of people helped into jobs.

Name badges should be worn by staff who will give their name in writing and on the telephone. The names of the local and area managers must be displayed in each office.

Customer satisfaction surveys must be carried out at a national and local level.

An easy-to-use complaints procedure must be set up and publicised in each office.

Details of help available from the Employment Service must be displayed in each local office and supplemented with widely available leaflets.

Figure 4.7 Job-seekers Charter

Investors in people

Given that a strategic plan identifies the future direction of a company, implicit within this is the need for staff training to help employees to cope with future needs of the business. **Investors in People** (IIP) is a national standard awarded to companies in both the public and private sectors which can demonstrate a commitment to training and developing their employees.

An organisation that wishes to achieve IIP must demonstrate to an assessor that it has achieved 24 standards or assessment indicators (see Figure 4.8) which link to a national standard that encompasses four key principles.

1   **Commitment:** 'An *Investor in People* makes a public commitment from the top to develop all employees to achieve its business objectives.'

   This means that there is a clear plan giving business goals and targets which is linked to a **staff development plan.** In addition, the plan and the targets are known by all employees together with their own personal contribution.

2   **Planning:** 'An *Investor in People* regularly reviews the training and development needs of all employees.'

   This involves identifying the resources required for training and development in the strategic plan and managers regularly reviewing and agreeing staff performance and objectives with their own staff.

Commitment

1.1 There is a public commitment from the most senior level within the organisation to develop people.

1.2 Employees at all levels are aware of the broad aims or vision of the organisation.

1.3 There is a written but flexible plan which sets out business goals and targets.

1.4 The plan identifies broad development needs and specifies how they will be assessed and met.

1.5 The employer has considered what employees at all levels will contribute to the success of the organisation and has communicated this effectively to them.

1.6 Where representative structures exist, management communicates with employee representatives a vision of where the organisation is going and the contribution employees (and their representatives) will make to its success.

Planning

2.1 The written plan identifies the resources that will be used to meet training and development needs.

2.2 Training and development needs are regularly reviewed against business objectives.

2.3 A process exists for regularly reviewing the training and development needs of all employees.

2.4 Responsibility for developing people is clearly identified throughout the organisation, starting at the top.

2.5 Managers are competent to carry out their responsibilities for developing people.

2.6 Targets and standards are set for development actions.

2.7 Where appropriate, training targets are linked to achieving external standards and particularly to National Vocational Qualifications (or Scottish Vocational Qualifications in Scotland) and units.

Action

3.1 All new employees are introduced effectively to the organisation and are given the training and development they need to do their jobs.

3.2 The skills of existing employees are developed in line with business objectives.

3.3 All employees are made aware of the development opportunities open to them.

3.4 All employees are encouraged to help identify and meet their job-related development needs.

3.5 Effective action takes place to achieve the training and development objectives of individuals and the organisation.

3.6 Managers are actively involved in supporting employees to meet their training and development needs.

Evaluation

4.1 The organisation evaluates how its development of people is contributing to business goals and targets.

4.2 The organisation evaluates whether its development actions have achieved their objectives.

4.3 The outcomes of training and development are evaluated at individual, team and organisational levels.

4.4 Top management understand the broad costs and benefits of developing people.

4.5 The continuing commitment of top management to developing people is communicated to all employees.

Figure 4.8 Investors in People: assessment indicators

3   **Action:** 'An *Investor in People* takes action to train and develop individuals on recruitment and throughout their employment.'

This means that new recruits participate in an **induction programme** on recruitment (see page 289) and undertake any training required to help them settle in as quickly as possible. Any changes to a person's job should be identified together with any associated training needs.

4   **Evaluation:** 'An *Investor in People* evaluates the investment in training and development to assess achievement and improve future effectiveness.'

This involves managers in reassessing the investment in training and the use being make of new skills in relation to business goals and targets. It also involves taking into account staff feedback on how appropriate and useful individual training activities were for their own personal and job needs.

When the organisation is confident that it can meet all the standards an assessor, appointed by the local Training and Enterprise Council (TEC), visits the organisation to interview staff and examine the training records. Interviews are held with a cross-section of staff at all levels in the organisation and holding a wide range of job roles – from the cleaner to the MD's secretary! Interviews are held either on a one-to-one basis or in small groups. The assessor then issues a report which states that the organisation has either

• failed to meet the standards

• nearly met the standards – in which the assessment decision will be deferred until the organisation has put right the areas on which it failed

• succeeded in meeting the standards – the assessor will then make a positive recommendation to the TEC panel that the award should be given.

All the standards must be met for the company to be presented with the award. Failing in one area means a deferment.

IIP is not awarded once and forever! Holders of the award are revisited every three years and reassessed to ensure they are maintaining the standard laid down.

North of the border with IIP

Investors in People was launched in Scotland in 1994, a year later than its introduction in England and Wales. The assessment system in Scotland is slightly different as the accreditation panel comprises senior managers from organisations that have already achieved the award.

Throughout the UK more than 2,000 organisations have obtained the scheme

and more than 18,000 are working towards it. However, take-up of IIPs nationally has been mainly by large companies – smaller organisations are less likely to think it is appropriate. For this reason, the training standards body is currently reviewing the targets with the aim of proposing different ones for organisations of different sizes.

Keywords

The important keywords from this chapter are given below. Check that you know and understand the meaning of each one – look back to the relevant pages and check the definition of any that you are at uncertain about.

Annual General Meeting
accountability
board of directors
chairman
chief executive/managing director
Charter Mark
conceptual skills
core business
effectiveness
efficiency
executive directors
governing body
human skills
Investors in People
middle management
mission statement

networking
non-executive director
objectives
operating statement
operational planning
PEST analysis
quality standards
responsibility
senior management
short-termism
strategic planning
subcontractor
SWOT analysis
tactical planning
targets
technical skills

Examination practice

Short-answer questions

1 Identify two main differences between the role of chairman and that of the chief executive or managing director.

2 Explain the main purpose of a mission statement.

3 State clearly the difference between a strategic plan and an operating statement.

4 Identify two benefits for employees if their employer is working for an Investors in People award.

5 Clearly explain the difference between the role and responsibilities of
  a   a company chairman
  b   a chief executive.

6 Describe the role played by the board of directors in an organisation.

7 Describe three duties undertaken by company directors.

8 Identify four benefits of undertaking a PEST analysis.

9 Describe two ways in which a private company might demonstrate its commitment to quality.

10 Identify four factors which would be checked if a public-sector organisation applied for a Charter Mark award.

Definition questions

1 Explain clearly the difference between each of the following terms.
  a   executive director and non-executive director
  b   efficiency and effectiveness
  c   senior management and middle management
  d   strategic planning and operational planning

2 Write clear notes to explain each of the following terms.
  a   mission statement
  b   short-termism
  c   governing body
  d   quality standards

Essay questions

1 Some managers who are promoted prove unable to cope with the changed job role. Explain why this is likely to occur.

2 Your boss is considering submitting an application for Investors in People but is unsure what this means. Write an explanation which

includes the actions to be taken by an organisation for this to be achieved.

3   'Quality awards are only applicable to large companies.' Critically evaluate this statement.

4   Organisations which set out to pay good dividends are praised by the financial markets and criticised by the media. State why this situation occurs and the dilemma this may cause managers.

5   Clearly explain the duties and responsiblities of a company director. What qualities and abilities will be required to operate successfully at this level?

6   Explain the phrase 'divorce between ownership and control'. Why does this factor cause difficulties for small shareholders of public limited companies?

Case study

You work for Peacework, a charity that is actively involved in promoting environmental causes and international harmony. The general aim of the charity is to make the world a better place for the next generation.

The Chief Executive, Karen Denwood, is currently working on several aspects concerned with strategic and operational planning. The charity is concerned that donations have fallen during the past year and wishes to revise its approach to the public.

a   What points must Karen Denwood bear in mind when she revises her mission statement so that it has the maximum appeal?

b   Karen has decided to undertake a PEST analysis to identify the external factors she must take into account when devising the strategic plan. Under each of the headings – political, economic, social and technological – identify at least three relevant factors which might apply to the charity.

c   Explain how the operating statement produced for the charity will affect the work of the managers during the next 12 months.

Introduction

This chapter is concerned with the structure of business organisations. This relates to the way in which the business has been organised to accommodate the different activities which are carried out.

The type of structure affects the job of managers in the organisation and the number and type of activities for which they are responsible. It also obviously affects the working conditions of the employees and the way in which staff are expected to perform their jobs. In this chapter you will be introduced to the most usual types of structures and see how these can be displayed in a diagram known as an **organisation chart.**

However, structures are not fixed entities. They may change for a variety of reasons. The organisation may grow to a point where its existing structure is unwieldy and ineffective. Technological progress may change the way in which jobs should be handled and even result in completely new areas – such as a computer service section. Rising costs might force senior managers to review the existing structure to see if a **restructure** could bring savings.

This chapter therefore considers the reasons why structures may change and the effect of such changes on other aspects of work.

Organisational structures

Every type of business organisation has a definite structure which is known by all employees. If it did not, then no one would know what they had to do, who was in charge, who they should communicate with over certain matters or to whom they could turn for help. Life would be chaotic. The aim of a business structure is to enable the work to be undertaken in the most efficient and effective way.

The type of organisational structure which is the most suitable varies considerably from one business to another. A small family business is unlikely to be structured in the same way as a large general hospital, for instance!

The structure of an organisation will depend upon

- the size of the organisation

- the number of employees

- the business 'culture'

- whether it is in the manufacturing or service sector

- whether it is a local, national or international organisation

- the type of work with which it is involved.

Therefore all organisations are different. There is no right or wrong structure – provided that the way in which the company is organised helps people to do their work more efficiently, communicate with each other easily and assists the business to achieve its objectives.

However, in a large organisation there is likely to be more **specialisation,** ie each person will concentrate on his or her own specific job. For instance, accounts staff will only deal with financial matters. In a small organisation, finance may simply be one part of a manager's job.

Functional activities

You have already seen how senior managers decide the goals of the organisation and how the strategic plans are incorporated into operational plans and operating statements in chapter 4. The operating statements look at the contribution of each area of the organisation towards the overall aims and objectives included in the strategic plan.

Apart from the very smallest firms, it is usually necessary for there to be a definite structure in the organisation which divides up the work into **key areas** or **activities.** Ideally, all the related activities would be grouped together into units, divisions or departments.

The way in which the **groupings** take place will depend upon the type of organisation, the work it does and the area it covers. The groups may be classified in a number of ways.

- **By product** – a pharmaceutical company, for instance, could be grouped into drugs, toiletries and hospital supplies; a retail company could be grouped into groceries, DIY and furnishings. Most awarding bodies, such as the RSA, are grouped into divisions or departments which relate to different types of examinations or awards.

- **By process** – in this case, the organisation has departments based on the part of the process the staff carry out. In publishing, it is usual for there to be an editorial department, a design department and a production department.

- **By area** – many large retail organisations, such as Marks & Spencer and Tesco, are grouped by geographical area in this way.

- **By customer** – frequently the division here is between private individuals and businesses. This type of separation could occur in organisations such as BT and the high street banks, both of which deal with the different needs of business and private customers.

- **By function** – this is the most popular way of structuring an organisation, with employees grouped according to the work they do. The main divisions or departments usually relate to

  - Finance and Accounts
  - Production
  - Marketing
  - Human Resources (or Personnel)
  - Administration.

  Quite obviously, a firm that offers a service would not have a Production Department. Equally, many organisations today do not have a centralised administration function but have given each specialist area its own administrative responsibilities. The work carried out by each functional area is discussed in detail in chapter 6.

Just because an organisation is grouped or structured in one way does not mean that it will always stay like that! Companies which restructure may change from one type of grouping to another. This is usually undertaken because the company has changed its form over time and the current structure no longer reflects the most effective working pattern (or what is really going on!). If there are areas of serious duplication and overlap – or areas of neglect for which no one is really responsible – then a change in structure may be called for. This can lead to a significant rearrangement of the workforce and the systems and procedures which are in place (see chapter 8).

The organisation chart

The structure of an organisation can be shown most easily by means of an organisation chart. The chart usually gives the job titles of employees and their relationship with each other – it does not usually include people's names. Those at the top of the chart are more important and have more responsibility than those lower down.

As an example, DPTS is a small computer consultancy. There are two partners, David and Paula and they employ two consultants, Jane and Martin, and an administrator, Sajida.

On an organisation chart, the structure of DPTS would be shown as in Figure 5.1.

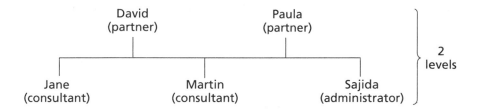

Figure 5.1 Organisation chart showing structure of DPTS

This shows that David and Paula are of equal status (they are on the same level on the chart) and they are *jointly* responsible for the consultants and for Sajida. At the same time, all the staff are on the same level.

If David was responsible for Jane and Martin, and Paula was responsible for Sajida, then the chart would be drawn differently. If Sajida was less senior than the two consultants, this would also be shown by changing her position on the chart – see Figure 5.2.

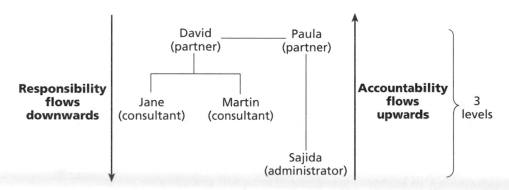

Figure 5.2 DPTS: an alternative organisation chart

The arrows on the chart show that managers or supervisors have **responsibility** or **authority** for staff who report to them, and that, in return these staff have **accountability** to their manager for their actions. These concepts are explained in more detail on page 182.

Levels in organisations

All organisations have different levels or layers. For this reason, people often talk about 'moving up a level' or 'operating at a different level' when they are talking about someone who has been promoted. You saw in the last chapter that there may be up to three levels of managers in an organisation. If you included staff as well, this would give four levels (Figure 5.3). Each level denotes a different type of role and a difference in the skills required. This links with the different skills required by different levels of managers which you met in chapter 4 (pages 142–3). Note that the shape is like a pyramid – there are fewer people at each progressive level.

The number of levels can vary considerably from one organisation to another. One with very few levels is normally called a **flat structure** whereas one with several levels is called an **hierarchical structure.**

The phrase 'passing it down the line' can refer to jobs and information passed down an organisation from one level to another – as shown by the lines on the organisation chart which denote **lines of responsibility.**

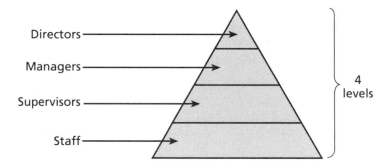

Figure 5.3 Levels in organisations

Types of organisation structure

Flat structures

An organisation with only two or three levels is known as a **flat** structure. The business is likely to have a relatively informal style or culture, as everyone will know everyone else. There will probably be good communications between bosses and employees. This should mean that they can respond quickly to changing situations and specific customer requests.

The difficulty with a flat structure is that as the organisation increases in size, the number of staff each manager has to supervise increases. A technical term for the number of people supervised is **span of control.** If this becomes too wide, then the manager's job becomes impossible and some subordinates may be virtually ignored.

As an example, imagine what would happen if, over the next three years, DPTS employed another 10 consultants. David and Paula would now be in charge of 13 people. They would also need office staff. If five more office staff were employed, the directors would be in charge of 18 people! They would then spend more time supervising the work done by other people than they would on doing their own jobs.

If David and Paula divided the staff into two halves, they would each have a span of control of nine people (Figure 5.4). Whilst this may be possible if employees are undertaking very routine or similar work (eg assemblers on a production line) it is almost impossible to supervise a large number of staff properly if they are involved in complicated work or very different types of jobs.

An added complication would be the fact that officially David could not give instructions to Paula's staff, nor could Paula give orders to those who report to David! In a small office, this would be unworkable – and would reduce flexibility and response times dramatically.

One solution would be to introduce another 'level' into DPTS as this would immediately reduce the span of control.

David and Paula decide to take joint responsibility for Jane, Martin and Sajida. They promote Jane and Martin to the position of senior consultant. Each is responsible for the work of five other consultants. All the office staff report to Sajida, who has been promoted to administration manager. The organisation chart of the company now looks like the one in Figure 5.5.

Line and staff functions
Without even thinking about it, David and Paula have divided up the operational or **line functions** of the organisation from the support or **staff functions** – simply by giving Sajida her own section.

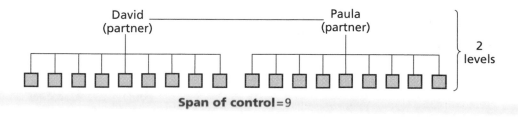

Span of control=9

Figure 5.4 Span of control at DPTS

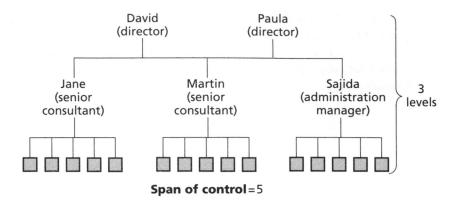

Span of control = 5

Figure 5.5 Span of control at DPTS Ltd after restructure

This type of division into areas is very common. Staff undertaking similar activities will need to communicate with each other regularly, will use the same type of systems and procedures and can operate more effectively as a team if they are grouped together.

Let us assume that, as time goes by, DPTS Ltd continues to expand. Four consultants have left and David and Paula decide that they now want to recruit *trainee* consultants who they can train in their own ways of working. They also appoint a financial manager, Gerry, and a sales and marketing manager, Brian. These managers are at the same level as the senior consultants who are now in charge of two separate areas. Martin is involved with software development and Jane is responsible for systems control.

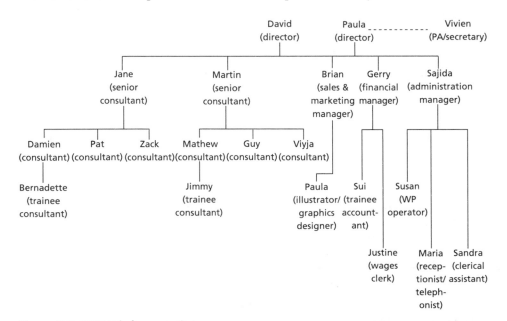

Figure 5.6 DPTS Ltd after expansion

At the same time they reorganise the office staff who now number six. In addition Paula appoints her own secretary/PA – Vivien. Because she does not report to anyone but Paula, Vivien is shown as linked to her by a dotted line. The organisation chart now looks like the one shown in Figure 5.6.

 ## Discussion point

1   As a group, discuss the advantages and disadvantages that there will be for staff working in an organisation of this size, rather than in the original DPTS structure.

2   An organisation chart only shows the 'formal' structure of an organisation – not the informal relationships. What difference do you think it would make
   a   to Martin if David played golf with Guy every Sunday morning
   b   to Pat if Damien, Zack and Mathew all went to university together
   c   to Maria if Vivien was a friend of her mother!

Discuss your ideas with your tutor.

Deputies versus assistants

A deputy is higher than an assistant – and therefore has a different position on the organisation chart.

Examine the chart in Figure 5.7. The deputy is directly below the manager – which means that if the manager leaves, the deputy could move 'up the line' and take her place. He would certainly be eligible to apply for the job.

The assistant, on the other hand, is to one side. This means that he is literally 'not in line for the job'.

Figure 5.7 Deputies and assistants

Hierarchical structures

A hierarchical structure is one in which there are many levels. It looks 'tall'. Each person has a narrower span of control. Jobs are more specialised – as an example, since the appointment of the financial manager, neither of the directors of DPTS will expect to be involved in this type of work, except to be kept informed as to how the company is doing!

Usually, the more hierarchical an organisation the more 'formal' it is. There will be more official systems and procedures which have to be followed and a greater number of written rules and regulations, eg

* official job titles and a specified **salary scale** for each 'level' of job

* a formal health and safety policy

* standard procedures laid down on hours of work, holidays, personal days off, punctuality, disciplinary procedures and so on

* an official interview procedure

* guidelines (or rules) on dress, customer service, layout of documents, methods of working, etc.

Why is all this necessary? There are two main reasons.

1 To ensure that the standards throughout the organisation will be the same – for customers and for employees.

2 To ensure that there is fairness to all employees – because they are all treated the same.

With a large number of employees this would be impossible unless some standards were laid down as different managers would respond to situations in different ways – and this would lead to problems.

Hierarchical structures are often called **pyramid structures.** This is because the shape is like a pyramid if you take into account the fact that at each level downwards in the organisation there will be more employees. The more

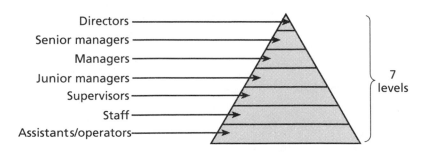

Figure 5.8 A hierarchical or pyramid structure

hierarchical, the steeper the pyramid. Compare the slope of the pyramid in Figure 5.8 with that of the organisation with fewer levels in Figure 5.3.

Max Weber, a German sociologist, called organisations with a hierarchy of authority and a system of rules **bureaucracies.** Today the term is often synonymous with red tape and officialdom.

He considered that bureaucracies occur when organisations become very large and complex as they need complicated systems for activities to be controlled. Typical bureaucracies are the civil service and local government – as well as large-scale private companies.

There are several problems with hierarchical structures, which are exacerbated in a bureaucracy.

- Because everyone has to follow rules and procedures, decision-making can be slow.

- Employees may feel stifled and frustrated in that they cannot show any initiative or introduce anything new.

- If there are too many **levels of authority,** they may be so far distant from 'the boss' that they feel more like a number or a cog in a wheel than a person with a distinct role to play in helping the organisation.

- They may also feel that the **lines of communication** (see page 186) are so long that it would be hopeless trying to influence anything not in their own particular area. Their own boss can effectively 'block them' in making their voice heard elsewhere.

- There might be a strong desire by middle or senior managers to want to impress the boss by telling him or her what he or she wants to hear, rather than the truth – in the hope that this will improve their own chances of moving up the organisation.

All these problems can result in a management decision to implement **delayering** (Figure 5.9). This term is used when an organisation removes at least one layer from the organisational structure (see page 205).

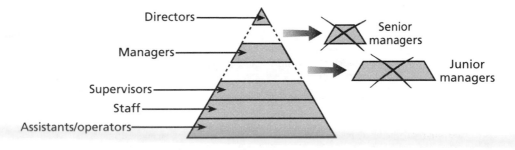

Figure 5.9 Delayering in a hierarchical structure

Empowerment at BAA

BAA (formerly British Airports Authority) is developing a different way of coping with the problems of being big. It has introduced a programme called 'Freedom to Manage' which is designed to enable employees at all levels to make as many decisions as possible on their own, without referring problems upwards. Training is given to employees to make sure that they know the range of decisions they can take –

and the areas over which they have more control.

'Empowerment' is one of the buzz-words of the 1990s – but often seems to employees to be a way of making them take more responsibility than they feel they are paid to handle. Instead, the aim at BAA is to remove frustration from both staff and customer by giving employees the power to make more decisions themselves.

Matrix structure

A different type of organisational structure is called the **matrix structure.** This is less common than a hierarchical or flat structure, but is becoming more popular. In this structure people report to two bosses – one of which is a line manager and the other a service manager. In other words, this structure integrates line and staff functions.

It aims to group people by skill or key area rather than by their position in the organisation. This is usually because a key area may often cross one or more departments.

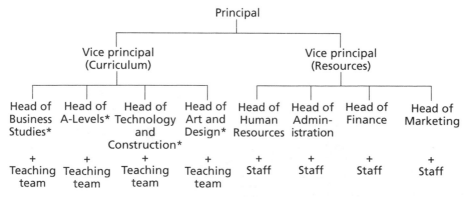

*Lecturers in each department mainly teach on courses in that department, eg Business Studies staff would teach accounts, law, business studies, etc. to students on business studies courses

Figure 5.10 Matrix structure – with departments in a hierarchical format – in a college

As an example, a university or college may have a matrix structure in which a number of related courses and staff are grouped into separate departments in a hierarchical format with deputy heads and heads (Figure 5.10). These are the line functions. However, all departments are supported by other sections which are concerned with the operation and maintenance of organisation – such as Finance, Administration, Human Resources (Personnel), Marketing and Student (or Customer) Services, ie the staff functions.

The matrix structure in business

In the business world the matrix structure is used when specialisms are important, and is frequently found in organisations that deal with specialised 'one-off' projects, such as civil engineering companies. For example BOMAC, a civil engineering company, is 'bidding' for three different contracts – motorway construction in the UK, building a bridge abroad and a high-rise banking building in London. Think of these bids as projects A, B and C. If the company is awarded each project, it decides on the project team in each case – comprised of experts who can see the project through. These experts need the support of the main functions of the organisation – finance, personnel, design and development – and the heads of each project will be in constant contact with the major function heads – about costings, staffing and design. The project teams would continue to work on the project until completion when the team would be disbanded. A new team would be formed to work on a different project when the next bid was won.

This can be shown on an organisation chart as in Figure 5.11. Trace the dotted lines to see which person each project manager contacts regularly.

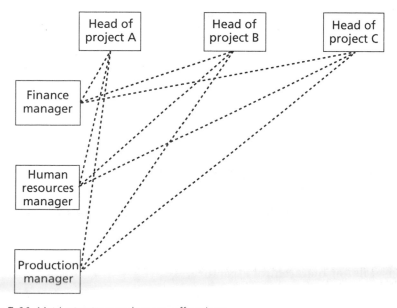

Figure 5.11 Matrix structure used on one-off projects

Advantages of a matrix structure

- Everyone makes the best possible use of individual specialist skills.

- Service departments such as Finance can have specialist staff to support the main teams.

- New teams can be formed and easily included in the structure.

- Old teams can easily be removed from the structure.

 Discussion point

1 As a group, discuss the *disadvantages* of the matrix structure. Think of

- possible problems of communication between staff in all the various areas

- the drawbacks of specialising in just one area – with no opportunity for staff to get wider experience.

2 You are employed by a small television production company which, you are told, has a matrix structure.

a Why do you think such a structure has been chosen for this type of company?

b Make a rough sketch, showing what it might look like.

A final note on organisation charts!

Organisation charts are drawn up for several reasons.

- The chart immediately shows the overall structure of the organisation and the way it has been grouped, eg by product, geographically or by function (see page 170).

- All staff can see clearly to whom they relate and to whom they are accountable.

- Managers can see the staff for whom they are responsible (ie the chain of command).

- The number of subordinates per manager is usually indicated (ie the span of control).

- The number of 'levels' in the organisation is shown – this shows whether there is a flat or hierarchical structure.

- The labels or descriptions for individual roles and functions give an indication of the type of work carried out or areas of responsibility.

However, organisation charts have benefits and drawbacks.

Benefits

- The chart can highlight problem areas – such as a manager with an unrealistic span of control or a person who is expected to report to different managers.

- The chart will show how many line functions there are and how many staff functions there are. Remember that line functions make money (ie Sales and Production) whereas staff functions are supportive (ie Finance, Human Resources, Administration). There should therefore be more emphasis on line than staff.

- Staff can check to whom they should refer a certain matter or problem.

- The chart can be projected into the future to give an indication of the human resource planning required, eg the number of vacancies which might occur in the future, areas of growth/decline, etc. (see chapter 6).

Limitations

- The fact that the chart shows the company as unchanging – in reality things may be changing all the time. Unless an organisation chart is updated regularly, it may be useless as a reference document.

- Organisation charts do not show the informal links between different people within the organisation.

- The chart does not usually show the formal lateral links between one function and another.

- There is no indication of the organisational culture, the style of management nor who has the most power and who the least!

- Staff can jump to incorrect conclusions by looking at the chart if they simply measure their potential by the distance between themselves and the boss. There may even be disagreements about the formal 'placing' of different members of staff.

- The chart may give the wrong idea of how the organisation operates in practice, eg by ignoring the informal lines of communication.

As a simple example of how misleading a chart may be, think of the amount of power held in some unexpected quarters! The security staff have the power to order you from the building if they wish – either because of a danger or because they want to lock up. An office junior can cause havoc by refusing to do some urgent photocopying because something else has cropped up. Computer services engineers can create problems if they don't cooperate with you if your PC fails, etc. Whatever you do, therefore, don't assume that you should only be pleasant to those in positions of authority in the organisation – the only safe route is to be nice to everyone!

● Other aspects of organisation structure

The actual structure of the organisation is not as important for employees as its suitability for the organisation and its objectives. However, some broad assumptions can be made in relation to certain aspects of people's jobs.

Responsibility, accountability and delegation

Responsibility relates to an employee's duty to undertake a task or assignment which he or she is given. The onus is the same whether you are talking about the security guard's responsibility to protect the organisation from intruders or the filing clerk's responsibility to keep the filing cleared or the chairman's responsibility to chair the board meetings.

Accountability is the duty of all staff to do the work to the best of their ability and to report back on the results.

Delegation relates to passing on work to other people and entrusting the responsibility of carrying out a task to someone else.

There are two key points to remember.

* You can *never* delegate ultimate responsibility if that task was originally yours. If your teacher invited a guest speaker for a session, but the result was total mayhem and confusion, then your teacher would take the blame, not the guest. This is because your tutor has responsibility for your class during the hour you are taught and cannot delegate total responsibility for this to anyone else. However, you could reasonably expect people to carry out their own responsibilities if they have agreed to do it for you and everything has been prearranged properly beforehand (see delegation below).

* Managers are accountable not only for their own work but for the work of their subordinates to their own boss. You first met this concept in chapter 4. What it means is that if managers choose to delegate to their own subordinates, then that is fine, but again they cannot delegate overall responsibility for the smooth running of their own section. If you make a mess of things, then your boss will ultimately get the blame!

Delegation and authority

You might well wonder why any managers take the risk of delegating anything! However, it would be totally impossible for a manager, supervisor or administrator to carry out personally all the tasks for which they are responsible. The skill lies in deciding what to delegate and how to do it.

- The worst possible case is when a manager tries hard not to delegate anything. Not only will he or she be likely to get in a mess trying to control everything personally, but staff will be frustrated because they never have the opportunity to prove that they are capable of dealing with responsibility.

- The next example (perhaps even worse) is when a manager delegates without any instructions or interest in the tasks staff have to do. This can cause extreme stress and confusion as there is little, if any, guidance and leadership from the top.

- Another problem arises if a manager delegates the responsibility for doing a task without the authority to carry it out. For instance, if you were asked to find some important information but everyone you asked said that you had no right to receive it, you would have a serious problem. If, however, the manager had cleared the way for you in advance, then the work would be both challenging and interesting.

The benefits of delegation
If delegation is done properly, it has several benefits to both manager and subordinate.

- It is essential for the organisation to operate effectively.

- It enables jobs to be done 'at the correct and most cost-effective level'. It would be ridiculous, for instance, for a manager paid £40,000 a year to lick envelopes for a mail shot when this could be done by someone being paid £8,000 a year. In addition, the manager could be more gainfully employed doing something else of which the junior would not be capable.

- Delegated duties stretch employees and give them the opportunity to develop new skills and abilities. This increases morale and improves motivation and job satisfaction (see also chapter 7).

- Delegation can be used as a form of training for coping with higher level tasks. This gives employees the opportunity to demonstrate that they are suitable for promotion.

However, in many cases delegation goes wrong – often because the basic guidelines are ignored.

Guidelines for delegation
Managers may be frightened to delegate because

- they believe that delegating will mean they lose control

- they are worried staff will make a mess of the job *or* they fear a member of staff would do the job better than they would

- they consider they haven't time to explain what is required – a common cry is 'it's quicker to do it myself'

- they think staff will object to the additional work
- they consider their staff are overloaded already
- they don't know where to start.

Generally, if everyone is overloaded already or if staff would object to taking on additional tasks, then there is something seriously wrong with the organisation of the section – and this may need reviewing first (see chapter 8).

So far as possible failure is concerned, to delegate properly means adhering to some broad guidelines so that success is, as far as possible, built into the delegation process.

1 The delegated tasks must be appropriate for the staff member selected in terms of scope and responsibility. Delegation is *not* a method of getting rid of tasks you do not want to do!

2 The selected staff member should be carefully briefed on what, exactly, he or she has to do. A check should be made that the instructions have been clearly understood. Obviously, at higher levels in the organisation, staff will be expected to use their own initiative to a greater extent and may therefore receive a rather more 'woolly' brief than at junior level.

3 Authority must be delegated also, so that everyone concerned knows that this particular person has the responsibility to carry out the task and the authority to make the necessary organisational arrangements.

4 Control and monitoring of progress should be carried out by the manager. It should not be so tight that the employee feels that he or she cannot make a move without permission, neither should the impression be given that any queries or feedback sessions are a nuisance! A good balance is 'get on with it as far as you can, let me know if you have any problems' – and then check up on progress at a later date. It is useful if clear boundaries are specified so that the member of staff knows the degree to which he or she has freedom of action and the areas which would be outside the remit.

5 Training should be given where necessary to enable the subordinate to cope with the task.

6 Good communication is vital at all stages of the delegation process so that

- the employee receives clear instructions on what he or she is doing
- all other staff affected are also informed promptly, so that they know about the change of responsibility
- monitoring is undertaken with tact and sensitivity
- feedback is positive and the employee is encouraged to do his or her best.

7 Once all the necessary systems are in place the employee should be left to get on with the job. It is important for the employee's confidence that he or she is left alone to some degree – if individuals feel that their manager has little faith in their ability, then this is likely to promote a feeling of inferiority and lack of confidence. Managers who believe in their staff can often achieve great things!

Delegation and organisation structures

In a flat structure one manager may have a large span of control. Delegation will then be essential for all the work to be done effectively. It is possible to do this on a semi-formal basis with nominated staff being made responsible for certain key activities with accountability to the manager concerned.

In a hierarchical structure it is the manager's responsibility to delegate, but there may be more scope for abuse of the system. For instance, the 'willing workhorse' might be given many jobs and the 'slacker' very few. Given that job roles and job descriptions are usually more precise in a hierarchical organisation, it is likely that staff know at the outset the type of work they will be expected to do. In a bureaucracy there may actually be rules and regulations which *prevent* people from operating above their normal level. In this case, the concept of formal authority becomes extremely important.

In a matrix structure the danger is that tasks will be delegated from different directions – because, in effect, each person is accountable both to a line manager and to those operating with staff responsibilities. A famous management concept is **unity of command.** This means one person should have only one boss. In reality it means that directions from managers should not conflict. In a matrix structure there are two dangers.

• Employees are given conflicting instructions from different managers.

• Employees are given too many tasks to undertake because each manager delegates in isolation from the others. If all perceive one person as being a 'willing workhorse', then that person could quite well be submerged in work very quickly indeed.

Close liaison between managers to prevent these problems is essential.

Global Ford

In December 1994 the Ford Motor Company announced one of the largest restructures ever. At that stage Ford comprised two similar organisations – one in North America and one in Europe. Ford had felt this was essential given the different markets – Americans have traditionally liked large, gas-guzzling cars, while Europeans are more restrained. They prefer smaller and more economical models.

However, recently not only had markets become more similar but also Ford had identified overlap, waste and poor communication which were reducing profits. It therefore announced a merger of the two operations to create Ford 2000. The number of levels within the organisation would be reduced from 14 to seven and five transatlantic vehicle centres are to be opened – four in the USA and one Anglo-German centre which is to be based both in Britain and Germany.

This, in effect, introduces a matrix structure as managers will not only report upwards within the vehicle centres but also will report to an executive from one of the functional departments of Manufacturing, Purchasing, Marketing and Finance.

 Discussion point

1   Individually, draw an organisation chart to show the new Ford structure. Then compare your chart with others in your group.

2   What do you consider were the disadvantages of the 'old' Ford with 14 levels?

3   Critics of matrix structures have argued that they lead to a confusion of accountability and internal conflict. As a group, discuss what is meant by these statements.

4   The aim of car manufacturers of the future is to make and design a 'global car' which will not need any modifications to be sold worldwide. Discuss why this is their aim.

Lines of communication

Lines of communication in a business can be both **formal** and **informal** – just as they are in your own college. The vast majority of communications between your tutor and yourself will be formal – related to teaching sessions. However, if you bumped into a tutor who taught you last year and chatted to her about how hard or easy your course was, this would be an example of an informal communication. Indeed, your current tutor might later be surprised to find information being received from that particular source!

However, there are different types of formal and informal communications, in addition to the ones mentioned above! An effective organisation uses *all* the methods of communication available to ensure a smooth flow of information in all directions.

Formal communications

You can draw lines of communication on an organisation chart. These can be **vertical** or **lateral.**

Vertical communications include the following.

- **Downward communications** – those which are sent 'top down', ie issued by senior management. These may be

  - statements giving information
  - instructions on work which must be done
  - persuasive or motivational messages to staff in general or certain people in particular (eg to congratulate them on a particular achievement).

  A major problem is making sure that a communication keeps its proper meaning if it is sent down through several **levels of authority.** If the message is 'translated' by four managers before it gets to the workforce, its original meaning may be lost.

- **Upward communications** – those which are sent 'bottom up', ie sent from staff to managers or from supervisors to upper levels of management. These may be

  - feedback on new systems and procedures
  - the response to surveys or suggestion schemes
  - information on the progress of work or views of staff.

  The problem for staff is that any information which is considered critical or negative by a poor manager may be construed as threatening and may be blocked without going any further. Good managers, however, will value contributions from their staff as this is the only way in which they can monitor and improve the way in which work is carried out and its effects on the people concerned.

- **Quasi-vertical communications** – those where staff may deal direct with senior management or vice versa – jumping several normal layers of authority. The most common example is trade union negotiations, where staff views are represented to management and vice versa. Trade union representatives may comprise ordinary staff members who will then be negotiating with a representative from senior management. Another example may be quality circles which report direct to senior management or staff information sessions held by a senior executive. Normally, unless there is a specific reason to exclude them, these type of sessions will include representatives from all levels of management – otherwise the concept may be unnerving for members of the management team who are excluded and unsettling for their staff.

Lateral communications are those which take place horizontally across the organisation. They are usually in the form of information or requests from one department to another, eg from Finance to Sales or from Production to Human Resources. Such communications are absolutely essential for the smooth running of the organisation as a whole because they **coordinate** the work of different sections.

Informal communications

These are routes for communication within the organisation by which messages can be sent and received. They mainly link to the network of friends and acquaintances within an organisation who make informal contact. Because, in most companies, everyone knows somebody who knows somebody else, news can travel all around the organisation by this means – usually known as the **grapevine** (Figure 5.12).

The grapevine will be used to give news and commentary on events – and will often beat the formal system! People may therefore receive major items of news informally first – and have time to speculate on the implications – long before they are told formally! All managers need to be aware of this when planning when to 'go public' with major announcements. Unless they do this simultaneously, it is likely that the second word gets out in one area,

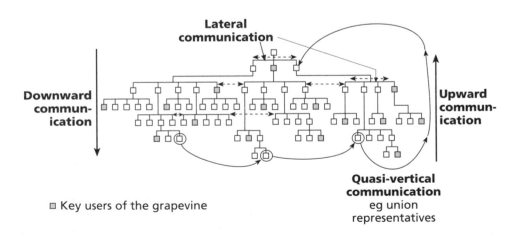

Figure 5.12 Forms of communication in an organisation

the information will spread like wildfire. Clear, accurate information is required to prevent rumours spreading out of control.

Managers can use the grapevine for their own benefit by planting or 'leaking' an idea and then waiting for it to spread. They can then see the reaction. If staff are in favour, they can then confirm the rumour. If staff are strongly against, they can deny the allegations. You may like to note that this is frequently done by the government, which will leak information to the media – and then wait for public reaction to the story before confirming or denying it!

Networking – an import from the US

Networking is becoming more and more common in Britain – but still not to the extent it is found in the USA. Networking is a method of developing contacts for personal benefit – normally those with similar interests. This means getting to know people, communicating with them about joint interests, making sure they know what you want – in other words trying to further your interests, even at social events. The wider your network and the more powerful people it includes, the better.

Whilst these are traits and tactics which do not seem to come as easily to the British as to Americans, there can be benefits. In some parts of the US few organisational vacancies are ever advertised, but filled through networking contacts. Chatting in the right jargon may help – if your organisation is downsizing you out, then you can talk about your new employability prospects and empowerment potential!

Lines of communication and organisation structures

Quite obviously, the more hierarchical the organisation, the longer the lines of communication will be. Therefore the greater chance of distortion as communications flow upwards and downwards in an organisation. In a flat organisation staff may have the opportunity of almost a daily informal chat with the boss – who can therefore keep 'tabs' on what is going on more easily. In a hierarchical structure it is all too easy for senior managers to lose their grip on what is really going on – as they have to rely on their own juniors to provide the information. This is often known as the **ivory tower syndrome.** The accuracy of the information will depend upon the individual manager concerned and the culture of the organisation. If an individual manager is blamed and chastised the second anything goes wrong, he or she is likely to be more secretive than if the organisation operates an 'open culture' or if the senior executive would rather his or her staff tried and failed, rather than did not try at all.

The flow of information is even more complex in a matrix structure as lateral communications are more pronounced. This can actually facilitate information handling for senior managers as they are receiving it from two sources – their functional managers and their project or support managers. If the information does not agree, then they can easily ask for more details!

The disadvantage can be information overload – when so much information is being received that it is difficult to sort out which is relevant and important and which is not. For that reason, the job remit of each manager must be clearly defined beforehand.

Organisation culture

Organisation culture refers to the 'atmosphere' in a company and the type of standards and values it favours. Here are some examples.

- Is there a formal or informal atmosphere? Would a member of staff address a senior manager as Mr/Ms X or by his or her first name? Are there any informal communications or events which involve both senior management and staff?

- Is the organisation relaxed or on a knife edge? What are response times like? Is the company in a state of constant crisis – always trying to meet deadlines – or is life far less rushed?

- Is the organisation traditional or modern? What is the furniture and decor like? This can be affected by the work carried out, the type of customer or the age of the senior management!

- How do staff dress? Are jeans and T-shirts acceptable or does everyone wear a suit or uniform? Or is it somewhere in between? A television production company and the law courts give two very different pictures!

- Are there a great many rules and regulations or is innovation and flexibility the key to progress? Compare your local authority or hospital with the offices of a software magazine for young readers!

- Is the focus on task accomplishment or people skills? Are people given precedence and are their needs high on the list of priorities for managers – or are they merely considered a means of getting the job done?

- Is the organisation at the leading edge of customer care, environmental issues and stakeholder concerns? Or does it ignore such pressures until it is forced to change by law?

- Are managers and staff encouraged to make suggestions and try new things – thus encouraging open communications throughout the company? Or is there a strong blame culture which prevents people changing anything – for fear of getting it wrong – and cultivates closed and secretive communications between rival groups?

Generally, it is considered that the more the culture of an organisation accords with a person's 'natural style' the more he or she will enjoy working there. You might think that no one would like to work in a formal organisation where there are many rules and a strict dress code – but you would be wrong! Some people are happier when they know exactly what they have to do and how to do it – and are unnerved by having the freedom of action and expression others enjoy. Despite this, there is clear evidence that in a rapidly changing environment, the organisation that has a flexible, informal and open culture is more likely to thrive than one that has not.

Culture and organisation structure

It is easier for an informal culture to prevail in a flat or matrix structure than in an hierarchical structure. However, as an organisation grows, this becomes more difficult to achieve. Richard Branson, for example, is a typical example of an 'informal executive'. In his early days he held business meetings on his houseboat and insisted his executives dressed informally and sat around on easy chairs rather than at a formal 'board table'. This type of approach is obviously more difficult today. However, by dividing Virgin into different operating units, still of a relatively small size in contrast to the whole, it is more likely to remain achievable.

From Big Blue to Big Red – and back again!

A few years ago the computer giant IBM was in serious trouble. From its previous high position as a key supplier of computer hardware and software it had slipped alarmingly and made a record loss. A key reason was identified. The culture of IBM – nicknamed 'Big Blue' was always to 'please the boss'. This had resulted in many middle managers being less than honest about the problems of selling IBM products when reporting to senior managers.

However, the truth came out when the financial accounts were published. The result was a complete restructure and reorganisation of the company to promote a more honest, forthright and flexible approach. It seems to have worked – IBM today is once again making healthy profits – in 1995 amounting to US$4.1 billion, the best profit since 1990.

Even so, Louis Gerstner, the Chief Executive responsible for downsizing the workforce by 86,000 people in three years, has been criticised by the US media – along with several others – because of the overall effect on the American labour market.

Salary grades

Generally, people at the same level in an organisation receive comparable salaries (pay rate policies are discussed in chapter 7). However, for there to be harmony amongst employees there must be some parity between those at the same level. In other words, the pay system must be *seen* to be fair.

Most organisations adopt a pay structure which reflects

- the type and degree of responsibility to be undertaken by the job holder

- the seniority of the job holder.

In the public sector, in particular, there are usually different grades of jobs and **incremental** scales which operate for each grade. A new employee will be appointed at a point on the scale in accordance with his or her previous experience and qualifications and will then move upwards, usually by one increment each year. Pay will then reflect seniority and experience. In some organisations, incremental awards may be given on the achievement of specified qualifications.

In the private sector the situation is more fluid. Most wage agreements today are organised on a local basis. However, there must be perceived fairness in the system – and for this reason job grading is usually carried out.

Job grading ranks jobs in relation to each other, based on their content. A common system in use is called the HAY-MSL profile which incorporates areas such as knowledge, problem-solving and accountability. A newer US version ranks jobs in relation to the amount of conceptual skills or vision required. It argues that it is more difficult to make successful long-term plans than short-term plans – therefore those involved with corporate strategy and policy-making should be paid the most. It is then possible to scale other jobs in relation to the time scale over which they are expected to make decisions. Senior managers would operate on a five-year model, middle managers on, say, a one-year model, supervisory managers would be operating with a six-month time scale and those lower down may only be interested in what they might be doing tomorrow morning!

To set up a pay structure, various other factors need to be taken into account in addition to levels.

- The type of work carried out, eg degree of difficulty or danger.

- The location of the work and/or whether extensive travelling is required.

- The type of hours – whether these will be 'normal' or consist of unsocial hours.

- Any other forms of bonuses or benefits which may be earned.

- Traditional differentials between different areas.

The first two reasons give a clear indication of why work on an oilrig or in the middle of Alaska is well paid! If it were not, no one would be tempted to do it. It is also usual for people to be paid more if they work in London, as the cost of living is higher. This additional payment is known as *London weighting allowance.*

It is also often customary for those who work on bank holidays or overnight to receive a higher rate than those who work standard 9 am–5 pm hours – because of the havoc this can play on their family and social life.

Bonuses and benefits can include

- bonuses linked to increased productivity or company profits

- the ability to purchase shares at reduced prices

- commission payments, based on sales

- pension scheme, company discounts, a company car, expense account and private health scheme – all can influence the basic wage rate

- increases based on payments by results or performance-related pay (PRP). This type of increase is linked to awarding above-average productivity or ability. In the case of PRP, it may then be possible for people at the top of the incremental scale to increase their earnings if they can prove exceptional performance.

The term **differentials** relates to the difference between jobs. It may, for instance, be the case that in an organisation computer operators earn more than clerical staff. If, however, clerical staff were ever regraded, than this could erode or destroy the differential unless the computer operators were also regraded. Eroding the differential may be deliberate, if the company is trying to standardise its pay rates. However, the situation needs handling with care as it is unlikely that the computer operators would be too happy with the idea!

From time to time even the best grading schemes need reviewing to take into account changes which affect the structure of the company and the jobs done by individuals. One innovation in some organisations is to reward teams who work together and produce good results. When a company restructures (see pages 203 and 208) a review of pay grades is normally essential. It goes without saying that a key factor which must be borne in mind is current employment legislation. This aspect is covered in chapter 7.

Local health trusts empowered to decide pay

The NHS is traditionally known as one of the most hierarchical structures in the world. Decisions are made in Whitehall and transmitted to managers in reams of paper containing instructions, circulars, bulletins, guidance notes and memoranda. This is neither cost effective nor good for employee morale.

To solve the problem more power has been given to the local health authorities. This has reduced the need for huge numbers of civil servants at the Department of Health and regional health authorities have also been shaken up and downsized.

The most radical decision has been to give local employers control to decide pay and design flexible reward packages for staff. This is a complete change from the old system of deciding pay centrally. It will enable employers not only to design pay packages to reflect the roles and responsibilities of staff but also enable them to attract the best staff they can.

Other differences between organisations

Before you start to examine ways in which companies may change their structure or ways of working to improve their efficiency, it is first important to note the other areas in which organisations differ.

Patterns of work

Not only does the structure of organisations vary considerably from one company to another but so may the patterns of work of the staff, eg

- the amount of team working and the degree of autonomy given to each team

- the degree of centralisation/decentralisation

- whether there is shift work or **flexitime** or variable hours for staff

- whether there is a predominance of full-time, part-time, permanent, temporary or casual workers in the organisation

- whether staff can work from home.

The way in which people work has changed over the past 20 years. The usual 'pattern' was for the majority of jobs to be full time, probably held by men (especially at senior level) and for job security for life to be an understood component of employment. Today things have changed dramatically.

- There has been an increase in female workers at all levels.

- There has been an increase in the number of part-time jobs.

- There has been increasing job insecurity – 'jobs for life' is an outdated concept. Most people see themselves as having several jobs or even several careers in a working lifetime.

- There has been an increase in flexible working arrangements, eg
  - **freelancing**
  - **homeworking, teleworking** and **hot desking**
  - **job sharing**
  - **temporary** and **casual work.**

Why have these changes occurred? A combination of factors has caused the change – and again PEST analysis highlights the reasons.

- **Political** – increasing unemployment means the government will welcome any initiatives which reduce unemployment figures and get people into work (as this also reduces benefits and increases taxes). Job sharing means two people are employed rather than one. Freelance work and temporary contracts mean claimants have to sign off benefits. Employment legislation (see chapter 7) has tempted many companies to increase short-term or freelance contracts. In many cases those contracted are not eligible for employment protection.

- **Economic** – the cost of living and current wage rates are such that most young couples cannot cope unless both of them work, even after the birth of children. Companies struggling to reduce costs in a competitive environment will look for alternative and cheaper methods of employment to reduce their wage bill. They will be particularly interested in any method which improves efficiency and does not negatively affect quality. Short-term contracts and casual staff can be hired only when needed – there is no ongoing financial commitment as there is with permanent staff (see also chapter 7).

- **Social** – today it is accepted that women will work and have careers. Working couples and those on unsocial hours insist that organisations are open longer to serve their needs. No longer is it acceptable for shops to close at 5 pm, for instance. In addition, rising customer expectations and increased leisure time have increased the demand for many services to be available out of hours.

- **Technological** – new technology has enabled more people to work from home or from a distant location and has reduced the skills required in many occupations (eg check-out operators no longer need to be able to add up!). New technology has also assisted decentralisation in that people are capable of doing more operations on their own when helped by a computer.

Team working

Team working is discussed in more detail in chapter 8. It refers to people working in coordinated groups where everyone pulls together to achieve a result. At this stage it is enough for you to realise that team working is

- more prevalent in flatter structures

- a good way of motivating staff whilst reducing costs.

Centralisation/decentralisation

These principles can be applied to the whole organisation or to specific functions.

In relation to the whole organisation, a centralised company would have a remote head office which gives instructions to geographically remote units. The degree to which managers of these units have to follow the 'rules' is dependent upon the culture of the organisation. In some companies, almost everything has to be referred to head office for approval. In other cases, individual managers have more scope for using their own discretion.

Apart from specialist areas such as retailing and banking, this type of control is now considered inefficient and ineffective as there is a danger in people giving orders who are out of touch with what is really going on. In addition, the cost of running a head office is very expensive. For that reason, most production organisations now operate from the main manufacturing base.

In relation to a particular function, centralisation is when an operation is carried out centrally for the whole organisation. Examples can include

- printing and reprographics

- filing

- data inputting

- word processing.

Usually this is only cost effective if there is a very large demand for a high-quality service.

Advantages of centralisation

- **Economy of scale** – if everything is concentrated in one place, it is possible to instal better and more expensive equipment.

- **Standardisation** – only one set of procedures is required and duplication can be avoided.

- **Specialist staff** – staff can be specially trained (or professionals employed) to ensure that they are capable of dealing with the work required.

- **Cover for absence** – tasks will not be left to accumulate because the person who normally does the job in a department is off sick or on holiday.

- **Centralised costing systems** – these can apportion the cost amongst different organisational users.

- **Quality output** – quality is more easily controlled and is unlikely to be different throughout the organisation.

Disadvantages of centralisation

- **Low morale** – it can be tedious for staff to work in a highly specialised environment rather than to use a variety of skills.

- **Inflexibility** – the service may only be available if standard procedures are followed, and these may not allow for emergency requests.

- **Increased bureaucracy** – the danger is that the service providers start to dictate terms to users, rather than being keen to meet their requests.

- **Duplication** – individual departments may start to set up their own systems and facilities to get around the disadvantages of dealing with a central provider.

For these reasons centralisation has been declining in popularity in many organisations. In some cases work has been devolved to departments, such as word processing. Technological developments have assisted this process quite considerably with the advent of computer networks and PCs. In other cases, work is contracted out, eg in the case of printing (see also page 124).

Flexible working

The increase in flexible working has led to different working patterns. Traditionally, people were employed on full-time permanent contracts of employment. Today there are several variations on that scheme and fewer and fewer people are working under a contract of employment which is permanent. Many people are now temporary workers or work under a fixed term contract.

Permanent full-time employment

This is where employees work for a set number of hours per week under a contract which has a start date but no definite end date. The contract will end either when the employee leaves (voluntarily or through compulsory redundancy) or retires or when he or she is dismissed.

Temporary work

This occurs where employees are given full- or part-time work for a limited number of weeks, months or years.

Work under a fixed-term contract

This is the case if employees are given full- or part-time work which not only has a definite start date but also a definite end date.

Casual work

Casual workers also have flexible working hours. However, it is normally the employer who dictates what the hours are – and the casual workers are offered work only when the employer needs them – not necessarily on a regular basis.

Zero hours contracts?

A recent development has been the introduction of zero hours contracts where employees are kept on the books but are not guaranteed any specific hours of work. One example is the fire service where 'retained firefighters' are often used to provide additional cover in emergency situations. Several universities have the same arrangement with some of their teaching staff. Hotels also often keep lists of catering staff who can be used to fill staffing gaps at short notice during busy seasons.

Shift work and unsocial hours

Many organisations have traditionally operated 'round the clock', eg manufacturing industries which work a **shift system,** hospitals, the police, the media and high-class hotels. Organisations today which open for longer hours include retail stores and leisure organisations – from pubs and clubs to leisure centres. All need to find ways to employ staff around the clock.

The traditional method was a shift system – either a three-shift system of eight hours for five days or a two-shift system of 12 hours for four days or a different variation which suited the individual organisation.

More recent variations to broaden hours of work without necessarily employing more staff have included job sharing and flexitime.

Job sharing

Job sharing enables people who do not wish to work on a full-time basis to gain all the advantages of being a full-time employee. They simply 'share' their job with someone else. Not all jobs are suitable for job sharing – usually senior and middle management jobs are exempt as the amount of information which would need to be coordinated between the two staff would be too great. In addition, the style and strategy of the department might be continually changing depending on who was in the office when! The other disadvantage, of course, is that staff could 'play' one manager off against the other! However, this does not mean that all such jobs are *automatically* unsuitable – each case should be judged on its merits.

Generally, however, most staff and supervisory jobs are quite suitable and there are definite advantages for both the post-holders and the employer.

The employer is able to

- retain qualified and experienced staff who may otherwise leave if they cannot work part time

- cover the post during sickness and holidays

- arrange for cover during peak times of activity

- arrange for the post to be covered for longer hours (eg from 8 am to 8 pm with each person working six hours a day)

- benefit from the joint skills and experience of both employees

- benefit from lower absenteeism as domestic arrangements can be made for times the job sharer would not be in work

- benefit from a greater number of applicants for each job.

Employees benefit because

- there is a wider variety of jobs to choose from and career opportunities available than those usually offered on a part-time basis

- job sharers can give each other mutual support during difficult times

- job sharers can arrange to cover for each other during times of unavoidable absence

- staff who job share are free to pursue other interests during non-working hours.

However, there can be problems with the scheme unless it is carefully managed.

- Managers of job sharers could, theoretically, have twice as many staff to control.

- If staff training is required, then it may be that *both* members of staff must attend.

- Communication problems can easily arise unless the job sharers are allocated 'overlap time' and are committed to the success of the mutual job.

- Job sharing allows each to blame the other if something goes wrong.

- If one person is far more competent than the other, that person may find he or she is always doing the majority of the work or all the difficult tasks simply because other people save up requests until the best sharer is on duty!

Flexitime

If a flexitime system is in operation, staff will be expected to work during **core time,** eg between 10 am and 4 pm. The time before 10 am and after 4 pm (eg between 7.30 am and 10 am and between 4 pm and 6.30 pm) is known as flexitime. If some staff are available throughout the whole time, then this gives total cover of 11 hours a day (Figure 5.13).

Figure 5.13 Flexitime system

When staff choose to work their flexitime hours depends on their individual preferences – and whether they are a 'lark' or an 'owl'. Some organisations do allow staff to build up some 'credit hours' by working all the flexitime as well as the core time hours and taking a day off in lieu but they normally put some limits on this. Staff cannot work flat out for six months and then demand three months off!

Rather than a conventional flexitime system, some organisations work a 'flexi year' by which employees are asked to work a certain number of hours per year rather than per week. The advantages to the employer include cover for longer hours without paying overtime, less need to employ temporary workers in traditionally short-staffed times such as the summer months and fewer employee absences. The employee has more opportunity for planning other leisure or work activities. However, disadvantages include the difficulty in coordinating staff cover and in forecasting exactly what time is to be worked and what time is to be taken off over a full year period.

Advantages of flexitime working

- Travelling problems are eased by allowing staff to travel outside peak travelling hours.

- Employees with families are allowed to work around school times, etc.

- Timekeeping is improved as there can be fewer excuses about being 'caught in the traffic' or having to leave early to catch the only convenient bus, etc.

- Morale can be improved by allowing staff some say over their working hours.

- Efficiency (and customer care) can be improved by allowing the workplace to be covered for longer periods of time. Some staff might find it easier to work in the quieter periods of the day such as first thing in the morning or last thing in the evening.

- Overtime may be reduced.

Disadvantages of flexitime
- The checking of individual work hours can cause an increase in administration (and therefore an increase in costs).

- There can be problems with having to schedule all important meetings, etc. within the core hours to make sure that all staff can attend.

Homeworking/hot desking/teleworking
Homeworking refers to working at home – whether this is routine manual work such as filling envelopes or highly skilled work such as would be undertaken by an architect or designer. A recent survey suggests that in the UK there are 662,000 homeworkers; 179,000 men and 466,000 women. The majority are **self-employed** or work in a family business, although 113,000 are employed by an outside organisation.

In some cases manual skills are needed – for packing, assembling, painting or hand finishing garments. In others, clerical or selling skills can be used. One engineering company employs three home-based sales staff: a firm supplying library books has its entire workforce of 30 staff based at home.

However, there have been developments in homeworking particularly in relation to new technology and a recent survey found that, of a random sample of 1,000 employers, one in 20 employ staff who work at home using information technology. They are generally known as teleworkers. The highest percentage is that of management and computer consultants and secretarial or administrative staff, closely followed by data entry clerks and training and education specialists. Other teleworkers include researchers and sales or marketing staff, accountants and finance workers and writers, journalists and designers.

Hot desking is found in companies where staff do not use the office as a permanent base (either because they work from home or are often travelling). One desk is usually allocated to four or five staff to use when they visit the organisation to attend meetings or seminars. One benefit to the organisation is that of reduced space which can be extremely cost effective, particularly in expensive city areas.

It is envisaged that over the next 10 years teleworking will expand considerably. There may be no need for people to visit an office at all – meetings can be attended through computer conferencing systems. This will have the result of vastly reducing the overheads of many large organisations.

It's a good job, really!

A survey by Home-Run, a London organisation that gives advice to homeworkers, has blown to smithereens the myth that people who work from home are lonely and are only there because they cannot get a proper job.

Today, of the 5 million people who are self-employed the majority work from home. People like being self-reliant and having a flexible daily routine. Many enjoy higher incomes because they save on overheads. However, there are some costs. Insurance is essential – and a legal requirement if any staff are employed. Office set-up costs average £2,141. The downside? Domestic interruptions, lack of feedback from a boss and having to be constantly self-motivated were given by some. Others missed the office gossip. But the trend is increasing – high redundancy rates, advanced telecommunications and modern technology have meant more people every year reject the office in favour of desk at home.

Freelancing

Freelancing is almost the next step from homeworking or teleworking. If you work at home for one company, why not work at home for several? Or, if you need to work 'on site' for a company, why not sell your skills to individual buyers, rather than just one?

A freelance is someone who is self-employed and who does not sign a contract of employment, as such, with an organisation. Instead, he or she contracts to undertake a particular job or task. When the contract is completed, the two part company, unless the contract is renewed.

Highly skilled freelance workers are much in demand, and this method of employment has frequently been common amongst artists, writers and photographers. Many journalists are freelance – selling stories and articles to newspapers or magazines which will buy them. The more well-known the writer, the higher price he or she can usually ask for an article. The same applies to graphic designers and photographers. A newspaper, therefore, can utilise the skills of a far greater number of staff than it actually employs – by supplementing its own articles, stories, graphics and photographs with work submitted by freelancers as well.

There are several advantages to an organisation which employs people to work at home.

* Less space is required in the workplace (this can save a considerable amount of money in city areas where overheads are high).

* Additional workers (on temporary contracts) can be hired easily when required.

- Greater flexiblity is possible – a range of skills can be hired which would not be feasible to employ on a full-time basis.

However, an organisation that employs teleworkers would, of course, normally be expected to supply the required equipment, and this has cost implications.

 Discussion point

As a group, debate the differences for employees who work from home rather than work in the office. See how many you can think of!

Changes in structure and reasons

Many organisations are moving away from a hierarchical structure towards a flatter or matrix structure. In many cases this is to do with streamlining the organisation, eg by delayering or **downsizing.** In other cases the original groupings are out of date or inefficient.

There are several reasons why a company may decide a different type of structure would be more appropriate.

- The firm has grown so that the original structure is too messy and disorganised. There are then problems in communications, replication of work and it is difficult to determine who is responsible for what.

- Increasing costs and low profits have forced a review of the structure. Usually these point to a poorly structured organisation which has ceased to operate efficiently to achieve corporate objectives.

- Changing technology has changed the way work is carried out by departments. It may even mean that some employees can work from home, linked to the organisation by computer.

- The firm has entered new markets or has diversified into other areas. Many firms have restructured around their move towards a global approach. For example, a company which has expanded to cover worldwide markets may restructure from a product structure to a geographical structure. This would mean, for instance, that specialists for each type of area (in relation to language, culture, regulations, etc.) would work together.

- Specialist areas are contracted or expanded to allow for a different balance of work. For instance, a product line which is in decline may be absorbed into another product-based department, or one which is expanding may be set up as a separate section in its own right.

- Specialist areas are linked in a matrix structure to enable each separate section to benefit from centralised functions required by all sections, eg finance, marketing or distribution functions (see chapter 6).

Problems connected to growth

Inappropriate structure

You have already seen how growth affected the computer consultancy DPTS. What would have happened if DPTS had not restructured as it grew larger? In summary, the problems would be likely to be

- increased inefficiency as people were unsure of their job roles and responsibilities

- people getting blamed for areas of work over which they had no control

- low motivation and morale of employees

- inconsistent and arbitrary decisions made by different people

- overloaded managers and supervisors with little work passed on or delegated to subordinates

- people working at cross-purposes because they were each doing a similar job from a different perspective with no coordination

- late and incorrect decisions because of lack of information or a clear brief

- slow response times to clients.

For all these reasons, it is essential that rapidly growing or rapidly changing organisations continually review their structure to check it is appropriate for their current activities.

Growth of a monster

Studies have shown that although organisations often become more hierarchical as they increase in size, there is a check on this process. It is very unusual, therefore, to find an organisation with more than about seven or eight levels, even if there are 10,000 employees!

However, today seven or eight levels would usually still be considered too many because of the associated problems. These include

- too many staff in senior (and expensive) positions

- a replication of administrative and support staff throughout the organisation as each department has vied with each other for its own 'share' and other areas have grown unchecked

- slow communications as information is passed up and down all the layers of the organisation

- distorted messages as information is 'interpreted' at each stage before being passed on

- lack of accountability and 'ownership' of decisions as each can blame someone else for any shortcomings

- lack of new initiatives and innovation because of the number of hurdles to jump before anything new can be implemented.

A method of solving these problems in many companies has been to downsize or delayer. The first relates to reducing the size of the company, the second to removing or reducing the size of certain organisational 'layers' – normally those of supervisory or middle management levels. This would make a flatter structure. In other cases a restructure is decided which changes the specialist areas. However, any type of change has effects on the remaining executives and staff who are left in the organisation.

The effect of delayering

For executives
- An increased span of control (ie more staff to supervise).

- A broader range of tasks to undertake.

- A wider range of responsibilities.

- Reduced costs of operating the section.

- More rapid communication feedback.

- A reduction in delegation options but an increased necessity for its application (see page 182).

For staff
- More opportunities for taking responsibility.

- Greater necessity for team work to get jobs done (see page 359).

- Fewer promotion prospects.

- More impersonal supervision by management.

- Less opportunities for guidance/discussion with individual manager.

Problems connected to costs or reduced sales

A problem for any organisation is rising costs. If costs increase, this then reduces profit. If sales fall, this has the same result. The net outcome is that the organisation has less money to spend on overheads as profits are squeezed tighter and tighter. Something then has to be done to reduce costs and/or increase sales – preferably both!

In most organisations the greatest proportion of money goes on the salary bill – sometimes as much as 70 per cent of total expenditure. Savings on staff, therefore, make economic sense – even if this is not good news to the employees. Other cutbacks can include closing unprofitable divisions or regional offices. This is usually carried out alongside a restructuring exercise and sometimes accompanies a change of job roles for the workers.

Downsizing at Littlewoods Pools

Littlewoods Pools encountered problems when people transferred their affections to the National Lottery instead. Littlewoods was a typical case of an organisation suffering from increasing costs and lower sales.

The company's answer has been to close its Glasgow centre, invest in technology to streamline coupon-handling and, in all, cut around 600 jobs. In Glasgow 318 jobs will be lost, the remainder to be made up of 280 job

losses from part-time and casual workers employed in Liverpool and Birkenhead.

Changing technology

The advent of new technology has resulted in many companies restructuring in different ways. Initially, many organisations formed their own centralised computer departments which controlled all the computerised activities undertaken by the organisation. This was in the days when mainframe computers dominated.

The advent of personal computers and networks has meant that technology can be utilised departmentally. However, the expertise required to maximise the potential of technology has removed much of the autonomy of individual managers as they may be extremely reliant on the cooperation and ability of computer staff to design systems and procedures which meet their needs.

Technology has, without doubt, improved communications and information flows throughout the organisation. This has also removed some control from managers as lateral communication (between staff in different departments) is much easier with the advent of electronic mail.

Production, purchasing and finance are all becoming heavily dependent on different forms of computerisation. Robots may have taken over some of the more monotonous, dirty or dangerous jobs, and the work of six employees may now be possible by one person plus a computer. Automation has become possible in many areas (such as coupon-handling at Littlewoods). In many cases this has led to a considerable amount of downsizing in many organisations with a proportionate reduction in staff and in the number of levels in the organisation.

Banking on success?

Over the past five years, over 100,000 jobs have been lost in banking as counter clerks, accounting and clerical staff have seen their jobs replaced by technology. Automated teller machines (more commonly known as cash machines), deposit machines, telephone banking and computerised accounting systems have caused most of the damage.

The result has not just been a decrease in the number of staff employed but **deskilling** generally, as computers take over more and more of the skills traditionally required by staff. Banks argue that technology has enabled them to concentrate on customer service and provide staff with additional skills – as well as increase profits and dividends to shareholders. Those who have been made redundant might have a different tale to tell!

Changing markets

As you have seen, changing markets and changing product lines can mean a complete rethink – especially if the organisation is structured along these lines rather than in relation to functional activities.

Many business organisations have restructured to take account of growing overseas markets and corporate plans which look towards future developments on a global scale or operating in different markets – either in terms of products or geographically.

A final word about patterns of work

In many cases restructuring and downsizing has been facilitated by different patterns of working. Options such as contracting out facilitate downsizing. Hiring freelance (self-employed) staff to cover specialist areas and temporary staff to cover areas of temporary need are commonplace. Increased teleworking possibilities also reduce the number of employees required on a particular site.

The effects of restructuring

For executives

- Different work responsibilities – normally a greater workload in areas of expansion. Those who were responsible for areas of decline may be made redundant or put in charge of a completely new section.

- Different staff to supervise – usually restructure involves a number of staff transfers from one section to another.

- Different systems and procedures to follow, related to new or amalgamated work areas.

For staff

- The transfer to a new section can be traumatic as it will involve a change of work routine, change of boss and change of colleagues. Even staff not transferred could find themselves working alongside different colleagues.

- New or different responsibilities. In some areas promotional opportunities may be available.

- A general upheaval with uncertainty about the new job role and retraining required for some staff.

The downside of downsizing

In a recent study carried out by Mercer Management Consulting, investors appeared more attracted to firms which were growing than firms which were downsizing. Whilst downsizing might be a trend, only 24 per cent of companies managed to change direction from cost-cutting policies to profitable growth. Sixty-six per cent of companies became caught in a downsizing spiral – downsizing either twice, three times or more.

Mercer Management argues that this is caused by companies 'taking their eyes off the customer'. Instead of focusing on areas for development, they continue to concentrate on their internal structures and processes. By the time they have downsized for the second or third time, they have simply nowhere else to go – and have destroyed their ability to grow.

Keywords

The keywords on which you should concentrate in this chapter are given below. Check you understand the concept in each case.

accountability
authority
bureaucracy
casual workers
core time
delayering
delegation
deskilling
differentials
downsizing
downward communications
flat structure
flexitime
freelancing
grapevine
hierarchical structure
homeworking
hot desking
increments

job sharing
lateral communications
levels of authority
line functions
organisation chart
organisation culture
pyramid structure
quasi-vertical communications
responsibility
restructure
salary scales
self-employed
span of control
staff functions
teleworking
temporary work
unity of command
upward communications
vertical communications

Examination practice

Short-answer questions

1 Identify three disadvantages of a hierarchical structure.

2 State three effects of restructuring on company employees.

3 What is flexitime? Identify two advantages and two disadvantages of this system.

4 State two benefits and two drawbacks of centralisation.

5 Describe teleworking. Why might some employees prefer this method of working?

6 Organisation charts cannot always be relied upon for information. Give three reasons why this is the case.

7 State two disadvantages of downsizing.

8 Identify four reasons why an organisation might change its structure.

9   Identify four reasons why managers should be encouraged to delegate.

10   Describe three different lines of communication which usually exist in business organisations.

Definition questions
1   Explain clearly the difference between each of the following terms.
   a   a hierarchical structure and a flat structure
   b   vertical communications and lateral communications
   c   responsibility and accountability
   d   lines of authority and lines of responsibility

2   Write clear notes to describe each of the following terms.
   a   delayering
   b   restructure
   c   delegation
   d   span of control

Essay questions
1   Many managers are reluctant to delegate. State why this is the case and give the benefits to both manager and employee if delegation is done properly.

2   Identify the benefits and drawbacks of job sharing from the point of view of
   a   the organisation
   b   the employees concerned.

3   Some management writers consider that successful organisations are those which do not keep altering their structure. State why this might be the case. Include in your answer the positive and negative effects of restructuring on all staff in the organisation.

4   'A successful manager will utilise all the lines of communication at his or her disposal – but for different reasons.' Explain what is meant by this statement.

5   What is meant by the term 'organisation culture'? Identify how the culture may affect the structure and operation of a business organisation.

6   An organisation which restructures may have to review its salary grades. Describe the factors which must be taken into consideration for the outcome to be considered 'fair' by the employees.

Case study

Bob Taylor started a small furniture business 12 years ago. It grew larger and larger with more and more employees. Bob invested in new machinery and equipment and concentrated on increasing specialisation in the workforce. He thought he had the answer until he started receiving complaints of poor-quality products from customers. Coupled with this was a sharp increase in absenteeism in the workforce.

a   Bob had tried to retain a flat structure but now considers this might have been a mistake. Explain what is meant by this type of structure and the disadvantages which may be encountered.

b   If Bob restructures the organisation to make it more hierarchical, what effect is this likely to have on the people working in the company?

c   Identify why increased specialisation may have been a contributory factor to increased absenteeism.

6   The functions of business

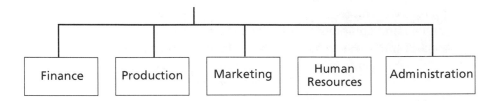

Figure 6.1 The functional activities of companies

Introduction

In chapter 5 you saw the way in which different businesses are structured and now know that despite the differences in levels and sizes, all large organisations have to be divided in some way, normally relating to the key areas of the organisation.

Despite the different groupings possible, the vast majority of companies are structured into functional activities. Broadly these usually cover the areas of finance, production, marketing, human resources and administration (Figure 6.1). Even in cases where these functions are not the predominant structure, then they are required in some form or another to support the operation of the specialist areas.

Understanding the range of activities covered by each of these areas and the way in which they interact is essential if you are to appreciate how they combine to further company objectives and affect the work of those employed in the organisation.

A word of warning! No two organisations are the same. What follows is therefore general guidance on the type of work and activities undertaken by each function – but it is quite likely that the organisation for which you eventually work will be entirely different!

Finance

All organisations need resources in order to operate. All need to make a profit in order to survive – and to pay for the resources they need. A healthy profit will leave enough to invest in future expansion of the business. A loss can be disastrous and certainly cannot be sustained for any length of time.

For these reasons the work of the Finance Department is critical to the future success of the organisation. Basically, the operations carried out by Finance include

- obtaining additional finance

- advising directors on investment decisions

- recording all receipts and payments

- preparing costings

- monitoring budgets and reporting variances

- producing **cashflow** forecasts

- producing continuous financial information for management

- controlling the level of debts

- producing **statutory accounts**

- paying wages and salaries (unless this is contracted out).

In addition to clerical and administrative staff who undertake routine tasks relating to recording financial transactions (usually on computer), the following specialists will also be employed.

- A **financial accountant.**

- A **management accountant.**

There is also likely to be a financial director who will be involved in financial decision-making at board level. His or her task will be to give the best advice to the directors based on the financial information and forecasts produced by his or her staff.

This will probably include decisions such as the best source of finance for new projects and involve a series of calculations to see if the projects are a worthwhile investment. This is done by calculating the potential return on capital invested. If this is greater than the cost of obtaining the finance, then the project will usually go ahead.

The financial accountant

The financial accountant is employed with the main remit of preparing the statutory accounts which the company has to produce each year. The word 'statutory' means they are a legal requirement. As you saw in chapter 1, under the terms of the Companies Act 1989, all limited companies have a legal obligation to produce a **balance sheet** and **profit and loss account** each year to a specified format. Most also produce a cashflow statement as well. Smaller, private companies can elect to produce only abridged or abbreviated accounts. The results and the report must be filed with the Registrar of Companies each year. In addition, large companies must have their accounts audited each year (see page 9).

The job of the financial accountant is mainly to prepare the balance sheet, profit and loss account and cashflow statement from information contained in the books of account for the year. Today the task has been made easier through computerisation – there is a variety of accounting programmes on the market though a large organisation may have its own tailor-made software.

The information contained in these accounts is very important for both shareholders and creditors, though all stakeholders may take an interest. In the case of a public company, the accounts may influence the future share price – as shareholders will be less likely to want to keep their shares if profits are falling.

The company will also use the accounts as a key source of information when deciding future plans and objectives – though, as you will see, the information contained in the accounts should come as no surprise to the senior managers!

You may like to note that a small organisation is likely to **contract out** the requirement of producing statutory accounts to a specialist firm. There are many firms of registered chartered accountants in every town in Britain, who undertake this work for small firms – from sole traders to small-scale limited companies. Outside accountancy firms also undertake consultancy work and auditing for their clients (see page 124).

Financial reporting

At the recent meeting of J J Cole Ltd, the Chairman reported that the financial situation of the company had improved considerably over the past 12 months. This was obvious from the balance sheet and the profit and loss account, which showed a **net profit** of £42,000. The purchase of the new warehouse had substantially improved the **assets** of the company and **liabilities** were less this year as the

number of **creditors** had been considerably reduced. The level of allowable **credit** to buyers had been reduced resulting in a reduction in **debtors** and an increased **cashflow.**

Reserves from retained profits now amounted to over £17,000 which would easily cover the level of forecast **bad debts** and **interest** payments on the bank loan.

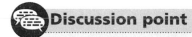

Discussion point

As an administrator, secretary or PA you will almost certainly be involved in meetings and discussions relating to the financial situation of a company. The above article comes from the chairman of a private company reporting to a group of shareholders – but what is he talking about? Go through the list of financial terms in Figure 6.2 carefully. Then, with your tutor's assistance if necessary, translate his statement making sure that you know what each part of it means!

Asset This is used to describe anything of value held by the company, such as stock, buildings or equipment. It also includes any money held as cash or in the bank and any money owed to the business by its customers. Assets can be divided into **fixed assets** and **current assets.** Fixed assets are those which cannot be turned into cash without virtually closing the business, such as motor vehicles and premises. Current assets are those which change as transactions take place, eg stock, debtors and cash.

Balance sheet A summary of the assets and liabilities of the business at the end of a financial year. It is a 'snapshot' of the financial position of the business on a particular day.

Capital The money invested in the business.

Cashflow The movement of cash both in and out of the business. Cashflow allows for the fact that not all buyers will pay on time (and will therefore become debtors). Any cash receipts are also included.

Credit A situation where goods or services are provided and there is a delay before the account is paid.

Creditors People or organisations to which the company owes money, eg suppliers of goods. Creditors are a liability because they represent a debt which must be paid.

Debtors People or organisations which owe the company money. Debtors are an asset because they represent money owing to the business.

Financial year Businesses summarise their financial situation on the same date each year. The date is known as the end of the financial year.

Liability The money the business owes to its suppliers or other organisations, eg a bank loan. These are debts which must be repaid.

Overheads Payments for items that do not go into creating the final product or service but are necessary to run the business, eg consumables, heating and lighting.

Profit The surplus from trading left over at the end of the year when all expenses have been paid. **Gross profit** is the amount earned from sales when the cost of purchases has been deducted. **Net profit** is the amount left when all expenses have been deducted. **Net profit before tax** is the amount of profit before corporation tax has been paid.

Profit and loss account A summary of all the transactions that have taken place during the year, for both income and expenditure. The difference between the two gives the profit or loss. A profit and loss account gives the final net profit before tax after expenses have been deducted.

Reserves Profit which has been retained by the company rather than paid out to shareholders as dividend. A level of reserve is usually set aside to offset a future cost, the details of which are not yet known, or towards new projects in the future.

Figure 6.2 Financial terms

The management accountant

The problem with financial accounts is that they are historic documents. They use past transactions to give a report on past performance. It is hopeless for the directors to find out today that they had serious problems last June!

For that reason management accountants are employed by virtually all large organisations. They undertake a key role in keeping management informed *on a daily basis* of the financial health of the organisation.

They do this by reporting on all the investment projects being undertaken and also on whether financial targets are being met in accordance with the financial plan.

Financial plans in business are always accompanied by a **budget.** Indeed the budget *is* the financial plan in that it identifies all the financial targets of the organisation over a stated period. A **master budget** is prepared after different sections of the organisation have given information on their own forecasts of costs and revenue, eg

- The sales budget will include the number of units forecast to be sold and the selling price of each. Against the expected total revenue will be set the costs of selling the goods or service, eg advertising, promotion and distribution costs.

- The production budget will take into account planned sales for the period. Budgets will also be prepared to take into account stock levels, work-in-progress and raw material requirements.

- Budgets for services are prepared by other departments, eg Administration, Human Resources and Computer Services.

- Budgets for policy areas are prepared for top management, eg for research and development or capital expenditure. They will take into account the long-term strategies of the business and are often calculated over a longer period.

- The cash budget is very important as this shows the proposed effects of all the other budget activities on the organisation's cashflow. If a deficit is predicted, then the budgets would have to be adjusted or an overdraft or loan would have to be arranged. If a surplus is forecast, then plans must be made to invest the money to obtain a good return, rather than leaving it lying idle in a current bank account.

Budgets are not treated as 'fixed items' but must comprise an element of flexibility to allow for unexpected changes and development. For instance, sales cannot always be forecast accurately – one line might suddenly prove more popular or profitable than another and it may be cost effective to switch resources to focus on this product.

It is the management accountant's job to keep management informed of any variances from the budget, ie occasions when there is a notable difference in actual performance from forecast performance. In this way managers can then make informed decisions as to the best way to proceed.

Overnight financial information

Many large retail stores have used information technology to completely reform their financial decision-making processes. Computerised checkouts identify levels of sales per item per day at stores throughout the country. This tells managers which goods are selling well and which are not. It also influences future buying and stock levels. Stock can be transferred from one store to another to meet a shortage, certain lines can be the focus of special displays if they are 'sticking', or marked down as special offers. Lines which do not sell above a certain level will be discontinued as the cost of stocking them is not worth the return. However, the ability to check stocks, order them quickly and note stock levels has increased so much through computerisation that large supermarkets can afford to offer far more choice than in the past.

Not only are stocks being transformed but so are monetary transactions. Today everyone is used to being able to pay for their shopping by credit card, debit card, cheque or cash – and obtain an itemised receipt. Tesco introduced its extremely successful Clubcard, which also relies on a swipe system and has now extended this to offer Clubcard Plus – a card which gives customers its own-label banking facilities as well – at interest rates far better than most high street banks! The system is being offered in conjunction with NatWest – and all through the developments of electronic transaction processing and banking.

The importance of costs

Management accountants must be aware of how much it costs to produce an item or offer a service. Only then can they calculate whether making the item is profitable, and, if so, the most profitable quantity to produce. They do this by calculating estimates to a unit of a production and building up a **standard cost** for a particular item. The standard cost will include both **direct** and **indirect costs.**

- Direct costs are those costs actually incurred as a result of making the product or offering the service, eg raw materials and the labour involved.

- Indirect costs relate to the overall costs incurred by the organisation such as rent, heating and lighting which cannot be attached directly or solely to one particular job. By using a process of apportionment and allocation a standard overhead rate can be applied to each job.

It is obviously important for management accountants to be aware of any changes to costs. Costs may fall, for instance, if a cheaper supplier is found or if a component is substituted by a cheaper one. Costs may rise because of inflation or because of a shortage of certain raw materials. Many organisations use costs to determine the selling price (called **cost plus pricing**). In this case, as costs rise, the selling price will also increase.

Break-even analysis

A useful technique for decision-making which involves both costs and sales is known as **break-even analysis.** This technique is applied by managers who use information on costs and projected sales to work out the level of sales that will be required to recoup the investment and move into profit. The technique can also be used to inform other decisions as you will see below.

Break-even analysis is based on the assumption that some costs are fixed and others are variable.

- **Fixed costs** do not vary with output. They are incurred regardless of the level of production. They include general company overheads, eg heating, lighting, rent and most staff salaries. Fixed costs are usually indirect because they cannot usually be allocated to a particular job.

- **Variable costs** vary with output, eg raw materials, packaging, sales commission payments, casual staff taken on when production increases and workers paid on piece-work rates. Variable costs are usually direct as it is possible to allocate them to a particular job.

When fixed and variable costs are added together, the result is the **total cost** of production for that particular item.

In the long run, all costs are considered to be variable, ie over a number of years, electricity and other bills will rise, staff will obtain salary increases, the workforce may be increased or decreased, etc.

A third category of costs, not included in break-even analysis, is **semi-variable costs.** These are items which have both fixed and variable components. A good example is a fax machine which has a fixed component (the line rental) but also a variable element – as charges are made for each fax transmitted. Therefore the more the fax machine is used, the more this cost will increase.

A break-even chart is shown in Figure 6.3. Fixed costs are shown by horizontal line A because they do not change. On the chart they are shown at £3,000 no matter how much output is produced. The total cost line is shown by line C. This is rising because it includes variable costs (shown as B).

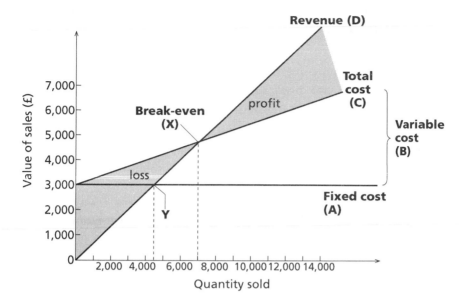

Figure 6.3 Break-even chart

The projected revenue line from sales is shown at D. At the point where this line crosses the total cost line (X) the company will break even – and cover costs but not make a profit. By extending this point downwards towards the output line you can see that 7,000 units would have to be produced. Any sales above that point result in profit, whereas any output below that point would result in an overall loss. You may like to note that if times are difficult, a company could operate for a short time if it just covered its fixed costs (ie Y, at 4,500 units) – but obviously the organisation could not sustain this level of activity for long.

The chart can be used to answer questions such as the following.

- What level of production would produce a profit if costs increased or were reduced?

- What level of sales would be required if prices were increased?

- What would happen to profits if demand fell or increased?

However, a break-even chart gives only a rough approximation – and is highly dependent upon accurate cost/revenue data. It also makes several assumptions about costs and revenue which do not always agree with the real world. However, as a basis for first-level management decisions it has a practical value which should not be dismissed.

Discussion point

1   With your tutor's help if necessary, try to identify all the costs involved in teaching you for each hour of your course! Remember to divide your list into direct and indirect costs. The number of indirect costs might come as a surprise if you do it properly!

2   Assume that on a particular course each student is worth £2,000 in income to a college. The fixed costs of teaching the course are £16,000 and the variable costs are £800 per student. Calculate the number of students required for the course to break even. (If you are learning about spreadsheets as part of your course, then this exercise is very easy indeed to do with the help of a computer!)

3   Why, in a school or college, might some staff salaries be counted as fixed costs and others be counted as variable costs? Discuss your answers as a group.

Production

The key element in all manufacturing organisations is that of production. Without any goods there is nothing to sell; if there is nothing to sell then it is impossible to make a profit. However, more importantly, the items that are produced must be in demand, supplied on time and of good quality.

Whether goods are produced for the industrial market or the consumer market, the production function does not stand alone. Closely allied to production are

*   **research and development (R & D)**

*   **purchasing** and **stock control**

*   **distribution.**

These may operate as part of the production function or as independent departments or divisions.

Research and development

R & D may also incorporate design and/or production planning. It is the first stage in translating the demands of consumers or the ideas of designers into new or modified products for the market. The scope for R & D varies from one organisation to another, depending upon the type of product(s) being produced, eg

*   Pharmaceuticals companies invest very heavily indeed in R & D to stay one step ahead of their competitors. They concentrate on finding,

developing and testing potential new drugs for the market both for common complaints and potentially fatal illnesses, such as Aids.

- Designers who work for motor manufacturers not only develop new cars for the market but also 'concept' cars for exhibitions. They are involved with such aspects as appearance, safety features, fuel economy and environmental factors – air bags and catalytic converters are both relatively 'recent' additions to cars.

- Food manufacturers employ technologists whose job is concerned with developing new 'ready' meals, new methods of packaging and new ways of cooking food. In recent years the food industry has spent a considerable amount of money developing a wide range of products based on non-traditional dishes as Britain's consumers have developed a taste for more exotic foods.

- In the electronics industry, R & D specialists are currently working on designs for digital televisions (which will give the same quality picture and sound as you would receive in the cinema) and CDs to replace video tapes. The CDs would also be of the same high quality and would record using a computer linked to the digital television!

The work of R & D generally covers two areas.

- **Industrial design** – this concerns the appearance of the product and the way consumers use it.

- **Engineering design** – this relates to the performance of the product.

If computers are used as an example, then the development of the laptop relates to industrial design and the development of faster chips and processors relates to engineering design.

The job of the designers is to produce a prototype which

- works

- meets the expectations of consumers

- can be produced at a price consumers will be willing to pay.

R & D specialists may also be involved with developing new production processes or utilising technological advances to find new ways to manufacture new products. The general aim of industry is to produce high-quality products more quickly and more cheaply, year after year.

Computers and R & D

Many organisations use **computer-aided design (CAD)** to help them to design new products. CAD packages can be used to develop anything – from a design for a chair to a jet airplane! These packages enable the designer to sketch basic shapes and then vary the dimensions, angles and size of certain parts as they wish. The product can even undergo stress testing by computer. In some industries CAD packages are linked to **computer-aided manufacturing (CAM)** or **computer-integrated manufacturing (CIM)**. For instance, in the carpet industry, a new design can be planned using a CAD package and the tufting machine which produces the carpet can then be pre-set and controlled to produce the new design by computer.

New products for the millennium

R & D can be involved in anything from the redesign of an everyday article such as a jug kettle or a nailbrush to a high-tech product for the next generation. Inventions currently being developed or launched include the following.

- The Advanced Photo System – APS. Cameras use transparent magnetic strip and store information about each shot which is then 'translated' by the processing equipment to give the best results. Negatives are a thing of the past. Cameras are more expensive than ordinary models and range from £60 to £170. Film

and processing costs are also higher but ruined photographs should be a thing of the past.

- A TV camera that records burglars on home video recorders. If you are viewing the latest video when a visitor calls, you may find yourself suddenly seeing Uncle Fred's face pop up on screen rather than Kevin Costner!

- Digital television (see page 221). This will be followed with digital interactive television which will eventually include 'movies on demand' for viewers!

The production function

Methods of production

The method(s) of production to be found in an organisation will depend upon the type of product being made and the size of the average order. There are basically four main types of production process.

- **Job production** – where each product is virtually a 'one-off' item, eg designer fashions, luxury cars, shipbuilding and the aerospace industry (such as satellites). Job production is suitable when output is low, repeat orders are rarely received and staff will need specialist skills. The second Severn Bridge – which cost £330 million to build and opened in 1996 is an obvious example!

- **Batch production** – where whole batches of products are made, eg bread, books and magazines, furniture, pharmaceuticals, food and cosmetics. Batch production requires a high degree of planning, although the batch does not have to consist of totally identical products as some variation is allowable (for instance, a bakery could produce a wide variety of loaves all at the same time).

* **Flow production, continuous or process production** – where a product is produced continuously using a technological process, eg gas, paper or oil. In many plants the process goes on continually – 24 hours a day, seven days a week. The job of production operatives in this case is to monitor the process, the output and the operation of the machinery.

* **Mass production** – where large number of identical products are made on a production or assembly line, eg cars, household appliances, office equipment and consumer electronics. In most cases the majority (if not all) of the components used are 'bought in' and simply 'put together' on the line.

This type of production is famous for the dissatisfaction and boredom experienced by those who are employed in performing the repetitive tasks involved. It was 'invented' by Henry Ford, who wanted his Ford cars to be produced identically and cheaply – and has often been called 'Fordism'. In the 1960s and 1970s, the constant strikes and problems in motor manufacturing meant that new methods for assembly were investigated – primarily by the Swedish company Volvo and several Japanese companies. The Japanese operate a different type of system –

sometimes referred to as **lean production.** This involves more flexible production methods (so that variations on the basic product can be made) and more commitment by workers who operate as 'teams' responsible for undertaking a variety of jobs – and checking upon the quality of each member's input. This type of production is now used by most motor manufacturers as the motivation and productivity of staff *and* the quality of the product are improved.

Organising production

Production can be divided into two areas.

- Planning.

- Control.

In reality both areas overlap although it is usually easier to consider them separately at the outset.

Production planning

After a product has been designed, its manufacture must be carefully planned. This will involve such considerations as

- the type of raw materials that will be required

- whether these should be made or bought in

- the number and type of machines which will be required

- personnel requirements, including skill levels

- method of production or assembly

- time and cost of production

- packaging and storage required.

The role of the planners is to ensure that all sections will operate at optimum levels and no bottlenecks or idle capacity will occur. The services of a production engineer will usually be required to determine the work process or layout of the production area in addition to the machines, equipment or tools required, tolerances needed and rate of work which can be expected. Techniques such as work study and method study may be used to determine 'standard times' of production.

It is the job of production planners to liaise closely with other departments – particularly Purchasing (to ensure raw materials and components are available) and Marketing (to ensure that realistic specifications or delivery times are quoted). In many organisations there is a history of antagonism between Sales and Production – both of which struggle to understand each other's problems.

Production control

Once the plans have been made and the manufacturing process has started, it is vital that controls are in place to ensure that the planned production targets are met or, if they are not, why they are not.

The controls in place to ensure this include the following.

- **Progress control.** Progress chasing means checking that planned output is as scheduled, otherwise the cause of the problem has to be found, eg machine breakdown (often called **downtime**), substandard raw materials or labour problems. The problem must be solved *and* production schedules readjusted to try to make up for lost time.

- **Quality control.** Traditionally, quality controllers were employed to check the standard of the finished product, either by examining each article or by random sampling. Many companies today have instigated either quality circles or **total quality management (TQM)** system. **Quality circles** are teams of employees from across the workplace who meet voluntarily and informally to discuss improvements that can be made. TQM broadens this approach still further by implementing certain standards, methods and procedures across the whole of the organisation to ensure quality – and is often known as the **right first time** approach. This is often extended to suppliers who must also conform to these systems (see below).

- **Stock control.** This relates to the supplies of raw materials and components which must be constantly available to ensure that production schedules are not interrupted. An alternative to holding large (costly) stocks is the **just-in-time (JIT)** method of operating which evolved from a system operated by large organisations in Japan. In this case, rather than shop around for the cheapest supply the aim is for the buying company to develop a group of 'preferred suppliers' – who are stakeholders in the success of the product. The seller will then produce and deliver the goods virtually on demand and the buyer can also demand high-quality standards. Many buying organisations insist that their suppliers hold an international quality standard such as ISO 9000 or the British standard BS 5750 (see page 158).

  Operating a JIT philosophy means the company is not involved in high storage costs nor with carrying outdated or unwanted stocks. It is particularly popular with motor manufacturers which are often surrounded by a whole array of satellite supplier companies that produce a range of components from windscreen wipers to tyres.

- **Machine utilisation control.** This controls the use of the machines to ensure that none is overloaded or overused without being checked and maintained. Because machine breakdowns can be critical, many organisations have a maintenance plan which shows the dates on which machines will be out of operation for inspection and servicing.

Do note that there are strong links between production and finance in relation to **cost control.** Both material costs and labour costs must be kept to budget levels if the original budget for the costs of production is to be met.

Production and computers

Automation and computers have changed many of the functions of production workers. Not only can the products themselves now be made by a completely automated process and controlled by computer (see CIM, page 222) but traditional jobs may now be done very differently, eg

- robots can be used to undertake work which is dirty, dangerous or extremely repetitive

- quality control may be undertaken automatically by machine – many machines that produce components are automatically programmed to check the end product within a specific tolerance

- progress chasers now receive much information either on computer VDU or computer print-out – and can check on progress without moving from the spot.

Truly made to measure!

Not yet available in Britain, a service available to American Levi jeans customers is a new development in the application of computers, robots and associated customer service. Quite simply, customers walk into a Levi outlet, are measured for jeans and then go home. Meanwhile, their measurements are entered into a computer, transmitted to Levi's

Tennessee factory where a robot promptly makes up the jeans and posts them.

Needless to say 'job production' jeans are rather pricier than the normal 'batch production' type – even with the help of the robot. But you may well long for the customised type the next time you try to squeeze into a pair you really meant to diet into instead!

Purchasing

Even a company operating with a JIT philosophy needs buyers who can assess the quantities which are required and when. Purchasing is often a centralised function because it is generally cheaper to buy items for the organisation as a whole, rather than to have individual departments 'doing their own thing'. For that reason, office supplies and even photocopying equipment may be provided through a centralised purchasing function.

The purpose of a Purchasing Department is to ensure that supplies of the correct materials, of the right quality are available as required. The purchase must be made at the most economic price (which is not necessarily the cheapest price), bearing in mind the needs of the organisation, possible gluts and shortages, storage space available, possible deterioration, obsolescence and delivery dates.

A further function of the Purchasing Department is to standardise items wherever possible so that bulk purchases can be made – for products as diverse as machine oil and paper. The Purchasing section will also be responsible for any contracts taken out with suppliers or preferred suppliers – the terms under which these are agreed and the re-evaluation of such contracts if these terms are not met. All items delivered are usually inspected upon delivery and this is usually the role of those directly employed in stores or stock control.

Do note that many raw materials used in the UK are purchased from abroad. Purchasing Departments are not, therefore, simply concerned with ordering from within the UK and may also be concerned with import restrictions and regulations and have to be aware of exchange rate fluctuations which may affect the cost of the supplies.

Close links between production and purchasing are vital. Any changes to products or production schedules can easily mean an adjustment is required in the type or quantity of raw materials required.

Computers and purchasing

Goods can be purchased by computer and paid for by computer using **electronic data interchange (EDI).** EDI was initiated in the 1980s by the retail and motor industries, both of which wanted fast communication systems with their suppliers. All orders and invoices are communicated by computer to companies on a worldwide basis. Because orders can be processed very quickly, EDI is another method of reducing the amount of stock that needs to be held and the associated storage costs. Some buyers even send the invoice they think should be issued to the supplier – who has to challenge it if it is thought to be wrong.

Payment is made by specific computer terminals which are nominated as the payment terminals and access is available only by means of a smart card and a personal security code. The payment computer communicates simultaneously with both the bank of the supplier and purchaser so that the money is transferred from one to the other – together with a computerised acknowledgement.

Bread and tyres – ordered by computer!

Two large UK companies who use EDI are Tesco and Rover. Tesco claims that 95 per cent of its orders and 60 per cent of its invoices are transmitted as EDI messages. Rover trades electronically with over 270 suppliers, each of which is given between 12 hours and one week to deliver goods. However, in an emergency the delivery time has been as short as 40 minutes!

Distribution

Whilst distribution is also mentioned under marketing, there are obvious links with production. The scope of the distribution function can vary from a small transport section which subcontracts all its transportation requirements to haulage companies or distributors, to a medium-sized operation where goods are delivered in the organisation's own vehicles to a major distribution facility – with depots or warehouses all over the UK controlled by a central distribution facility. In this case you may find experts in **logistics** working for the company – specialising in calculating the most economical and cost-effective routes to use.

Again bear in mind that many goods may be exported. In this case the Distribution section may be known as Shipping and Exporting – specialising in the completion of exporting documents and preparing goods for travel by sea or air. Conversely, the company may subcontract its shipping requirements to an international haulage contractor or export agent who will complete all the paperwork on its behalf.

Distribution and computers

Computer software to deal with scheduling and sequencing problems has been available for many years, but today's versions bear little relation to those used in the past. However, it can still need human input to adjust or refine schedules, to take into account emergencies or other non-programmable events, such as bad weather or unforeseen traffic delays.

Marketing

The management writer Peter Drucker defined marketing as 'looking at the business through the customer's eyes'. The Chartered Institute of Marketing defines marketing as 'the management process responsible for identifying, anticipating and satisfying customer requirements profitably'.

Marketing, therefore, is more than just a 'department' within a firm. Equally, it is more than just a range of jobs or techniques for finding out what should be made and how it should be sold. Marketing is a philosophy – or company orientation – which means that the whole organisation is committed to satisfying the needs and wants of its customers. It includes everyone in the organisation – from the receptionist or switchboard operator to the reprographics section. The needs of the customer are paramount.

You may like to think of marketing as a two-way process.

- Outward-facing – finding out what customers want, need and why.

- Inward-facing – finding out what the company can do to satisfy those needs and wants.

Marketing mix

The **marketing mix** comprises all the 'ingredients' or variables which apply to marketing. The easy way to remember these is to think of them as the 4 p's – **product, price, promotion** and **place.**

- **Product** relates to the variety on offer, quality, features, brand name, style, packaging, durability, guarantee or warranty, after-sales service.

- **Price** includes the basic price, discounts, credit terms, competitors' prices, special allowances and trade-ins (such as occur with second-hand cars).

- **Promotion** covers advertising, personal selling, sales promotions, publicity, public relations and merchandising.

- **Place** relates to distribution channels, the sales force, geographical coverage, transport methods, location of shops and depots, stocks held, freight and insurance required.

All these factors are discussed in more detail in the pages which follow.

Marketing strategy

A successful company has to consider

a what business are we really in

b how and why are the needs and wants of our customers changing?

Failure to answer either correctly can have serious implications on future sales.

Discussion point

A company produces two computers, one for the business market and one for the home market.

a In what way do you think the marketing mix will vary in each case?

b How will the product mix vary, and why?

c How will the promotional mix vary, and why?

d How will the price vary, and why?

If the same organisation exports its business computers, how will this affect its distribution mix?

You may wish to complete this section before you decide upon your answers!

Market research

Market research is carried out to assess

- the potential of new products

- customers' views of existing products.

The company can carry out market research itself, but is more likely to employ market research specialists, as you saw in chapter 3. Designing questionnaires, for instance, is a skilled job – so is analysing the results.

Market research can involve either primary research or secondary research methods. Primary research is original research (eg asking someone their opinions). Secondary research (or desk research) means looking up statistics and relevant facts in relation to the product or potential/actual market.

Primary research

This is usually carried out by means of surveys. These are based on questionnaires or interviews which may be conducted face to face, by telephone or by post. Postal surveys have the lowest response rate – but this is improved if an incentive is offered, such as a prize for the first 50 opened.

'Closed' questions are usually asked with a range of alternatives specified. This means the completed survey can be 'read' by optical character recognition. The survey can be carried out to consolidate 'needs analysis'. This is an analysis of gaps in the market which may have been undertaken through secondary research.

Other methods of market research include test marketing a product in a particular area and measuring the results, setting up a consumer panel (Boots does this) or using a testing panel. The latter is often used in the food industry – and may comprise employees who can obtain a 'sample meal' if they complete a survey afterwards. One hosiery manufacturer used its female employees to test market new brands of tights and stockings before putting them on general sale.

The sample of people surveyed must be large enough to give significant results and representative of the **key** customer. It is no good surveying pensioners, if you are trying to find out about Levi jeans! Samples may be considered by gender, age, socioeconomic grouping or ethnic grouping – depending on the product being surveyed. A company usually knows the profile of its existing and potential customers and will use this to identify those who are suitable in relation to their age, gender and income.

Secondary research

There is a vast number of data sources – from current customers and their past orders to economic data published by the government and major newspapers. Data can be purchased – from company databases to statistics covering consumer expenditure and the market share of different companies together with competitors' prices both by region and product group.

The advantages and disadvantages of using primary or secondary research methods are shown in Figure 6.4.

	Benefits	Drawbacks
PRIMARY RESEARCH	Many sources Mainly held in company Relatively cheap Limited answers	Can be slow May be misinterpreted
SECONDARY RESEARCH		
Personal interviews	Accurate More flexible Misconceptions rectified	Expensive Slow Permit bias
Postal questionnaires	Cheap Wide coverage	Low response rate Construction difficult
Telephone surveys	Not intimidating Quick Misconceptions can be rectified	Impersonal May be confused with telephone selling
Consumer panel	Range of views Regular updating	May not be totally honest

(Note: composition of panel important!)

Figure 6.4 Market research – the advantages and disadvantages of different methods

Discussion point

1 A college is thinking of putting on more courses for the unemployed.

   a What secondary data could it use to find out if there is a need for these type of courses in the locality?

   b How could staff find out whether their ideas for the content of the course would help students to find a job?

2 A newspaper publisher wishes to survey potential readers. What representative samples do you consider would be suitable if the publisher was producing

   a the *Financial Times*

   b the *News of the World*

   c the *Daily Telegraph*

   d the *Daily Mirror?*

The product

Product planning and development may take place as part of the marketing operation – or as part of production. Much depends upon the product or service offered. For instance, a car manufacturer may have a key 'research and development facility' linked to production, whereas a wallpaper manufacturer may link its design skills with marketing. Product planning is linked to translating the needs and wants of the customer into

- completely new products

- changes to existing products

- extensions to an existing range of products

- taking an existing or adapted product into a new market, eg from a home market to an overseas market.

The **product mix** is the range of products produced or services offered by an organisation. These may be variations of a product (eg cars) or different types of products (eg toiletries and cleaning materials). In some cases a firm may produce only one product or offer only one service, though this is relatively rare.

Product life-cycle

Products vary in terms of their life span. Bread has changed little over the years, whereas hit singles can be out of favour within three months of release. Generally, five stages are recognised (Figure 6.5).

- **Introduction** – sales are low as are profits at this stage. Marketing costs are high. There may be few competitors.

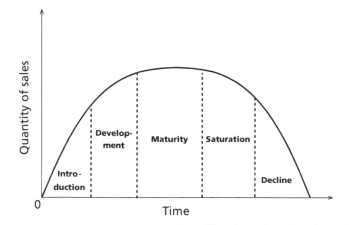

Figure 6.5 Product life-cycle

- **Development** – sales are rising rapidly and competition may be increasing. The company may be aiming for the mass market. Profits are rising towards their peak level.

- **Maturity** – sales are rising more slowly, profits have levelled off. There is maximum competition.

- **Saturation** – sales have fallen and profits have reduced. The mass market is satisfied and has turned to new products.

- **Decline** – sales fall, profits are low or even zero. The product is withdrawn from the market.

Companies often try to relaunch existing products to extend the life-cycle, eg by 'new improved' versions (think of washing powder!).

Product differentiation

Companies use a variety of methods to make their products different from their competitors. These include distinctive packaging, brand or trade names and advertising slogans (eg Guinness, Coca-Cola and Fairy Liquid).

Market segmentation

By dividing a market into segments and meeting the needs of different types of customers, a company can either specialise in one area or charge different prices for different types of products. (Think of cars – estates, saloons, sports cars, hatchbacks – and airlines – charging for first class, business class and economy – and giving a different type of service in each.)

Brushing up the product life-cycle!

One way of increasing sales is to reduce the product life-cycle – by persuading consumers they need to replace products more often. In one industry this has resulted in sales increasing from 60 million to 80 million a year. The product? The humble toothbrush – or not so humble these days, with bendy handles and specially shaped bristles. Our concern with dental hygiene is such that a range of subsidiary products has also increased – from floss to mirrors to special interdental brushes.

Given that toothbrushes cost on average about 10p to make – and sell for around £1.50 the industry has seen a major boom in profits. Increased advertising to promote consumer guilt about the state of their teeth is working. The market is growing at over 5 per cent a year as we throw away our toothbrushes ever more frequently.

 ## Discussion point

1   At what stage of the product life-cycle do you consider each of the following to be?

   a   digital televisions
   b   mobile phones
   c   microwave ovens
   d   the Internet
   e   electronic typewriters
   f   newspapers

2   Identify two similar products and identify how they have been differentiated to attract different customers.

3   How would you relaunch a singer who had been out of favour for some time?

4   Discuss how packaging can be used to influence customers' perceptions of a product.

After-sales service

The degree and type of after-sales service depends on the products produced or services offered. At its most basic level it may comprise handling queries or complaints. Anyone who buys a tin of beans is unlikely to refer it back to the manufacturer very often! However, the situation is very different for producers of technical equipment and machinery. Washing-machine manufacturers, for instance, not only issue the product complete with guarantee but also provide a repair service for customers.

For highly complex machinery and equipment the organisation may have a separate Technical Service section to which detailed queries and problems are referred. The section may employ mechanics and engineers who may be sent worldwide to carry out repairs and improvements. This is particularly the case if a machine breakdown would cause serious problems for a customer. A large computer organisation, such as IBM, which provides mainframe computers to industry, has on hand specialists to deal rapidly with hardware faults because of the problems and costs associated with system failure.

Pricing

A company considers many aspects when deciding what price to charge.

- The type of product being produced.

- The price of other products in the company's range.

- Company image and the income group of their key customers (compare Netto with Sainsbury, Rimmel with Estee Lauder, or Ford and Porsche). Note that many producers deliberately use 'prestige pricing' as a strategy.

- The number of competitors and their prices (think of paperback books, records, magazines and newspapers).

- Price sensitivity of the product (ie the extent to which demand is likely to fall if the price increases).

- The stage in the product life-cycle. A product may be offered at an initial, tempting lower price when it is first introduced in order to gain a large market share. This is often known as **promotional pricing** or **penetration pricing.** Conversely, some products are launched at high prices – and only fall when competitors enter the market.

- The costs of production. Mass production means products can be produced far more cheaply – technically advanced products are therefore often launched at quite a high price (eg colour televisions). The price falls as demand increases and economies of scale become possible.

- The costs of distribution and additional services, eg offering special customer service or after-sales service.

Promotion

The promotional mix is the mixture of different methods that can be used to promote the product. The main forms of promotion are

- advertising

- personal selling

- sales promotions

- publicity campaigns.

The aim of promotional methods is often identified by the acronym AIDA.

- Draw **Attention.**

- Create **Interest.**

- Develop **Desire.**

- Enable **Action** to be taken.

Advertising

Products and services are advertised daily in the press, on television and commercial radio, by direct mail, in cinemas and outdoors – on hoardings and public transport. By far the most widely used is the press, which accounts for about 70 per cent of all advertising. The second most popular is television.

Many companies (and politicians!) employ the services of advertising agencies to design and produce their advertisements. Apart from the technical expertise and creativity required, agencies will also know the laws relating to advertising and the codes of practice to be followed (see chapter 3).

Advertisements are designed to either **inform** or **persuade,** though some do both. A persuasive advertisement sells an image whereas an informative advertisement is more concerned with facts. Again, packaging and branding are used to good effect to ensure rapid customer recognition and association.

The choice of media depends upon

- the type of product

- the extent of coverage required

- the geographical distribution of the product

- the cost.

All media have advantages and disadvantages – and these will be carefully considered by the agency. Effectiveness can be measured in various ways – from reference numbers on return coupons in the press, to customer service checks on where people first heard of the product or service, to increases in sales volume.

Direct mail is an increasingly popular method of advertising or promoting a product, service or charity appeal. A vast number of computer databases are for sale which enables companies to target those people they think might be interested in a particular product with a direct mail shot to their homes.

Personal selling

Some products need personal selling, especially in industrial markets where specialist expertise is essential. In this case, the price may also be negotiated as well as the terms of payment and the after-sales service offered. Good sales representatives know the market, keep in touch with their customers and are always on the look-out for new sales opportunities. Representatives can be grouped on a product, customer or geographical basis – the latter being the most common. Their performance is often monitored closely and many representatives receive commission or bonus payments for above target sales.

Fast Moving Consumer Goods (FMCGs), eg groceries, are unlikely today to be sold by representatives. Suppliers are usually in touch with retailers by telephone or computer. Instead of representatives, merchandisers are employed to visit stores and set up displays or undertake sales promotions.

Sales promotions

These include offering free samples, point-of-sale demonstrations, special discounts, competitions and special offers. The aim is to draw the customer's attention to a new product or encourage or stimulate sales of slow-moving items. The aim is to increase sales not only during the time of the promotion but also afterwards – although sales are likely to drop below their peak level.

Special promotions can also be offered to dealers to encourage them to push a product – sometimes by offering bonuses and prizes and the use of special display materials.

Publicity and PR

Free publicity is obtained by all companies through stories which are regularly passed to the media – the aim being to keep the name of the organisation and the brand name in the public eye. (Richard Branson and Virgin have to be top of the list for maximum publicity stories in any given year!)

Other organisations obtain publicity through sponsorship – often of sporting events or concerts. Another method is to donate money towards a special project – this may be an academic or research project – or a charity which is 'linked' to the company in some way (eg Mothercare supports Great Ormond Street Children's Hospital).

PR is usually coordinated by a public relations officer who is responsible for a wide variety of activities to assist customer relations and to ensure the company image remains untarnished. A typical approach is to promote the company as caring, quality conscious, a fair and just employer, concerned with the community and about the environment. Alternatively, as you saw in chapter 3, a specialist organisation may be used.

Publicity campaign

This is where a range of different promotional methods take place at the same time – often to launch a new product or in an attempt to revive sales. Direct mail shots can be combined with press and TV advertising, publicity stories and special offers and point-of-sale promotions – all to 'blitz' the consumer over a short time span.

Discussion point

1   Identify three products which
   a   are suitable for advertising on television
   b   are more suitable for advertising in the national press
   c   are suitable for advertising on local transport.

2   Marks & Spencer has always been very conscious about its company image. Can you identify four ways in which it uses PR to create and maintain this image?

3   What factors would concern you if you were deciding upon the price of
   a   a new chocolate bar
   b   a new perfume or aftershave
   c   a luxury holiday?

Place

Distribution is a key element in the marketing process. For products to be sold, it is said they have to be available at the right time, in the right quantities, at the right price and in the right place (and you might add, in the right condition)! Distribution is the means by which goods are made available to the customer.

The range of outlets is variable, but must be chosen carefully – as must the 'channels of distribution', ie the number of intermediaries involved between the manufacturer and the consumer (Figure 6.6). In some cases goods are sold direct (eg Next Directory) or through one agent (eg Avon cosmetics or your local milkman). In other cases goods are sold direct to the retailer, or through a wholesaler. Some goods are available generally (eg groceries) and others only through specialist dealerships (eg cars).

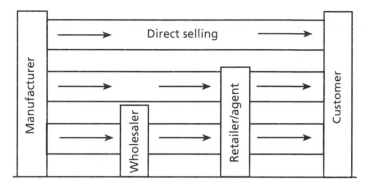

Figure 6.6 Channels of distribution

Distribution is concerned with stocks and storekeeping, warehousing, packing and loading, transporting and processing the orders, as well as selecting the best channel of distribution. This will depend upon the type of product, eg whether it is large or small, fragile or perishable; the service offered by competitors; the type of intermediaries and their cost; the needs of the customer.

Specialist distribution companies exist for transporting all types of loads – from frozen foods to urgent spare parts wanted on the other side of the world. Today many companies prefer to keep low stocks of goods and have prompt and urgent deliveries whenever they wish. They may order by computer and expect a delivery the next day. This reduces the cost of warehousing as well as the potential cost of buying goods which will not sell. Customers today do not expect to wait long for goods to arrive – if this is the case they are likely to take their custom elsewhere.

The direct approach

A new type of selling approach for the 1990s has been 'direct'. Not only do we have Direct Line Insurance, which sells its motor insurance straight to the consumer, and First Direct, the telephone banking company, but we now have direct-sale cars. Daewoo, a South Korean company, launched a new way of selling cars in Britain in 1995 and has since scooped 1 per cent of the market. With no sales representatives, no 'extras' and a money-back guarantee

for three months, Daewoo, it seems, cannot go wrong.

The aim of these companies is to cut out all intermediaries and pass on the savings to the consumer. The next prediction is for direct shopping – view the goods on your TV or computer screen, ring the store with your order and your goods will be packed and delivered. By 2010 shopping trips might be a thing of the past!

● Human resources

The transition from personnel to human resources

The terms 'human resources' and 'human resource management' reflect the new face of personnel management in the 1990s. Whereas in the 1960s and 1970s 'Personnel' was a centralised operation dealing in the recruitment and selection of workers, negotiating with trade unions and involved in supervising welfare, the enterprise culture of the 1980s has seen a shift towards a decentralised human resources function involving individual line managers. Many experts are in favour of this change. They consider it is a recognition that the workforce is one of the organisation's most important resources. It would therefore make sense if this was managed mainly through line managers in the same way other resources are managed. Only line managers have in-depth knowledge about their staff and the requirements of their departments and are therefore in the best position to manage their staff to reach their objectives as well as promoting the development of the required skills and expertise.

However, critics of the new style of human resource management argue that decentralisation has mainly been to achieve cost reductions. Given the downsizing of many organisations and the general fall in union power, it has been possible to achieve savings by reducing the size of the personnel function. This is made even easier if the organisation has also contracted out many of its activities (eg wages and salaries), employs temporary, casual or fixed-term staff or hires freelance workers to cover many areas. This reduces the number of permanent full-time staff and the amount of administration required. Staff have also been given more responsibility for their own training and development which they negotiate with their line managers.

The facts and figures bear out this argument to some degree. The job market in the 1990s is very different from that of the 1980s. The number of males in full-time work fell to an all-time low of 1.4 million between early 1990 and 1993 and there has been a huge increase in part-time jobs and temporary vacancies. However, the 'style' of human resources in any organisation (or whether there is still a substantial personnel function) will depend upon

- the size of the organisation

- the categories of workers it employs

- its approach to its employees.

It is not therefore possible to make any judgements about a company's style of human resource management based simply on the way the organisation is structured!

The human resources function

The human resources function of an organisation has an outward-facing and inward-facing aspect, in a similar way to marketing.

- Outward-facing relates to its role in relation to the outside world including prospective employees, trade union organisations and other stakeholders.

- Inward-facing relates to its role towards the management of the organisation and its responsibilities in relation to the needs of current employees.

This section examines the outward-facing role of human resources and the way in which it relates to the management and culture of the organisation. Its responsibilities in relation to the needs of current employees are covered in chapter 7.

Human resources policies

The human resources policies of an organisation not only determine its 'human face' to the outside world but also provide guidance on procedures for managers. This is important because whilst certain aspects of human resources will be determined centrally for the whole organisation, individual managers have a responsibility in relation to their own staff in areas such as appraisals, training, promotion, welfare, disciplinary action and handling grievances. An organisation which has well thought-out and fair human resource policies will not only be able to recruit the best staff but, generally, be able to retain them as well. This aspect is dealt with in more detail in chapter 7.

Specific areas where policies will be formulated by senior management include

- human resources planning

- recruitment and selection

- promotion

- remuneration (eg wage and salary rates)

- industrial relations

- redundancy.

In addition, it is usually the remit of at least one senior manager to advise management on employment legislation and changes which will affect the employment of staff, or their conditions of service (see chapter 7). Usually, too, contracts of employment are drawn up, issued and retained centrally and staff records are kept centrally and updated as required – subject to the terms of the Data Protection Act (see page 318).

Human resources planning

The major aim of human resources is to ensure that the organisation has the best possible people in place to do their jobs. This usually means ensuring that

- there are highly skilled people in essential areas

- there are competent and able managers in charge of specific areas

- there is a mixture of young, enthusiastic staff and older, more experienced staff

- skill gaps and shortages are known and action taken to remedy the problem (eg through a **skills audit** – this matches existing skills against those which are needed and can be used to inform staff training policies)

- manpower planning is carried out. This means identifying areas where there may be gaps appearing (eg through retirement) and looking at able employees who would be eligible for promotion (see chapter 7). Documents used to inform this process include the organisation chart (see chapter 5) and feedback through the appraisal process. However, in most companies there is an agreement that the actual appraisal documents are treated as confidential between line manager and employee.

Recruitment and selection policies

The aim of recruitment and selection is to ensure that the organisation's need for staff is met by attracting suitable applicants for a job in the most cost-effective manner and that as far as is possible, the most suitable applicant is selected, with due regard for current employment legislation.

An ethical company will have a clear policy on recruitment, which is likely to include specialist training of all managers involved in any part of the recruitment process, but particularly in relation to equal opportunities policies. It will also include such aspects as

- standardised layout for advertisements

- guidelines on the sources of recruitment to be used for particular jobs

- a specified closing date for applications

- a specified procedure for shortlisting candidates

- a set procedure for interviewers

- the requirement for any interviewers to disclose any relationship they have with any of the candidates.

Most ethical companies will not allow interviewers to consult referees unless the candidate is a serious contender for appointment. It used to be the case that references were not taken up unless a candidate had received a job offer, but today many are requested in advance to save time. However, applicants can insist that no reference is taken up with their current employer unless a firm job offer is being made – in which case the offer is likely to be made 'subject to suitable references'.

Promotion policy

Some organisations have a policy whereby only junior positions are filled from outside. This enables internal candidates to compete for promotion. Other organisations have a policy of advertising both internally and externally. In this case all candidates apply in the same way, regardless of whether they are internal or external. (Further details are given on page 282.)

 Discussion point

> As a group, discuss the advantages and disadvantages of promoting an internal candidate as opposed to recruiting 'new blood' from outside the organisation.

Pay policy

You have already read about salary grades in chapter 5. The grades which have been determined by the organisation will have been agreed subject to the pay policy in operation.

Organisational policy may vary on this topic, eg

- There are clear incremental scales for each job. Post-holders are appointed according to age, experience and previous qualifications at a specific point on the scale and move up each year until the top of the scale is reached. Promotion would mean a move to a higher-level scale.

- There are no clear scales but those appointed are nominated a salary relating to other people doing similar jobs and with a similar level of experience.

- There is no policy at all! People are paid according to 'scarcity value' – the more important they are perceived to be, the more they earn!

The danger with the last approach (which is only likely to survive for any length of time in a very small organisation) is that the company can easily break the law. The Sex Discrimination Act 1975 (as amended by the Sex Discrimination Act 1980) and the Race Relations Act 1976 (as amended by the Race Relations (Remedies) Act 1994) make unlawful the direct or indirect discrimination on grounds of gender or race. The Equal Pay Act 1970 (as amended by the Equal Pay Amendment Regulations 1983) enforces this still further in relation to wages and salaries.

To prevent any problems, most organisations undertake a job grading or evaluation exercise at regular intervals when jobs are 'scored' under a variety of key factors such as skill, responsibility, mental effort, physical effort and working conditions. The aim of job evaluation is to arrive at a ranking of all jobs in the organisation to which pay rates can be attached in a systematic and rational way.

However, other pressures operate which can mean that job evaluation, on its own, is not the only means by which pay rates are determined. Some pressures are external to the organisation, others are internal.

External factors

- Union activity – traditionally the most powerful unions extracted the highest pay awards for their workers. It is still the case that non-unionised or fragmented workers (eg in hotels, shops and restaurants) are paid low rates.

- Custom and practice – where different groups have traditionally been paid a higher rate for a particular reason (which may be historic).

- Labour market and the scarcity effect – every job has a 'market rate' where demand and supply prevails. The greater the shortage of qualified specialists, the higher the market rate is likely to be.

- 'The going rate' – a wide range of information is published on pay scales. These compare rates across an industry and across different jobs. Other sources include job advertisements, employment agencies and Job Centres. All of these can be used to inform an organisation (and its current employees!) of the average rates in the area for a particular job.

- The type of job – and whether pay is a strong motivating factor or not.

Internal factors

- The culture of the organisation – whether staff are seen as an important resource or a means to an end.

- The profitability of the organisation (and its future prospects) – the amount that the company can afford to pay.

- Incentive schemes – whether there are other schemes in place to supplement basic pay, eg bonuses, payment by results, commission, etc.

- Fringe benefits – whether indirect benefits can be 'earned' by or awarded to employees, eg holiday pay, sick pay, pension, company car, subsidised canteen, cheap mortgages, etc.

- Performance related pay – in some organisations this is linked to an appraisal scheme. Employees with exceptional performance can be awarded additional pay awards to a specified level.

Industrial relations

The term industrial relations is generally used to describe the interface which exists between management and trade unions. It covers areas such as specified structures and procedures (eg collective bargaining, disciplinary and grievance procedures, equal opportunities policies) and the methods by which the management and unions discuss and negotiate specific issues within the workplace. In the main, both parties usually wish to resolve disputes and obtain a compromise solution as quickly as possible, although this may not always be possible.

Trade unions today are vastly different from those which existed in the 1960s and 1970s for a variety of reasons.

- A succession of laws under Margaret Thatcher's administration of the 1980s steadily removed power from the unions. Whereas the majority of people disliked the strong union power of the 1970s, many people now consider that the balance has swung too much in the opposite direction, with some employers offering sweat-shop wages and very poor working conditions.

- Only 33 per cent of the workforce belong to a union, although unionisation is higher in the public sector (62 per cent) than in the private sector (23 per cent).

- Blue-collar union membership is still falling – 40 per cent of union members are manual workers, 32 per cent are skilled or white-collar workers and 28 per cent are professionals.

- Most unions now recognise part-time workers – a sensible move if they are to avoid further decline. Union membership has fallen overall from 12.2 million in the late 1970s to 7 million by 1995.

However, many unions are now following the US example of exerting more subtle pressure on organisations by concerted attempts of 'corporate campaigning'. American unions have hired PR and advertising agencies to attack companies publicly who don't play fair with their workforce. The aim is to bring pressure to bear on the company through influencing public opinion. The TUC – the Trades Union Congress – which is the central organising body for trade unions, considers this idea may replace and be more effective than strike action and is holding a conference on the strategy during 1996.

Collective bargaining

This term is used when one group of people negotiates with another about rates of pay, conditions of employment, disciplinary procedures or productivity agreements. In the past, most bargaining was undertaken at national level and covered all workers in an industry (eg the miners). Today local bargaining is more common and can take account of regional differences. Most settlements are linked to productivity 'deals' with the aim of increasing efficiency and output per worker. The subsequent reduction in costs helps to fund any pay award.

If negotiations break down, a union must ballot its members before taking any action. Usually strike action is the last resort because the members lose pay – few people can afford to strike for long. Instead the union may recommend

- a 'go slow' (where everyone works at a slow pace)
- a work to rule (where only legally required duties are carried out).

If there is still no agreement, and a majority of members are in agreement, then strike action may be taken.

No post today

The number of strikes in Britain has fallen dramatically from its peak in the 1970s. However, strike action reminiscent of those days was caused in 1996 by a disagreement between the management of the Royal Mail and its 160,000 workers – represented by the Union of Communications Workers. The argument was about changes in working practices, which both sides said were needed, but there the agreement ended. Management wanted to introduce flexible team working in a lean, commercial, enterprising organisation. The union wanted a five-day week with shorter hours, a single grade of delivery worker, and argued that team work would be unworkable in a sorting office. It also argued that public service should be the main objective.

One of the key problems is seen to be the Post Office's status as one of the last public corporations. This stops managers going against public-sector pay guidelines or competing internationally. It also enables the government to scoop up the profits each year. Both management and unions are united in their resentment of the percentage of profits taken by the government – £296 million in 1996 – which they argue should be reinvested in the industry to provide new technology and new service.

Discussion point

1   Discuss, as a group, whether you consider trade unions have any useful role to play in the 21st century.

2   **a**   Businesses were worried about the threat of a Royal Mail strike – particularly the Direct Marketing Association. Why do you think they were so concerned?

 b   What alternatives are available to business which mean that a Royal Mail strike is less problematic in the 1990s than it was in the 1970s?

 c   According to the union, postal workers were suffering from 'long hours, low wages and low morale'. What advantages might be gained from Royal Mail privatisation? Discuss your answers as a group.

Redundancy

Redundancies are an unpalatable fact of the 1990s. Much has been written about the shock and distress caused to employees and the difficulties and guilt felt by managers who have to tell employees that they are being made redundant. In some organisations this has led to stress counselling programmes being introduced. Many trade unions have negotiated redundancy packages for their members, which means that the employer will usually make payments in compensation above the legal minimum. The legal minimum was laid down in the 1965 Redundancy Payments Act (as amended by the Employment Protection Consolidation Act 1978), but is still very small – for instance, for each year of service between the ages of 22 and 41, the employee should receive one week's pay.

An organisation should have an agreed procedure for redundancy to comply with current legislation. An example of this type of procedure is given in chapter 7, page 300.

Human resources and management

The key role of human resources in relation to management policies is

* to influence the development of human resources policies

* to develop personnel objectives which relate to strategic planning

* to provide information and statistics which assist management to plan for future human resource requirements

* to provide information on the current labour market and pay rates

* to liaise with external organisations which can provide staff

• to assist staff to cope with change caused as a result of implementing a strategic plan.

Administration

The true definition of administration sees this as a support or service activity which assists the operational functions of an organisation. If this is taken literally, then finance and marketing and human resources are all classed as administration activities because the only operational functions of an organisation are production and sales (which make and sell the product). In reality, the term is used more generally to describe a range of activities in all areas which provide support. Therefore, if finance, production, marketing and human resources are the bricks to build the wall, administration is the cement which holds them together.

Traditionally, administrative functions were often **centralised** in an organisation. This meant that a central support or administrative unit provided all the services required. Today companies are more likely to see administration as a **decentralised** activity with each department having its own administrative section to serve its own needs. This is also more likely to be the case in small organisations which would not find a centralised section cost effective.

The major responsibilities encompassed by administration mostly cover **information and communications.** Both are the life-blood of any organisation and are critical to its effective operation. Information is required both for internal use and for communicating to stakeholders such as existing and potential customers, suppliers, shareholders, government bodies and other business organisations, eg banks and insurance companies. Unless it is accurate and up to date and communicated promptly by the most appropriate means, then it is unlikely to be any use. Indeed, it can be positively hazardous as decisions may be based on mistaken ideas.

Administration is another department, therefore, which is involved in outward-facing and inward-facing activities.

• Outward-facing – the production of documentation for external use; the transmitting of such information by mail and electronic means; dealing with correspondence; dealing with customers, clients, interviewees and other visitors; ensuring that standards of customer service are met.

• Inward-facing – the storage and reproduction of information; the finding and researching of required information; attending meetings and taking notes; the ordering and storage of supplies; the planning and monitoring of work; the development and monitoring of administrative systems and procedures to ensure that work is done on time and in a well-organised and methodical way.

In the same way that administrative staff will deal with inward- and outward-relating tasks, so they will also have to deal with a variety of internal and external customers. Those requiring their services may be from their own area or from any other department in the organisation. Customer service skills do not, therefore, just apply to dealing with outside visitors. The skill of administrative staff in dealing diplomatically with internal staff can be crucial – particularly when deadlines are running out and tempers are frayed. Administrative staff can be caught in the 'cross-fire' when there are conflicting priorities and a good administrator will need a considerable amount of skill to sort out the problem.

In addition to good personal skills, the best administrative staff are those who can use their own initiative in solving problems successfully. Busy managers do not have the time to spell out all the requirements of a task and yet will still have high expectations of the finished product! Good administrators will utilise all the sources of information at their command, remember individual idiosyncrasies shown by different managers, stay calm no matter what happens and will be quite capable of making sensible decisions which affect their area of work. Excellent administrators will even recommend improvements and implement these if they are agreed! Further information on administration is given in chapter 8.

Note that in chapter 3 you learned about the role of computer services. In some organisations this is an internal section which may be part of administrative services. If you have forgotten what computer services staff might do, turn back to page 121!

● The interaction of functional activities

Even though you have just been reading about individual departments and their various functions, in any organisation there is a considerable amount of interaction between these functional activities. For instance, there is no point having a Sales Department if there is nothing to sell. A Research and Development Department would soon go out of existence if the organisation stopped manufacturing products. If there were no workers, there would be no job for the Human Resources Department and so on.

As another example, marketing staff will need to liaise with

*   Manufacturing – about product schedules and customised orders

*   Despatch – for delivery dates

*   Finance – for costs to calculate prices and the budget available for advertising and promotion

*   Research and Development – about product planning and the requirements of the customer linked to technological progress and developments.

Discussion point

1   Give two ways in which you think each of the following departments *could* interact, eg the Research and Development Department could link with Marketing over (a) market research and (b) design of a particular new product.
   a   Production and Distribution (Logistics)
   b   Production and Purchasing
   c   Purchasing and Marketing
   d   Finance and Administration
   e   Human Resources and Finance
   f   Marketing and Administration
   g   Marketing and Human Resources

2   In small teams, identify the ways in which the departments of a large motor manufacturer will liaise over the development, production and launch of a new car. If possible, show your ideas on a flow chart from an idea for a prototype to the stage where the first sales are made.

   As a group, compare the different flow charts and discuss the results with your tutor.

Keywords

The keywords you should know from this chapter are given below. Check you can write a clear explanation for each one. Check also that you at least know what each abbreviation represents – then see if you can say what it means.

assets	liabilities
balance sheet	logistics
budget	management accountant
break-even analysis	market research
CAD	marketing mix
CIM	product life-cycle
cost control	profit and loss account
cost plus pricing	purchasing
creditors	quality circles
debtors	quality control
direct cost	research and development
direct mail	reserves
distribution	right first time
downtime	standard cost
EDI	statutory accounts
financial accountant	stock control
fixed costs	TQM
indirect cost	variable costs
JIT systems	variances

Examination practice

Short-answer questions

1 Your friend is applying for a job as a trainee administrator. What are the key aspects of the organisation with which he will be involved?

2 Identify three key activities undertaken by the finance function.

3 Explain how the human resources function will relate to other departments in an organisation.

4 State four main activities undertaken by the marketing function.

5 Explain the difference between (a) production planning and (b) production control.

6 Your friend is hoping to obtain employment as a trainee management accountant. Briefly explain the type of work with which she will be involved.

7 Identify four reasons why the interaction of marketing and production can be crucial to the success of an organisation.

8 Identify four factors an organisation will take into consideration when deciding the price of a product.

9 Briefly describe two different methods of distribution which might be used by a fashion chain.

10 Identify three activities over which the Human Resources Department would interact with the Production Department.

Definition questions

1 Explain clearly the difference between each of the following terms.
    a stock control and quality control
    b liabilities and assets
    c management accountant and financial accountant
    d fixed costs and variable costs

2 Write clear notes to explain each of the following terms.
    a product life-cycle
    b break-even point
    c marketing mix
    d balance sheet

Essay questions

1 ModComms plc is about to launch a new mobile phone on the market. Clearly explain the contribution that the marketing, production and finance functions will have played in its development.

2 The key role for administrators is to obtain and provide information on request to assist management decision-making. Explain this statement with particular emphasis on the role and responsibilities of administrative staff.

3 Explain what is meant by the term 'human resources policies' and give examples of at least two of these policies.

4 In what ways could the marketing function contribute towards the overall success of an organisation?

5 Explain why *costs* and *budgets* are so important to a company.

6 Today many purchasing operations have been revolutionised through *JIT systems* and *computerisation*. Explain both these terms and state how they can assist organisations.

Case study

Petersen Fabrics is a well-established company which designs and produces wallcoverings, coordinated bedding and curtaining. Erica Petersen, the managing director, has called a meeting of the board of directors to discuss the problem of falling sales which has meant that the organisation is unlikely to meet its targets for the year.

a Explain how key staff in the Finance section will have been able to keep Erica Petersen appraised of the financial situation.

b What role is Erica Petersen likely to expect the Marketing section to play in improving sales?

c Erica Petersen considers that a lack of communication and coordination between departments has been a substantial cause of the problem. Give an example of how this could affect sales.

d Why is departmental interaction essential for organisational success?

● Introduction

You have already read much about the managers in business – what they do and how much they are paid. But no business can operate if it is full of chiefs with no Indians! The most important part of any organisation is the staff who work there. A well-known management writer, Peter Drucker, considered staff the most valuable resource available. Machines, land and money, he said, were all limited in their capacity – a machine could produce so much, land could grow so much, money could buy a certain quantity of items. People, he argued, were different. They may do very little work if they are depressed or demotivated or they can achieve incredible feats. In other words, people are the only resource which is uniquely and totally flexible. It is management's job, in his opinion, to get the best out of staff so that the staff, the manager and the organisation will all benefit.

This chapter concentrates on the different ways this can be done. It looks at the needs of the staff in an organisation – why they go to work, what they expect from work and how managers satisfy these needs. It also examines the responsibilities of management from the point of view of current legislation, particularly that relating to employment and health and safety.

However, any relationship is a two-way process. Whilst managers might have certain responsibilities towards their staff, employees also make a commitment to the organisation when they sign the contract of employment. This chapter therefore also considers employees' responsibilities to the organisation.

● Individual needs and wants

Why do people go to work and, more importantly, what makes them work hard when they get there? Before you are tempted to answer 'money', stop and think! Human beings are complex creatures. Would you *really* prefer to work the night shift in a dirty, lonely or hazardous occupation – just for more money?

From this, you can easily deduce that whilst money is *one* factor which makes people go to work, it is certainly not the only one!

An overview of motivation

Before it is possible to decide what actions can be taken to **motivate** people, it is first necessary to consider what people look for or need from a job. Experts have changed their views on this over the years, and this has meant that theories have changed and developed.

Thinking about motivation

Try the quiz below to find out your views of people! Answer true or false to each of the following questions.

1 Making friends and working with others is important for employees.

2 There is usually a good reason for people's behaviour at work.

3 The majority of people enjoy being asked to contribute towards decisions made at work.

4 People enjoy being challenged as individuals.

5 The boss's attitude is very important – praise and recognition can work wonders for employees.

6 Most people are capable of achieving far more at work than they are given credit for.

7 No one would work if they didn't have to.

8 People don't like being given responsibility – they prefer to do as little as possible.

9 People are only interested in the quickest and easiest route to making money.

10 What people do at work is far less important to them than what they earn.

11 If people aren't supervised constantly, they will do as little work as possible.

12 Most people like to be told exactly what to do.

These comments are all linked to a view of management called 'Theory X and Theory Y' which you will read about on page 258. Score yourself now according to the instructions below and keep the result safely.

The first six statements are all positive comments about people. For each statement that you said 'true', count this as a 'Y'. For each statement you said 'false', count this as an 'X'.

The second six statements are negative and reflect a different view. This time score yourself the opposite way round – each time you said 'true', count this as an 'X' and each time you said 'false', count this as a 'Y'.

Now add up your X's and Y's.

Money, money, money
Early management writers, such as F W Taylor, took a basic view. They thought that people were only motivated by money and most workers were only capable of doing basic tasks. Constant supervision was essential and tasks should be kept as simple as possible. Only then would good quality work be produced.

Whilst this may seem harsh, it is more understandable once you realise that Taylor was involved with factory workers at the beginning of this century. At that time people were not used to the routine and discipline of working life away from their homes, and the majority had received very little education.

Human relations
In the 1930s, management theorists started regarding people more as individuals. The conclusion was reached that people's social relations at work were important and that boring, repetitive tasks were demotivating. It was felt people would respond to being given more attention and more responsibility, provided managers treated them with consideration and considered their needs.

Whilst this was felt to be an improvement in ways of thinking, critics argued that it was simply a more sophisticated method of manipulating employees. The aim was still the same, to make workers amenable to doing what management wanted them to do, with as little resistance as possible.

Human resources
Writers since the 1950s have approached the situation differently. They believe that motivation is complex because people are complex. What motivates one person at one time, does not work all the time and doesn't necessarily work with everyone. People are different and should therefore be treated as individuals.

Generally, most people arrive at work *already* motivated to do a good job and gain even greater satisfaction from doing a good job. It is therefore up to management to create a working environment where people can contribute to decisions and take responsibility for their own work as much as possible.

Do unto others?

An interesting finding from a study into motivation showed that some managers hold two contradictory views at the same time! For themselves, they believe the human resources theory is right, but they do not believe this applies to their subordinates! Hence they expect their own boss to challenge them and give them responsibility, but they do not do this for their own staff.

Another study showed that when managers are under stress, they are more likely to react negatively to their staff. You may like to think back to when you were at school and your teachers were under stress (or struggling to cope with a particularly difficult member of the group) to see whether you think this theory applied then.

 Discussion point

As a group, discuss whether you would hold different theories on motivation about each of the following types of workers:

a   doctors
b   administrators or secretaries
c   car mechanics.

Discuss also whether such a difference is really valid.

Abraham Maslow's hierarchy of needs

Maslow was one of the first writers to consider people's individual needs. He designed this as a pyramid or a series of steps upwards (Figure 7.1). At the bottom are basic animal needs for self-preservation. If you think of yourself on a desert island, these would be the first needs you would try to satisfy! You would then probably look for a safe place to go – and this need equates with Maslow's second category, that of safety. Assuming you met this need, you would next want company – and would probably look around for other people.

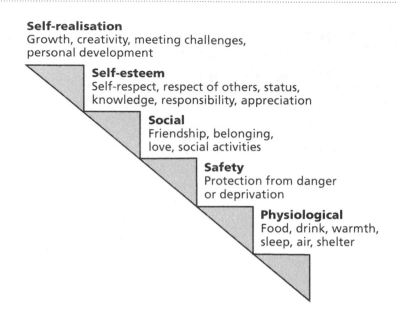

Self-realisation
Growth, creativity, meeting challenges,
personal development

Self-esteem
Self-respect, respect of others, status,
knowledge, responsibility, appreciation

Social
Friendship, belonging,
love, social activities

Safety
Protection from danger
or deprivation

Physiological
Food, drink, warmth,
sleep, air, shelter

Figure 7.1 Maslow's hierarchy of needs

In our daily lives most people have these three needs satisfied without too much trouble, so they look to satisfying their self-esteem needs. Self-esteem relates to our inner need for the respect of others through status, achievement and prestige. In other words, our need to 'feel good about ourselves'. Self-realisation is the top step. This means 'seeing how far we can go' – it is our constant need for self-development, new knowledge and experiences – to see just how much we can achieve.

Some writers have criticised Maslow's theory saying that most people do not systematically move up and down the steps. Apart from that, his theory is generally accepted as being a useful indication of the type of needs people have when they are at work, and which management can help them to meet.

Theory X and Theory Y
It is now time to look back at the answers you gave to the quiz on page 255 and to compare your result with the findings of another management writer, Douglas McGregor.

McGregor surveyed a large number of managers and supervisors and classified them by attitude as 'Theory X' or 'Theory Y' as in Figure 7.2.

The danger in this approach is thinking that managers are *either* Theory X or Theory Y. In practice most managers are a mixture, and, as you saw on page 257, in times of stress can take a more negative approach. There is an obvious danger for managers in assuming that all staff are either one thing or the other.

> **Theory X managers** believe that people dislike work and will try to avoid it. They must therefore be induced to make an effort – either by monetary incentives or by threats. Threats would work because people are anxious about job security. It is useless expecting people to be imaginative and creative – they are only creative when it comes to getting out of doing work!
>
> **Theory Y managers** consider that if the conditions are right and the goal or target is acceptable, then people enjoy work. They also believe that people want to realise their own potential and can drive themselves to work far harder than any manager can. Generally they feel that the majority of people are an under-used resource and could be encouraged to do more by involvement and participation.

Figure 7.2 Attitudes of Theory X and Theory Y managers

Motivation and hygiene

Frederick Herzberg was a management writer who undertook considerable research on job satisfaction. His conclusions are outlined below.

- Some factors at work actively cause satisfaction. Herzberg called these **motivators.** These were all related to the content of the job and the most important were achievement, recognition, work itself, responsibility, advancement and personal growth.

- Some factors at work, whilst not leading to actual satisfaction, cause *dissatisfaction* if they are not present. Herzberg called these **hygiene factors.** The most important were company policy and administration, supervision and relationship with supervisors, working conditions, salary, relationship with other workers and subordinates and personal life.

The key finding is that whilst motivators can create job satisfaction, improving hygiene factors will only *prevent* dissatisfaction. According to this theory, therefore, the organisation which redecorates the canteen or gives everybody a bonus will not make people work harder if the motivators are still missing. It will just prevent them becoming more dissatisfied.

Herzberg's theory led to many managers reviewing the content of people's jobs. This is covered in more detail on page 268.

Other theories, developments and conclusions

Many other theories which relate to people's needs and even the process of motivation have been carried out, mainly in the United States. A brief summary of the main findings is given in Figure 7.3.

Supportive management
(Rensis Likert)

Four different styles of management are

1 **authoritative** – power and directions come from above, threats are made, team work is nonexistent

2 **benevolent** – some opportunities for consultation and some rewards, but still threats and managers still seen as 'the boss'

3 **consultative** – discussions held on goals and some team work; communications quite good

4 **participative** – workers urged to be involved and committed to goals of organisation; upwards and downwards communications.

Productivity and absenteeism improve considerably from 1–4.

Immaturity/maturity
(Chris Argyris)

People at work are mature adults who are independent, have deep interests and behave in many complex ways. In contrast, in many organisations they are treated like children and expected to be passive, dependent and subordinate. This can lead to tremendous frustration among workers.

Expectancy theory
(Victor Vroom and Edward Lawler)

People's behaviour is affected by their perception of how they see the world and how they see the link between effort, performance and rewards. People are motivated when they believe that effort will lead to effective performance and that this will lead to attractive rewards.

Rewards can be **extrinsic** (outside the individual) such as pay or promotion, or **intrinsic** (within the individual), such as self-esteem and personal growth.

Figure 7.3 Some theories about management and motivation

All the theories lead to the same type of conclusions.

- Job satisfaction is important to individuals. It is created more through **job content** than by paying high salaries.

- Recognition is important. People need to feel they make a valuable contribution. Praise is important but so, too, are clear achievable targets.

- People enjoy seeing what they have created and achieved – this gives them positive feedback on the experience so that they are more likely to want to repeat it.

- People react positively to a challenge where they have to use some skill and judgement. They are capable of organising the work and enjoy taking some responsibility provided this is commensurate with their ability.

- Good supervision will encourage and extend an individual. Staff should participate in planning the work and setting the objectives.

- If the job is too complex to be done by an individual, people work better in teams with joint responsibility. This is preferable to breaking work down into small independent parts and giving each part to one person. (Team working is covered in chapter 8.)

Motivated to learn?

A MORI poll on learning surveyed 5,000 adults and children about their attitudes to training and learning. Although 75 per cent said they would work much harder at school if they had their time again, and 95 per cent believed 'you are never too old to learn new things', only four out of 10 thought they would take any type of course over the next 12 months.

Eighty-two per cent felt they needed to learn new things to do well at work and 93 per cent wanted the opportunity to study whilst at work. However, 98 per cent thought staff should be supported by their employers, especially on work-related courses, whilst only 33 per cent actually received backing by their employers.

The Campaign for Learning, launched as the first step to create a 'learning society' in the UK by the year 2000, categorised people into four groups based on their motivation for training.

- **Improvers** (who value learning and are receiving training).

- **Strivers** (who value learning but are not doing enough).

- **Drifters** (who are dissatisfied with their achievements but are not doing anything to change the situation).

- **Strugglers** (who see no point in learning and are not doing anything either).

No doubt you are an improver at the moment, but what will you be in five years' time?

Discussion point

Those who completed the survey said their reasons for not furthering their ambitions at present included personal responsibilities, lack of time and apathy. As a group, discuss the following.

1   Whether you would be likely to want to undertake training once you have a job and, if not, the reason you would give.

2   Why you think people do not always act in accordance with their beliefs (eg believing training is beneficial but still not doing it).

3   Whether you can identify one person you know in *each* of the above categories – and if this gives any further indication as to their motivation – or lack of it.

Factors affecting motivation

There are a variety of factors which will affect the motivation of staff in an organisation and their job satisfaction. These include

• the structure of the organisation

• the way the work is organised

• the organisational culture

• the **style of management** in general

• the style of their own manager in particular.

These factors are important because most relate to the motivational needs of individuals – rather than to hygiene factors. In any area, if problems are serious, continuous or cause frustration to employees, then **conflict** can ensue. This can manifest itself in several ways – from hostility between two employees, to open antagonism or a frosty atmosphere between employee and supervisor or to general disagreement between workers and management which is referred to the union (see Industrial relations on page 244).

The structure of the organisation

You read about the structure of organisations in chapter 5. What you may not have thought about very much is the way in which different structures might affect the people who work within them – particularly administrators or secretaries.

Hopefully you still remember that

• structures may be flat, hierarchical or matrix, that the more hierarchical the structure the more you would be likely to report to a line manager and have to follow rules, regulations and laid-down procedures

- structures can be based on functional areas, products, process, geographical area or customers. A complete restructure, which results in people working in different groups and for different managers and using new systems and procedures can be quite traumatic.

The type of organisation and structure you prefer will depend very much upon your own outlook and the type of person you are. If you like security, find rules and regulations comforting and want a job where there are many promotion possibilities, then you would be happy in a hierarchical structure. If, on the other hand, you are a creative free-spirit, who challenges authority at every move, you would feel stifled and repressed in such a structure.

The same applies to a flat structure – some workers would prefer the informality which often goes with such a structure. Others would resent the lack of promotion opportunities.

In a matrix structure – as in *any* structure – the main point is whether

- the structure is clearly defined – so that everyone knows what they are doing
- it shows clear lines of responsibility and accountability
- it *assists* the flow and organisation of work rather than impeding it.

However, even in an organisation where the structure is ill-defined and against your normal instincts, you may find that 'your patch' is fine! From this we can draw a few conclusions.

- If possible, it is always better that the structure 'matches' a person's individual traits and preferences (eg for formal rules or creativeness).
- Usually structure is less important than 'atmosphere'. This is usually termed **organisation culture** – see below.
- The main point is that the structure should be clear and help people to do a good job.
- People's individual experiences are more important than overall structure or culture.

The organisation of work

The more an organisation is well-organised, the more probable it will be successful and the more likely individual workers will have job satisfaction and be motivated.

It is easy to understand if you think of the opposite scenario. Imagine an organisation where everything is chaotic, papers are piled everywhere, no one knows what they are doing or for whom or why. No matter what you try to do to improve the situation, nothing seems to help. How would you feel? The chances are that very rapidly you would 'switch off' and either coast along or look for another job!

The reason for this is closely linked with Maslow's hierarchy of needs. People need to feel they have achieved something at the end of the day (self-esteem) and then want challenges which will stretch them (self-realisation). Both these needs are frustrated if the workplace is badly organised and nothing they can do will help.

Bear in mind that the structure should be designed to *assist* the organisation of work – which is why many companies are divided into functional areas such as those described in chapter 6.

Organisation culture
You met this concept in chapter 5. You may remember it relates to the style, formality, written and unwritten rules of the organisation. In chapter 5 the organisation culture and its structure were also linked together. If you need reminding, turn back to page 191.

Just like the structure, the more the organisation culture matches your own style of working, then the more easily you will settle into working there and the happier you are likely to be. If you love wearing jeans, working until late at night and dealing with the unexpected, then you are better off working in the media than in the local town hall! Equally, if you like things neat and ordered, fairly formal, with a clear way of working, then you would be better off in a local solicitor's office rather than working for the local newspaper.

Style of management
To a point, this is influenced by organisational structure and culture, but not entirely. People are far more affected by the style of their immediate boss than the managing director – unless they happen to be in senior management themselves! Therefore, if the culture of the organisation is open, friendly and informal with excellent communications, this will not help you very much if your own boss does not play by these rules. Equally, even in a very formal or staid organisation, if you had a wonderful boss who was friendly, sincere and concerned about your welfare, you may be very happy indeed.

The first point to remember is that no boss is perfect and all have 'bad days'. However, it is the overall style which affects people most. Probably the 10 *worst* traits shown by bosses include the following.

1 Taking credit for other people's ideas and accomplishments.

2 Not telling staff what is going on.

3 Being incompetent – and blaming their staff.

4 Allowing staff little or no autonomy .

5 Being sarcastic or deriding people's contributions, particularly in front of others.

6 Outright bullying and threats.

7 Being disorganised and a bad planner, so that deadlines are only met at the last minute or missed.

8 Showing no interest whatsoever in what staff are doing, thinking or feeling.

9 Being disloyal and talking derisively about staff behind their backs, and particularly to their boss.

10 Being erratic, so that nobody knows what to expect next.

All these make a job far more stressful than it otherwise needs to be – and distract everyone's efforts from what they should be doing. People are likely to become demotivated in this type of climate and do their jobs only reluctantly or grudgingly. In the worst cases, outright victimisation by a boss can make people ill.

Employment protection legislation and company grievance procedures are designed to prevent this type of abuse and are covered on pages 297 onwards.

Discussion point

1 As a group, decide on the 10 traits you would *most* like to find in a boss and then work out the effect this would have on your own motivation for a job.

2 What other benefits would you be prepared to sacrifice in order to get the 'perfect boss'?

3 Identify the advantages and disadvantages of working for a boss who is mainly Theory Y in his or her approach.

Working conditions and environment

If you attend an interview, it is usual for you to receive information about your working conditions. In other words, you will be told about your hours, holidays, pay and other benefits. However, the term **working conditions** can be viewed in a much broader way, especially if it is linked to staff attitudes and motivation. It then includes a wide range of issues, eg

- **physical environment**
- **job content**
- **terms of employment**
- **miscellaneous factors.**

You have already learned, from the studies of Herzberg and others, that deep-pile carpets are no substitute for an interesting job! You should also be aware that even an interesting job can lose its appeal if you have an unreasonable boss and are stressed because you have a heavy workload and unrealistic deadlines to meet. Therefore, it is the 'mix' of conditions which is important – and whilst no job is ever perfect, some mixes are more acceptable than others.

Physical environment

Given that the physical environment relates to hygiene factors, all the points below will help to prevent your actual dissatisfaction but will not motivate you to work hard every day. However, given an interesting job, these are the added benefits.

- Good lighting and ventilation.

- Spacious surroundings.

- Modern furnishings.

- **Ergonomically designed** seating and furniture.

- Modern equipment.

- Adjustable heating.

- Lack of noise.

- Clean, tidy and well-kept work area.

- Restful, coordinated colour scheme.

- Adjustable blinds at windows.

Quite obviously, all jobs cannot be carried out in this type of environment. A coal miner or motorway contractor might look at such a list with longing! In this type of job, where noise, dust, heat and risk are greater, or less controlled, people are usually paid more to compensate them (see also page 192).

Ergonomics is concerned with the relationship between people and their physical working environment. Imagine going on a self-catering holiday and finding yourself having to prepare meals in a poorly designed kitchen. The sink, cupboard and cooker are located on different sides of the kitchen. The work surfaces are too low down and the cupboard too high for you to reach with ease. Imagine your difficulties, the amount of walking about you would have to do and the discomfort you would feel bending and stretching!

This, quite simply, is an example of a working area without the benefit of ergonomics. Now imagine a poorly designed assembly plant or an office. How long would it take to assemble a printed circuit board if all the parts were haphazardly spread around? How long would it take to open the mail if there was no organised working area?

The science of **motion study** was first formulated by Henry Galbreth who, with his wife Lilian, was involved in early working practices. He even practised different ways of doing up the buttons on his waistcoat to find the quickest way of doing it! More practically, he looked at factory layouts and where things should be positioned to minimise time wasted on unproductive activities.

Today the science of ergonomics has moved on considerably from Galbreth's waistcoat! Not only are layouts considered important but also the height and design of furniture. Practical examples include

- the height of desks (for writing and keyboarding) and working tables (to prevent people having to bend or stoop)
- the design of chairs (to allow for movement and back support)
- the type of lighting (to avoid glare)
- the angle of keyboards (to prevent repetitive strain injury disorders – see page 315).

Employees who benefit from such considerations not only work more quickly and more easily because everything is at hand, but are also far less likely to suffer any physical discomfort or long-term ailments.

Further information on this topic is found under health and safety legislation on pages 303–318.

Job content

What makes a job interesting and challenging? As all people are different, it is likely their answers to this will also be different. One person might enjoy travelling and being out and about, whilst another would prefer a quiet office to work in. However, quite apart from the *type* of job, there is normally some agreement that people are happier when they

- are busy
- have a variety of tasks to undertake

- can plan the work themselves

- work with other people.

Equally, people are more likely to be dissatisfied when they

- are bored

- suffer constantly from factors outside their control, (eg bad planning by the boss which causes frequent, frantic activity)

- are 'oversold' a job at interview, so it is less interesting or stretching than they thought

- have to work alone for long periods.

At this point you can start to have sympathy with the receptionist in the luxury foyer who only has three visitors a day to deal with!

Some jobs are almost automatically interesting, others are much less so. For that reason, a system known as **job design** has been popular since the early 1970s to try to structure jobs in such a way that they are made as interesting as possible. This is usually done in one of three ways.

- **Job rotation** – a group of people at the same level rotate or change duties over a specified period. This allows people to learn new skills and makes the job less monotonous.

- **Job enlargement** – people are given additional duties to increase or enlarge the number of tasks they do. An assistant administrator, for instance, may be given the job of dealing with visitors as an additional duty once he or she has become used to more basic procedures. This will make the job more interesting because different duties are involved. Today this is also sometimes known by the term **multi-skilling.**

- **Job enrichment** – people are given more responsibility for their own work and allowed to make a more active contribution. In other words, their control over their own job is greater, they can make a wider range of decisions relating to what they do and how they do it. Being given autonomy means that people are made more responsible for the outcome – and job satisfaction and performance usually increases.

Of all three methods, Herzberg was a firm believer in job enrichment as the best, commenting that people do not become more motivated when two or three meaningless tasks are added to by even more tasks which are just as meaningless!

Discussion point

You work as administrator at a dairy where 200 milk delivery people are employed. The dairy boss is thinking of diversifying into other products such as eggs, orange juice, yoghurt, etc. and also giving the delivery staff the responsibility of deciding which lines to carry and in what quantity.

The marketing director thinks this move is unwise and wants to decide stock lines and levels centrally. He argues that the delivery people will not be interested in this aspect of the work – they simply want to do their round as quickly as possible and won't give the increased lines the care and attention they need to make them a success.

1 With whom do you agree, and why?

2 Look back at the notes on motivation on pages 255–261. Which management style does each of your bosses display?

3 a Now try to think of as many points as you can to support the *opposite* argument from the one with which you first agreed!

   b Why might thinking through both arguments in more detail enable a manager to make a more informed decision?

Terms of employment

You should find certain terms included in your contract of employment (see page 293). They should be pointed out at interview so that you do not receive any nasty shocks after you have agreed to accept the job! Usually they include

- your pay and any bonuses or commission payments

- your hours of work and any commitment towards flexible hours or overtime

- whether or not you will receive sick pay and on what basis

- your pension rights

- your holiday entitlement, both personal leave and statutory days

- any fringe benefits, such as luncheon vouchers or staff discounts.

Again, these are part of the realm of hygiene factors. Your terms of employment are only really of any use in comparison with other, similar types of jobs. On their own they will not motivate you to work harder if the job is less interesting. However, it is quite natural to look at the 'package' being offered and compare it with the one you are currently receiving.

Miscellaneous factors

If you ask a group of people what they most want from a job, they would doubtless list several other aspects than the ones discussed above. These might include

- job security

- friendly colleagues

- good promotion prospects

- reduced travelling time

- different hours of work.

All these *contribute* to working conditions – as it is obviously better to work with friendly people half an hour from home than it is to travel over an hour to be with a group of people you dislike! A reason for changing jobs, therefore, can be to improve any of these areas – to gain promotion, for instance, or to work more/fewer or different hours. However, a common issue facing many people today is job security. This is a major contributory factor to lowering stress and anxiety.

As you have already seen in previous chapters, the issue of change is high on the agenda of every organisation. Companies that do not change, do not survive. However, how they deal with this – and their track record in this respect – can be critical for employees. A company which values its staff and is a thriving concern will be a far more attractive proposition for employees than one which is going downhill rapidly or lays people off at a moment's notice. An organisation which shows little or no loyalty or commitment towards its staff can hardly expect very much in return. For that reason, how the organisation copes with change becomes very important indeed when it is linked to staff motivation.

Change and individuals

Change occurs to some degree in all types of organisations and has the potential to affect all the stakeholders in an organisation. However, out of all the groups, the employees are more likely to be affected to the greatest degree.

The more dynamic the organisational environment, the greater the likely rate of change. Some organisations operate in a relatively static or conservative environment (such as solicitors and funeral directors), others operate in a far more dynamic or entrepreneurial area (such as computer software houses or telecommunications companies). However, today there is virtually no organisation which is immune to change – so much so that some writers have commented that all organisations must be adaptive and flexible to survive, with a culture able to cope with constant change.

Change can be described as **reactive** and **proactive.**

- Reactive change is undertaken because external factors have created the necessity for change (see PEST analysis, chapter 4).

- Proactive change is undertaken by the organisation itself because it is seen as useful in its own right (see SWOT analysis, chapter 4).

In some cases, however, a combination of external and internal factors can interact to create the impetus for change.

The results of change

Change may result in

- new or modified corporate goals and strategy

- a different corporate culture

- restructuring of the organisation

- downsizing or delayering

- acquisitions or mergers – or demergers and franchising

- increased centralisation or decentralisation

- different production methods or processes

- different administrative procedures

- new product developments

- targeting new markets

- the introduction of new technology

- changes in staffing or job roles

- different patterns of working.

Research has shown that even planned positive changes such as moving house, getting married or having a family put people under stress. Negative changes – especially those which are imposed from above – can create distress, confusion and worry. For the employees in an organisation – at any level – change can be very stressful.

Problems for managers can be summarised as follows.

- Organisations need to change to survive.

- Many changes are imposed upon an organisation from outside – by forces outside its control, eg new legislation, technological developments, actions by competitors, social change, etc. The organisation therefore *has* to react to these.

- Staff vary in their ability to welcome or cope with change.

- For many people change is threatening – in terms of their lifestyle, status or job.

- Whilst senior managers may be enthusiastic about change and the possible benefits, staff may be less so – or even antagonistic.

- Middle managers may be particularly worried if change involves downsizing or delayering – as it is often these jobs which are at risk. Those who remain often have to cope with increased hours and responsibilities, a heavier workload, more staff to control, new systems and procedures and must also learn to help their own teams to cope with the increased or changed workload.

- Change can be managed so that people can cope more easily, but often this is mishandled or even ignored.

The management of change

Management writer Kurt Lewin analysed the process of change and identified three steps which must take place.

1 **Unfreezing** – creating the atmosphere or culture where not only is change accepted and supported but also is seen as desirable.

2 **Changing** – assisting people to adapt to new ways of working and to form new relationships.

3 **Refreezing** – reinforcing the permanency of the new methods and changed behaviours through a system of encouragement and benefits.

In many cases, creating a culture which actively welcomes change is one of the most difficult tasks for managers. However, studies have shown that change is most likely to be welcomed in organisations which foster a participative and adaptive culture and where management is consultative rather than authoritarian.

Management styles
H. Igor Ansoff and Edward J. McDonnell identified four different management styles of implementing change.

1 **Coercive** – top management imposes change. This is the quickest method but is likely to meet high levels of **resistance.**

2 **Adaptive** – change is gradual and introduced over a period. This takes time but is likely to meet low resistance.

3 **Crisis management** – everyone accepts change is essential even if the idea is disliked. Change is usually undertaken in a rush, may result in

failure, but this is as a result of lack of planning rather than staff resistance.

4 **Managed resistance** – change introduced on a flexible basis, with a reasonable time scale, with the key aim of fairness to all. This is the most difficult to achieve but the most likely to succeed.

The learning organisation

Modern management gurus such as Tom Peters and John Harvey-Jones have been instrumental in assisting organisations to cope with change. Studies have shown that organisations that have a culture and management style involving the following attributes are the most likely to manage change well.

- Group and team working is encouraged – often complemented by self-managed teams (SMTs) which set their own goals and targets and monitor their own performance.

- There is open communication at all levels and networking across the organisation.

- Employee welfare is high on the list of corporate objectives, but expectations of performance are high.

- There is a healthy respect for the customer with a strong emphasis on product quality and customer service.

- There is continual staff training and development.

- The company takes a holistic (wide-ranging) approach to problem solving – favouring collaboration and coordination instead of internal segmentation, competition and individual rivalry.

- New ideas and experimentation are welcomed. Solutions to problems are welcomed from all levels, with success rewarded and failure openly tolerated – mistakes are treated as 'positive learning experiences'.

- Bureaucracy is detested and the structure is as decentralised and as simple as possible. All employees are encouraged to share in the decision-making processes of the organisation.

- Change is viewed as an opportunity not a threat.

- The culture is one of pride in organisational achievements.

Some writers have termed organisations which view change positively and encourage continuous personal and organisational development as **learning organisations.**

Implementing change

There are two requirements for changes to be implemented successfully.

- Management must **plan** change.

- All involved must be helped to **adjust** to change. This often needs the assistance of those who are charged with
  - progressing the **task**
  - helping the **people.**

Those with good 'people skills' are most appropriate to select for assisting others to cope with the emotional aspect of change.

Planning involves the following.

- A careful examination of the problem.

- Consideration of the timing – both in relation to the announcement of the change and its implementation schedule. Often proposed changes may be secret at the beginning – when to 'go public' (and how) can often be critical. 'Leaks' through the grapevine are cruel and can lead to speculation and rumour .

- An analysis of the operational effects *and* the human effects.

- Consideration of how anxiety can be minimised through
  - good communication
  - sound human relations policies
  - retraining programmes
  - protection of jobs, earnings and status where possible
  - as little disruption to effective work groups as possible.

- Consideration of the most appropriate management style to use and the degree to which participation by others is possible.

- Examination of corporate culture and development of 'open culture'.

- Deciding the best method to use. This will depend upon the issue(s) involved, the numbers of people involved, the work carried out, the history of the organisation, the degree of confidence of staff in the management. Therefore, the method which will be suitable in one set of circumstances may be totally inappropriate in another.

The SWOT approach

You have already met this technique in chapter 4. It is useful for a SWOT analysis to be carried out before any specific changes are suggested or considered. Examining the **strengths** and **weaknesses** of the organisation and the **opportunities** and **threats** of external events enables managers to maximise opportunities and build on existing strengths.

The analysis may show that the implications of a change being forced upon the company from outside (eg new legislation) are not as severe as were first thought or that change can be 'staged' rather than implemented quickly or even that the degree of change can be less than was first envisaged.

The key issue is that the **benefits** of the proposed change *must* outweigh the **costs** – both financially and in human terms.

Type of change and implications

The next stage is for managers to differentiate between **basic change** and **fundamental change.**

Basic change relates to changes such as introducing different operating procedures or systems of working which may create short-term hassle and annoyance but can be managed relatively easily. Such changes are almost always **task-centred.** Examples include changing the design of forms, adapting to new rules or regulations for expense forms or changing a filing system.

Fundamental change involves more far-reaching changes which can cause long-term anxiety, worry or distress and can only be managed with difficulty. Such changes are both task-centred *and* **people-centred.** Examples include increasing the responsibilities of a job, changing the hours people work, changing the structure of an organisation, introducing new technology, restructuring the reorganisation or reducing the number of employees.

Each type of change should be analysed in relation to its potential impact on employees in areas such as

* job security (eg redundancy or reduced income)

* status (eg greater 'distance' from boss, loss of perks)

* prestige (eg loss of self-identity or self-worth – for instance, if learned skills lose their value)

* social ties (eg social life disrupted because of shift changes, work group/teams disrupted)

* personal anxieties (linked to fears of disliking or not being able to cope with new job or new procedures coupled to a natural fear of the unknown).

The natural reaction of most people when threatened is that of 'fight or flight'. Therefore, if such changes are imminent the reaction of employees may range from outright aggression/militancy to increased stress, lack of motivation, morale and productivity and possibly increased absenteeism.

Identifying barriers and resistance

One of the main threats to the success of a proposed change will be the degree of resistance which may be encountered from staff. This will be intensified if

- there is no confidence in management (perhaps because of an earlier fiasco!)

- staff perceive weaknesses in the plans

- poor communication has led to speculation and rumour

- there is no consultative process whereby staff anxieties can be discussed and problems resolved.

There is usually a range of reactions to suggestions for change, ranging from gratitude and acceptance, through subtle or obvious resistance, to open conflict and antagonism.

The barriers which trigger these are linked to **security.** Individually, people will be used to existing practices, loyal to current managers and teams and may not see the point of the proposed changes.

Overcoming barriers and resistance

There is usually no single 'ideal' solution for overcoming barriers to change. Too often, changes are seen as devised in corporate ivory towers and imposed on the workforce. They may appear ill-thought out and not take account of a range of possible options. Wherever possible it is sensible for managers to take soundings and obtain suggestions – preferably from those who will be personally involved. Although this takes longer, staff will be more likely to feel they 'own' the new procedures with which they will be involved.

Building support for change

When Japanese companies moved to the UK they involved a range of stakeholders in consultations about their methods of working. They considered this was essential because their working practices were very different from those with which their employees or suppliers were familiar. The aim was to remove tension and conflict and bring about a joint responsibility for the initiative.

Support can be maximised by

- open discussion of the issues involved

- making sure that all staff are clearly aware of the reasons for the change

- minimising changes that will affect job security and working relationships

- encouraging participation

- identifying the benefits for staff and overall improvements that the proposed changes will bring

- maintaining effective and accurate communication at all stages of the change process

- arranging counselling for those adversely affected.

Method of implementation

Some types of change benefit from a **pilot scheme.** This is a trial which may operate only over a limited area and involve a few selected staff – who can then feed back their views so that the process can be modified before overall implementation. The word 'pilot' implies that staff suggestions and feedback will be sought and indicates that there is a limited time scale to the event. This can often be another way of getting people used to the idea of change and persuading them that it will be beneficial. Changes which can be 'piloted' are often those involving new systems and procedures or new technology. This enables the 'users', as well as the expert designers, to influence the process.

However, some changes are inappropriate for piloting. A major company restructure can hardly have a trial run for several months beforehand! In such a case it is even more important that all the potential benefits and problems have been thought through beforehand.

The schedule for implementation should be circulated as widely as possible and, preferably, be accompanied by staff development and training programmes.

Monitoring the results

It is important that the effects of the change are monitored. Quite often there may be results and repercussions which were not thought of when the plan was conceived. Some of these may be beneficial, others may not be – in which case it is a poor management which will stick like glue to its original ideas. Often changes can be introduced in stages so that the new scheme can be modified as required. If the organisation operates an open culture where ideas for improvement are welcomed, this will make it easier for management to adjust the new systems without fear of losing face.

Ongoing evaluation

Any change can only gain benefits in the short term. In the long run there will be new factors which will impinge upon the organisation making further change necessary. A constant 'weather eye' on the internal and external environment affecting the business, plus ongoing evaluation of current systems and procedures will mean that further changes or reorganisation can be contemplated as required.

However, organisations and managers should resist the temptation to change for the sake of it – possibly dreaming up benefits they hope will accrue rather than giving careful consideration to the human cost involved. Change may occur for negative reasons when a new chief executive or manager wishes to take the 'new broom' approach and sweeps away many existing good systems together with those which really did need changing. Staff in a constant state of flux and worry are likely to be demotivated and dissatisfied. Managers must also realise that not all problems are solvable by making changes – some they just might have to live with!

Meeting people's needs

You have already learned a lot about people's needs – for information, security, interesting jobs, consultation over potentially worrying changes, and so on. In many organisations the key area concerned with employees is **human resources,** which you first met in chapter 6.

However, human resources is not just concerned with overall staff policy, it is also related to **identifying** and **meeting** the needs of employees. This can be done in a variety of ways.

Recruitment procedures

Individuals have needs when they first walk through the door of an organisation as a potential employee. They need to be given clear information on what the job will entail and their conditions of employment. If this information is too sketchy or too exaggerated, then many good potential employees may withdraw or, if they are employed, may fail to meet expectations.

A key human resource activity is therefore concerned with recruitment – and to help existing employees to benefit from a suitable new colleague. The methods by which this is done vary – a small organisation is less likely to have in place formalised application procedures.

Generally, however, for each vacancy, a series of procedures is carried out which may include

- deciding whether it is a 'replacement job' or whether the vacancy provides an ideal opportunity to change the job

- revising and preparing a **job description** or a job outline

- drawing up a **job specification** (in some organisations these are called person specifications or candidate profiles)

- deciding on the best source of recruitment

- advertising the vacancy (internally, externally or both)

- ensuring applicants receive full details of the job and relevant information about the organisation

- short-listing candidates according to set procedures to prevent bias

- carrying out interviews according to specified procedures

- determining the most suitable applicant

- notifying unsuccessful applicants.

The exact procedure followed in preparing the documentation which precedes an interview can vary considerably from one organisation to another. Below is given a general outline based on recommended personnel procedures.

Job description or job outline

A job description or job outline is the information document which contains basic information about the job itself and/or the role of the job holder. This usually includes

- the job title

- grade or salary level

- title of line manager

- description of duties and responsibilities.

It is usual for a job description to include a 'catch-all' phrase along the lines of 'such other duties of a comparable nature as may be required'.

This allows for flexibility and prevents the job holder from later refusing to undertake any additional duties on the grounds that they were not included in the job description. If this was the case, the organisation would be prevented from adjusting the content of the job to match changing conditions in the workplace.

Job specification or person specification

A job specification is a more detailed document which gives details of the characteristics that will be required by the job holder. It usually contains information on the **essential** and **desirable** attributes required by the successful candidate. Trained personnel officers often use either a seven-point plan or a five-point plan, although some organisations use their own headings. As an example, the seven-point plan divides attributes into seven sections – physical make-up, attainments, general intelligence, specialised aptitudes, interests, disposition and circumstances.

Once the essential and desirable characteristics have been identified under each heading, the advertisement is drafted. An example is shown in Figure 7.4. It is usual for organisations only to short-list candidates who have the essential characteristics. More discretion can be used over 'desirables'.

Sources of recruitment

These include

- Job Centres

- schools, colleges and universities

- careers offices and training providers

- selection consultants and employment agencies

- advertising in the national or local press

> # ADMINISTRATION ASSISTANT
>
> required for busy data communications company
>
> The successful applicant must possess an excellent telephone manner and have first-class administration skills. Experience of IT systems essential. } **Essential attributes**
>
> Preference will be given to candidates who have experience of Word for Windows 6 and 50 wpm+ typing. Most importantly, candiates need to be flexible and willing to undertake a variety of tasks. } **Desirable attributes**
>
> Salary negotiable depending upon experience.
>
> Applications in writing with CV to Digital Datacomm, Boston Avenue, Hightown HG4 5MP.

Figure 7.4 Job advertisement showing the essential and desirable attributes required of applicants

- advertising in specialist journals or magazines

- advertising internally (either by memo, including it in a staff magazine or placing the advertisement on a notice-board).

Each source has its advantages and disadvantages and is suitable for different types of jobs, with different skill levels and at different ages. An unskilled worker may be recruited easily through a Job Centre advert, a school leaver by contacting the careers office and a new managing director by employing a firm of selection consultants. General vacancies are usually placed in the press, in the most appropriate 'job section' for that particular vacancy and paper.

An effective job advertisement must contain

- brief details about the vacancy *and* the organisation

- details about *all* the *essential* requirements

- information about all the *desirable* requirements

- information on the conditions of employment

- information to candidates on how to apply. Larger organisations usually have a standard application form which must be completed. Smaller companies may request a letter with accompanying curriculum vitae (CV).

The success of the advertisement can be measured by the number and type of applications received. The more precise the advertisement, the larger the number of suitable applications which are likely to be received! One which is vague, or fails to include basic requirements, is likely to result in dozens of unsuitable applicants!

Short-listing

This is the process where all applications are carefully sifted with applicants divided into those who are

a highly suitable

b quite suitable

c unsuitable.

Most organisations limit the number of people they interview – otherwise the cost of the interviews can soar because of the time involved. If enough highly suitable applications are received, then only these applicants will be interviewed. Otherwise some applicants will also be called for interview from group **b**.

The interview

Interviews can take several formats, eg

* one interviewer, one interview

* a preliminary interview and a second interview

* a panel interview.

Interviewers should be trained so that they know how to conduct an interview to get the best out of all candidates and can make a fair assessment.

Experienced interviewers make certain that they are well prepared for the interview. The room should be suitable and there should be no interruptions. All relevant information relating to the job and the applications should have been studied beforehand.

A skilled interviewer is capable of

* helping the candidate to relax

* finding out as much as possible about the applicant

* probing to ascertain critical information on key areas

* identifying any 'gaps' or 'weaknesses' in the application

* conducting a courteous interview at which candidates can give of their best

* controlling an interview so that it keeps to time

* giving all the information required or requested by the candidate.

Most interviewers work to some type of checklist or grading form to help them to review the candidates fairly afterwards and come to the right decision. However, interviewing is an inexact science! It is often difficult for interviewers to calculate suitability objectively or numerically when many of their views are subjective. For instance, the interviewer may feel that the most well-qualified candidate may not fit in with existing staff.

To help assess suitability a range of tests may be used. These can include

- intelligence tests (eg IQ tests)

- aptitude tests, eg to test the ability to do a particular job, such as computer programming or clerical work

- attainment tests, eg typing or spelling tests

- personality tests. These provide a personality profile of candidates which can be used as an indicator of their suitability. They are usually used to confirm suitability, rather than as a definitive guide to recruitment.

All of these components, plus the written application and any references received help to inform the interviewer(s).

Career opportunities and promotion

In many interviews candidates ask about their opportunities for career development and promotion. Good organisations will have a policy which normally incorporates

- appraisal of and feedback to staff (which is linked to)

- staff development and training opportunities.

In this way, not only can all individuals benefit by working towards maximising their own potential, but the organisation also benefits through motivated and more skilled staff. These aspects are covered on pages 283–291.

However, the degree to which employees can progress their career within the same company can vary tremendously. A hierarchical structure obviously has more opportunities for promotion – because there are more levels – than a flat structure. Usually, too, a large organisation will have a greater range of opportunities than a small one. However, today many people expect to move around and work for several employers before they reach the pinnacle of their career. In fact, some positively enjoy this because of the variety and additional experience they gain – and can then take to their next job.

In chapter 6 you read about promotion policy. Staff working in large, hierarchical organisations may be particularly interested in finding out what they need to do to move up within their own organisation. Promotion policy again can vary from one company to another and can range from

- no external advertising if there are sufficient good internal applicants for a job

- internal applicants expected to compete with external applicants for all jobs

- no one can remember when the last person was promoted!

It is unlikely that a zero promotion policy will officially be in force, but some companies do give the impression that it is better to move outwards and upwards – and then even come back again at a higher level – rather than wait to be moved upwards and onwards!

If you are a candidate for promotion at some stage in your career, then the degree of formality with which your application is treated will vary considerably from one organisation to another. At one extreme you may even be called into your boss's office and simply offered a better job! At the other, particularly if the organisation has a formal or bureaucratic culture, you will have to go through a formal application process alongside other candidates, including external ones.

The problem in this case is that whilst the external candidates will only sell their good points at interview, everyone knows all about you! In addition, if the external applicants fail to get the job, no one will ever see them again. If you are rejected, then you have to put on a brave face to everyone the following day. In a good organisation you should receive feedback afterwards where you are told the areas in which you were considered lacking – and given advice about what to do to put things right.

Today, most organisations operate an appraisal system (see below) so that staff have this type of information well before they even think of applying for promotion. They then have a relatively accurate idea of their chances before they even put their name forward. This is a far kinder and fairer system than allowing people's hopes to be dashed unexpectedly. Rejection takes some time to get over and it is a reckless employer who would risk demotivating good staff needlessly in this way.

Appraisal schemes

In many organisations, the identification of staff development and training requirements is undertaken through an appraisal scheme. **Appraisal interviews** are usually held annually, between employee and line manager, and the content of all discussions is confidential. In cases where employees feel they might not obtain a fair interview with their line manager, it is usually possible to nominate a different person to be the appraiser.

Appraisal interviews are nothing new – they were around in one form or another in the USA for the best part of this century. However, it took until the 1970s before they were introduced in Britain – initially, for middle and junior managers in the private sector. Later they were adopted by the public sector.

Discussion point

1 Discuss the advantages and disadvantages of promoting an internal candidate, rather than recruiting from outside.

2 **a** Which do you consider would be the best source of recruitment for
    i a waiter
    ii an administrator
    iii a marketing director?
  b How would the recruitment and selection procedures vary in relation to each of the above jobs?

3 Many organisations issue job applicants with a copy of their equal opportunities policy which states that the organisation will not discriminate against applicants on the basis of race, ethnic or national origin, nationality, colour, sex, marital status, disability, sexual orientation, age or religious belief. In some of these areas discrimination is illegal – in others it is not. Which do you think are which? (You can check your answer later in this chapter – after you have read the section on employment legislation on pages 297–303.)

The aims of appraisals

Initially, appraisals concentrated upon employee traits, such as loyalty and commitment. The focus then changed to job performance – what people did rather than how they acted. Today the main emphasis is on job results and achievement and appraisal interviews are usually held to

- review past performance (often linked to success in meeting previous targets)

- review – and hopefully improve – job performance

- set new targets or performance objectives for the coming year

- assess training and development requirements – linking the needs of the individual with the organisation's strategic plans

- assess future potential or promotability

- assist employees to plan their career.

The structuring of appraisals

Good appraisals are carried out in a positive way by managers who have received some training in how they should be undertaken. Three styles have been identified.

- The 'tell and sell' approach – where the appraiser does most of the talking. This is generally the wrong approach to take.

- The 'tell and listen' approach – where the appraiser opens the interview and the appraisee then takes over.

- The problem-solving interview – where there is a frank and open discussion on the strengths and weaknesses of the appraisee followed by an agreed plan to move forwards.

A trained manager also knows the difficulties and dangers inherent in carrying out an appraisal, such as

- being overly influenced by recent events or the long service of the appraisee

- allowing a good or poor rating in one area to affect judgement in other areas

- 'playing safe' by giving a middle score to everyone

- overrating employees if a pay award is linked to the appraisal (see below) to avoid bad feeling afterwards

- avoiding discussion on sensitive areas or poor performance

- wanting perfection and making unfair criticisms and evaluations – this can destroy staff morale and motivation.

Employees can help by preparing for the interview. In many organisations a form must be completed beforehand and submitted to the manager two or three days before the appraisal is scheduled. This gives the manager prior notice of the areas the employee wants to discuss. The basic areas which must be considered beforehand include

- the work which has been done since the last appraisal – including areas the employee wishes to highlight

- any areas which have caused particular problems – with suggested reasons and positive recommendations for how these can be overcome

- an indication of which areas the employee would like to develop and/or move into

- areas of personal and professional development the employee would like to discuss.

The aims of the appraisal interview

The main aim of the appraisal interview is, of course, to maintain and increase staff motivation. An Institute of Personnel and Development (IPD) survey found that 60 per cent of employees were motivated by the experience. A well-structured appraisal is only part of the relationship between managers and their staff – it should not be the only time that managers and employees ever meet or talk about what is going on. However, it is the only time they may ever be able to step back from day-to-day problems and tasks and look at the overall picture together – with the manager listening carefully to the views and ideas of the employee.

Most appraisals involve some type of review against targets. It should be emphasised that this can only be done fairly if external factors are taken into account – as well as those aspects of the job which cannot be measured quantitatively.

The success of appraisals – and their value – depends to a great extent on the skill of the appraiser and his or her management style. If the appraisal ends in confrontation, then this is an indication that there is something far more serious taking place than a poor appraisal. Adequate time should be allowed for appraisals – between one and two hours per person is fairly normal – and there should be no interruptions. The support of top management is essential – if appraisals are loathed or feared by staff, they will not serve their purpose.

The use of appraisals?

Not all appraisals give employees a positive feel. The management writer Tom Peters was quoted as saying 'performance appraisal is the number one American management problem. It takes the average employee six months to recover from it'.

Whilst this may seem unduly negative, research by the IPD shows that about one third of companies use appraisals to decide pay awards and yet others use them to decide redundancies. Generally, the experts consider that pay should be separated from the appraisal process. It goes without saying that, in this case, employees will feel honour bound to defend or justify their performance – and only agree to low targets which they know they can achieve. However, others take the view that appraisal is only taken seriously when pay issues are involved and that those who are high performers are 'disadvantaged' when the review does not include a reward for their achievements.

Experts also criticise appraisals which measure targets in unsuitable areas. A hospital doctor who has achieved the fastest 'throughput' of patients is an obvious example – as doctors may be tempted to send people home early to meet their 'targets'. In the late 1980s and early 1990s, many people were sold inappropriate pensions by financial advisers trying to meet targets.

The main area where appraisals are considered successful is in the identification of training and development needs – provided, of course, that the organisation is then prepared to support or assist with the training and link personal development with new performance goals.

Successful appraisals aim to

- enable the organisation to identify where rewards (including promotion) should be allocated

- to discover the work potential of employees and, collectively, each section or department

- to identify the training needs which are required and link these to strategic planning

- to control and monitor performance

- to assist individuals with their own self-development (see below)

- to improve employee motivation by understanding and recognising their needs

- to check the effectiveness of current practices, eg recruitment and training.

Discussion point

1   In a study undertaken by Garland and Price, the success of female managers was attributed to luck or an easy task whilst the success of male managers was attributed to skill and hard work *by the majority of appraisers.*
    a   What do you think caused this view?
    b   What action could an organisation take to overcome findings such as this?
    c   To what extent do you think such views can ever be totally eradicated?

2   As a group discuss
    a   your views in relation to linking appraisals to pay awards (note that both advantages and disadvantages are mentioned above!)
    b   the difficulty (and dangers) inherent in setting performance targets for police officers.

3   Some appraisal interviews are recorded on rating scales, others on forms which simply include headings with explanatory notes.
    a   Which do you think would be most appropriate, and why?
    b   Can you see any benefits in operating the other system?

4   Discuss the advantages and disadvantages of being appraised by an independent senior manager (eg the human resources manager) rather than your own line manager.

Training

An organisation which is working towards, or has achieved, the Investors in People award (see page 162) will already have a specific policy for training and staff development. Employers must ensure that they do not discriminate when offering training on the grounds of gender, race or disability. Nor should there be any distinction between the support offered to part-time and full-time staff as this may be classed as indirect **discrimination** (see page 302).

An organisation can establish its training needs

- by carrying out a **skills audit,** which identifies which skills staff already possess

- matching this against the skills required to meet the strategic plan

- adding to this individual needs as identified during the appraisal process

- summarising the requirements (usually by department) in a staff development plan which is then approved by senior management.

Staff responsibility for self-development

Most organisations expect their employees to take an active role in their own self-development. They are expected to

- undertake self-assessment to identify the skills they have already achieved

- identify the skills they feel they *should* achieve (both personal and professional) and those they would *like* to achieve

- discuss their ideas with other people to gain more information

- discuss their ideas with their line manager to check their personal needs relate to organisational needs

- prepare an action plan to prioritise their training needs and set their own objectives

- be prepared to review this plan and their progress as part of their appraisal process.

You should note also that organisations do not necessarily expect to pay for expensive external courses. Some have facilities for training in-house, others will organise staff development activities if there is sufficient demand (eg on health and safety requirements). Training can take place 'on the job' or 'off the job'. **On-the-job training** is given to employees in their normal working situation (eg learning to use a switchboard or photocopier). **Off-the-job training** occurs when employees spend time away from their desk to receive specialist instruction. This can be in-house or at an outside organisation, such as an FE college, private training provider, TEC or specialist centre.

The aim of training

Training is given to

- provide new employees with the skills and knowledge required to perform their jobs effectively, in the minimum of time

- retrain existing employees when their jobs change or when new legislation requires a change in working practices

- enable newly promoted staff to cope with new responsibilities

- equip managers for changes in legislation, company policy or working practices

- help existing employees to keep up to date and to improve and extend their knowledge and skills

- improve organisational efficiency in all areas.

Types of training

Training needs vary both in relation to the type of training required and the level. People who have achieved a basic skill will normally wish to develop it, perhaps even to advanced level, whereas others are just starting out. In addition, their training will depend upon how long they have been working for the organisation and the type of job they do.

Induction

Induction courses are held for new employees. The aim is to quickly familiarise recruits with the organisation so that they become productive as soon as possible. Most induction courses comprise three elements.

- **A personal element,** which relates to company policy and procedures, conditions of employment, knowledge of the building, environment and people, individual responsibilities in relation to health and safety (see page 303).

- **An organisational element,** which relates to the history of the organisation, current structure, products and markets.

- **A job element,** which relates to the job itself and the duties required.

In many cases new employees are assigned individual 'mentors' at the same level as themselves to whom they can refer if they have any concerns. An example of a company's induction programme is shown in Figure 7.5.

Technical and commercial

Many organisations employing skilled workers operate training or apprenticeship programmes. These can include a training element off the job either on a one-day-a-week basis or a block release. The content can range from a motor mechanics NVQ course to an administration course.

INDUCTION PROGRAMME

Monday, 28 April 199-

Please report to room 342 at 9 am

0900	Introduction and welcome	Geoff Barnes Human Resources Manager
0915	Terms and conditions of employment	Joanne Gilpin Personnel Officer
0945	Health and safety and fire training	Barbara Whyte Health and Safety Officer
1030	Coffee	
1045	Company overview and major issues	Ken Jones Managing Director
1100	Current markets, aims and objectives	Nicola Wyatt Marketing Director
1130	Guided tour	
1230	Lunch	
1330	Company IT network and computer systems (hands-on session)	John Chang IT Manager
1445	Tea	
1500	Mentoring, training and staff development (plus allocation of mentors)	Joanne Gilpin Personnel Officer
1530	Departmental induction Transfer to own working area	Departmental heads
1600	Introduction to mentor and colleagues	

Figure 7.5 A company's induction programme

Supervisory and managerial

Higher level training is carried out by a variety of organisations to help to prepare staff who are promoted or appointed to supervisory or management posts. These include courses offered by universities, business schools, colleges and private organisations. Many organisations also run special internal sessions for newly appointed managers to help them to cope with their new responsibilities and/or how to manage staff.

Developmental training

Staff who wish to improve their career prospects may ask to attend a variety of courses. For instance, they may work towards a first or second degree (such as a BA or MBA) or ask for the company to support them in obtaining high-level professional courses, such as CIMA (for management accountants) or ACCA (for chartered accountants).

Specialist training

Specialist training courses may be held on a variety of topics, eg new software packages, first aid, fire fighting, telesales, customer service, delegation, etc. These can range from short courses lasting between half a day and a week to longer training courses leading to a specific qualification.

Many NVQ qualifications, for instance, can be acquired in the workplace with employees providing evidence from their own job. These may be supplemented by 'top-up training' carried out off the job.

 Discussion point

As a group, discuss each of the following aspects of training.

1 The advantages and disadvantages of undertaking a programme of training 'on the job' and 'off the job.'

2 How the effectiveness of a training programme can be evaluated.

3 How effective the idea of 'cascading' new information is likely to be. Cascading takes place when, for instance, one employee only is sent on an expensive training course with the remit of then teaching other staff what he or she has learned.

4 The benefits of training to the organisation as a whole.

Employee welfare

Traditionally, **welfare** was often 'managed' by central Personnel sections and included issues such as

- employee savings and loan schemes
- sickness scheme
- retirement training and pension advice
- recreation and sports clubs
- medical examinations, screening and medical facilities.

Recently, there has been a change of emphasis. Only the largest organisations are likely to have recreation or sports facilities – people mostly prefer to spend their leisure time away from work. Many organisations have also reduced medical checks and screening programmes to save money – and expect employees to make their own arrangements about their health care. Savings are likely to be organised through a salary scheme such as SAYE (save as you earn) and detailed pensions advice may be contracted out to financial advisers, linked to the company scheme for Additional Voluntary Contributions.

Welfare issues may be handled by a member of the Human Resources staff who gives advice and information to either line managers or staff on particular company policies or welfare issues and who is responsible for reporting the effectiveness of the systems to senior management.

Responsibility for welfare for many employees has been passed to their own line manager.

The heart of the problem?

The British Heart Foundation estimates that stress at work costs the average UK company with 10,000 employees 73,000 lost working days each year; the death of 42 employees a year aged between 35 and 65; lost production amounting to more than £2.5 million a year. Recently, a social worker successfully sued his former employer and won £175,000 compensation after claiming that workplace stress forced him to take early retirement – thus increasing the focus on stress as a health and safety issue, and something that companies would be wise to heed.

People's ability to cope with different levels of stress varies considerably. However, the 'modern organisation' with its flatter structure, increasing workloads and high rate of change is a major contributor to high stress levels. Trying to solve the problem is usually the remit of the Human Resources section which can undertake a 'stress audit' based on absenteeism and sickness statistics, to identify the areas that are obviously 'stressful'. Questionnaires may be issued to staff and employee health can be monitored over time. Relevant training courses include those which teach coping strategies or those which improve health and fitness. If all else fails, counselling services can be provided – expert counsellors such as those employed by Relate can be brought in to give confidential advice.

Areas which can be classified as welfare are now more likely to include

- salary issues, increments and bonuses

- interpretation and clarification of contracts of employment

- advice and information relating to grievance procedure

- advice and information relating to disciplinary procedures

- health and safety issues

- protection of personal information

- redundancy issues and policy

- dealing with stress

- company policies on areas such as loans, absenteeism, additional personal leave, compensation for accidents, holiday entitlement, payment for training, additional benefits.

It will therefore be up to individual line managers to decide whether to recommend that an individual is granted a loan, given permission to take additional leave (eg in the case of a family emergency) or should receive support to go on a training course. Provided that the manager stays within the bounds of agreed company policy, usually these types of issue are dealt with departmentally.

However, certain central policies are laid down in all organisations where they relate to statutory issues, ie where the company is required by law to comply with specified standards. Key areas, of course, are those relating to the contract of employment, employment legislation and health and safety legislation, which lay down responsibilities to which both organisations *and* employees must conform.

Legislation and the individual

The major areas which relate to employees in the workplace are those which concern

- the contract of employment
- employment legislation (including equal opportunities)
- health and safety legislation
- data protection.

Many aspects of employment and health and safety legislation are the result of European directives which are binding on all member countries, eg

- equal pay for men and women
- equal pay for work of equal value
- employee rights when a business is transferred to a new owner
- protection for employees made redundant or whose firm has become bankrupt
- freedom of movement of workers throughout member states
- health and safety.

Contracts of employment

The Employment Protection (Consolidation) Act 1978 (updated by the Trade Union Reform and Employment Rights Act 1993) covers the rights and responsibilities of employers and employees. These include

- the right to be given a written statement of terms and conditions of employment

- the right to an itemised pay statement

- the right to a statutory period of notice

- the right to choose whether or not to be a member of a trade union

- the right to maternity pay and to return to work after a pregnancy

- the right not to be unfairly dismissed

- the right to a redundancy payment.

There is a legal obligation upon all employers to provide all employees with a written statement of their terms and conditions of employment. This should be issued within two months of the commencement of the job. The information contained in the contract relates to the **express** conditions of that particular job. However, it is important to note that when you obtain a job, there are also **implied** conditions which are not included – they are taken for granted.

Relevant facts about the job
These include

- the name of employer and employee

- the title of the job or a brief job description

- the place of work

- the date the job starts (on a fixed-term contract the finish date would also be given)

- the rate of pay.

Express conditions
These include

- the normal hours of work and any flexibility or overtime arrangements

- the method of calculating pay, the system by which payment will be made and at what intervals (eg weekly, monthly)

- any probationary period which must be worked

- holiday arrangements and holiday pay

- sickness entitlement and notification requirements

- period of notice to cancel the contract (on either side) plus payment due on termination

- pension scheme details

- information on the company disciplinary and grievance procedures (if details are not given in the contract, then they should be enclosed or made available on request).

The contract is in force from the day the employee starts work. From that date its terms and conditions are binding on both employer and employee. The employer cannot summarily dismiss an employee without good reason (see below) and the employee cannot suddenly decide to take time off for no good reason either! Employees who do not comply with the terms of their contract will be subject to disciplinary action (see below). Employees who consider their employers have breached the terms of the contract can take their case to their union representative, enter into a formal grievance procedure or, as a last resort, appeal to an industrial tribunal. These aspects are covered below.

Implied terms

There are five additional conditions which all employers can reasonably expect of their staff, ie that they must

- be ready and willing to work (this means in person – an employee cannot send a substitute to do the job for him or her!)

- use reasonable care and skill

- obey reasonable orders

- take care of the employer's property

- act in good faith.

Most of these are self-explanatory, although some points should be noted. For instance, a young employee who refuses to conform to a company dress code might be subject to disciplinary action if this is considered to be a 'reasonable order' – whether or not he or she personally agrees with it. Equally, an employer is not allowed to give orders which would mean that staff had to break the law or which would put them in personal danger.

The term 'act in good faith' is meant to prevent employees from forgetting to disclose important facts about themselves (eg a serious health problem at interview), taking money on the side in bribes and back-handers, and disclosing confidential information to rival companies. Some contracts even contain a clause to stop employees from moving to work for a close competitor within a certain length of time after leaving, eg 12 months.

Equally, however, there are two implied terms to which the employer is bound, ie

- to treat staff reasonably

- to give staff the opportunity (rather than the right) to participate in and be consulted on certain company matters.

Changing the contract

A contract of employment can be changed with the agreement of both parties. However, employee choice in the matter may be somewhat limited! If your boss says that the only way he or she can keep you on is if you work an extra three hours a week for no extra pay, then you may decide it is more sensible to agree to a new contract than to lose your job! Alternatively, you may feel your boss is treating you unfairly and you should be able to do something about it. The action you could take if you had *any* complaint is limited by the time it takes for you to gain **qualifying rights** in law. These are shown in Figure 7.6.

	Qualifying period		
Claim	Nil	2 months	2 years
Equal pay	✔		
The right not to be discriminated against	✔		
Unfair dismissal for trade union reasons	✔		
Action short of dismissal for trade union reasons	✔		
Time off for ante-natal care	✔		
Contract of employment		✔	
Unfair dismissal			✔
Maternity pay			✔
Right to return to work after pregnancy			✔
Redundancy payment*			✔

*Starting on 18th birthday if employee began work before that date

Figure 7.6 Qualifying rights

Ending the contract

Equally, depending upon how long you have been employed by the organisation, you have a right to be given a certain period of statutory notice – just as you will find that you are also obliged to give notice of your intention to leave. In certain circumstances employers may waive their right to make you work your period of notice, but this must be by agreement. Legislation provides for minimum periods of notice to be given (Figure 7.7) but the contract may state that a longer time is required in certain cases. For instance, managers are likely to be issued with a contract which stipulates that they give a period of three months' notice – to allow the company time to find a suitable replacement.

Length of continuous employment	Period of notice
Less than 1 month	No period necessary
1 month but less than 2 years	1 week
2 years or more	1 week for each completed year up to a maximum of 12 weeks

Figure 7.7 Statutory periods of notice

Employment legislation

Employment legislation has been designed to cover unfair practices and discrimination, primarily in the workplace. These include such issues as

- failure to comply with the contract of employment

- equal pay

- sexual discrimination and harassment

- racial discrimination and harassment.

Some companies go further than the law in advising and monitoring working practices within the organisation, such as issuing clear guidelines on company policy on sexual or racial harassment. All companies are aware of the cost and bad publicity involved in having claims made against them. For that reason they are likely to

- have a trained member of staff to advise them on employment law – particularly as this is an area subject to constant change

- have formal policies on **grievance and disciplinary procedures** which give guidance to both staff and managers (the disciplinary procedure is usually included in a staff handbook and a reference to both disciplinary and grievance procedures has to be included in the contract of employment – clear procedures are essential to avoid claims of unfair or constructive dismissal).

- consult any represented trade unions over policies in these areas.

Grievance procedures

Grievance procedures are established to deal with employee complaints about unfair treatment. Most grievance procedures cover three broad areas.

- Money, eg mistakes in a pay packet or the calculation of pay.

- Work issues, eg a change in job content, time off, physical conditions, overtime, etc.

- Discriminatory or unfair treatment.

Generally, of course, it is hoped that any problems will be sorted out informally and amicably, but sometimes this is not possible. There are usually three stages in a grievance procedure.

1 An interview with the departmental manager at which all the facts are checked and, at which stage, the problem may be rectified. The employee has the right to be accompanied by a person of his or her choosing, eg a solicitor, union representative or colleague at this interview.

2 An interview at the next level of management, usually outside the department. Sometimes a joint committee of both union and management representatives is called.

3 An interview with a third party such as ACAS (the Advisory, Arbitration and Conciliation Service) if the grievance procedure allows for this.

Individuals who feel they were unfairly dismissed or were forced to leave (ie constructively dismissed – see page 300) have the right to take the case to an industrial tribunal for a final decision.

Retiring at 65!

Taking a case to an industrial tribunal is not always the end of the matter. Higher authorities exist – a decision can be referred to the Courts of Appeal or even the European Court of Justice. It was the action of one Hampshire woman, who took her case to Europe, which has dramatically changed women's retirement in Britain.

She appealed against a decision by South-West Hampshire Area Health Authority that she was being made to retire at 60 when her male colleagues could continue until they were 65 – and alleged discrimination. The

European Court found in her favour. Therefore, all organisations (and the government) were directed to change this policy and to offer pensions to all workers at the same age. As the cost of giving the state pension to everyone at 60 was too great, the government announced its plans to implement a move towards a common retirement age of 65 for all.

This has meant that whereas women today can retire at 60, and receive a state pension, in the future this will change. Everyone in Britain will have to wait until they are 65.

Disciplinary procedures

In a sense, these are the opposite of grievance procedures. In this case, it is the employer who is complaining because an employee has breached the terms of his or her contract of employment. Most organisations use the procedures recommended by ACAS in its code of practice, *Disciplinary Practice and Procedures in Employment*.

This code of practice recommends that disciplinary procedures should

- be formal and in writing
- state to whom they apply
- ensure that everyone has access to a copy of them.

They must also specify

- what disciplinary action may be taken
- which level of management has the authority to take such action
- that employees should have the opportunity to defend their position against any complaints
- that no disciplinary action should be taken without full investigation
- that no employee is dismissed for a single incident unless it is gross (very serious) misconduct
- that the employee should be provided with a right of appeal against any disciplinary action.

There are usually three stages to a disciplinary procedure.

1 Verbal warning for a minor offence.

2 Written (or final) warning for a serious offence or a repeated minor offence.

3 Suspension, demotion, transfer or dismissal for a gross (very serious) offence.

If an organisation terminates an employee's contract of employment without notice, then this is called **summary dismissal** or **instant dismissal.** This usually occurs if someone is found guilty of stealing, being drunk, attacking another employee or is in gross breach of their expected behaviour or the stated rules of the organisation – for instance, clocking in another employee is usually a dismissable offence. It must be made clear to all employees that such conduct would lead to instant dismissal.

Normally, however, dismissal only takes place when all other options have been exhausted – and there is still an appeals procedure to the top level of management. Usually, however, the first stage is to hold a disciplinary interview promptly after the offence to check on the validity of the claims and to give employees the opportunity to put forward their case.

Constructive dismissal

You may have heard of this term or read it in the newspapers. In a recent case, a library employee took her case against her employer to a tribunal. She alleged that her boss had bullied her for five years, denying her leave when her child was seriously ill, intercepting her mail, reprimanding her on many occasions, even though she had an intolerable workload, and then refusing her the opportunity to work part time when she wanted to care for a sick parent. On the day the parent died she was forced to work late. The pressure was such that she resigned from her job and she is now claiming **constructive dismissal.**

Constructive dismissal, therefore, is the term used when someone feels that they have been made to leave their job even though they did not want to. Rather than actually dismiss them, someone has made life so intolerable that the employee could not cope and was forced to resign.

Redundancy

Redundancy occurs when employees are dismissed because there is no work for them to do. Before this goes ahead, however, the management is likely to examine less painful alternatives. They may ask, for instance, for **voluntary redundancy,** where people (often near to retirement age) agree to leave. In other cases a system of **natural wastage** may be employed, where those who leave the organisation voluntarily are simply not replaced. Usually, **compulsory redundancy** is the final option. In most cases, this dismissal will be regarded as fair because the employer has little choice.

Other methods to prevent redundancy may be to reduce the number of part-time or temporary employees, lower the retirement age or introduce work sharing.

If redundancies are a possibility, then the organisation must have an agreed procedure which includes

- full consultation (eg with the relevant unions as soon as possible)

- full disclosure of information (eg as to why the redundancies are justified)

- the number and description of proposed redundant employees

- the total number of employees of that type in the organisation

- the proposed method of selection

- the proposed ways of carrying out the dismissals including
  - method of notification on payment and legal rights

- details of any additional incentives or bonuses offered to volunteers
- the time scale over which dismissals will take place
- information about counselling, retraining or opportunities for alternative employment elsewhere in the organisation.

The method of selection is very important. The management cannot just pick and choose the individuals they want to get rid of! Common policies include

- last in, first out (where the most recent recruits are the first to be asked to leave)

- last in, last out (where the longest serving employees are the first to leave)

- delayering – where a 'layer' of managers is removed

- efficiency criteria – where employees are judged on absence, time-keeping, work performance, disciplinary record.

If employees are offered suitable and equivalent alternative employment, which they then refuse, this may mean forfeiture of their right to redundancy pay. Minimum rates of redundancy pay are specified by law, but unions will always try to negotiate for additional sums to be paid.

Equal opportunities

Equal opportunities legislation relates to enforcing minimum standards of equality in relation to gender and race. It does not cover age, and the employment of disabled people is covered in a separate Act. Many organisations go beyond the letter of the law by implementing equal opportunities policies which cover a wider area than just gender and race. They may even be involved in positive action programmes which try to discriminate positively in favour of minority groups, though this is a debatable issue. Some members of these groups do not like to feel they are being 'advantaged' or 'patronised' in this way.

Pay

The Equal Pay Act 1970 (amended by the Equal Pay (Amendment) Regulations 1983) provides for equal pay for men and women and states that both must receive the same pay if

- they are employed on the same work

- both jobs are rated the same under a job grading scheme

- if the jobs are regarded as being of 'equal value'. In one famous case, a woman who worked as a cook in a shipyard canteen claimed her work was of the same value to the organisation as that of a man who was a shipyard worker.

This point is important where women are segregated into women-only jobs and have no one with whom to compare themselves, such as a group of female secretaries. The comparison could then be made in relation to the value of the job itself rather than against men doing the same job. However, the case would not be upheld if there was an important difference between the jobs or one employee is more qualified and/or experienced than the other.

A woman employee at a Brighton clothing firm was awarded £120,000 plus a £20,000 contribution from her employer when she successfully claimed sexual discrimination because a male worker was paid more than her. This was alleged to be a record settlement at the time it was made in 1996.

Gender

Discrimination can relate to more than pay. It covers recruitment, promotion, training, fringe benefits and any other relevant area in relation to employment. The Sex Discrimination Act 1975 (as amended by the Sex Discrimination Act 1980) attempts to prevent this from happening by forbidding any discrimination on the grounds of sex. It defines two types of discrimination.

- Direct discrimination, eg an advertisement for a male administrator.

- Indirect discrimination – when an employer asks for a particular requirement which particularly disadvantages one sex over the other, eg all applicants must be over 6 feet tall.

  However, an employer may be allowed to justify such a request in certain circumstances, particularly where it is a general occupational qualification (GOQ), such as in modelling or acting (where the part of Cinderella should obviously not be played by a male!). Other exceptions mainly relate to live-in jobs, eg the matron of a girls' boarding school.

Do bear in mind that sex discrimination can be against men as well as women! In 1996 a male police sergeant was awarded £16,200 by a tribunal for sexual discrimination. However, this is small compared with the £150,000 award to a female RAF officer who was dismissed for becoming pregnant.

Race

In this case the law is concerned with equality of treatment for people from different ethnic backgrounds. The Race Relations Act 1976 (as amended by the Race Relations (Remedies) Act 1994) forbids discrimination on grounds of 'colour, race, nationality or ethnic or racial origin'. Its provisions are very similar to the Sex Discrimination Act and both direct and indirect discrimination is forbidden unless there is a need for a GOQ or if the employer can justify it on other relevant grounds.

Discrimination and victimisation

The Acts try to protect people who have claimed discrimination at work from being **victimised.** Examples of discrimination include isolation from colleagues, constant reprimands, demotion or down-grading and redundancy.

The Disability Discrimination Act 1995 seeks to prevent discimination against disabled people in the same way as the Sex Discrimination and Race Relations Acts seek to prevent discrimination against women and ethnic minorities.

Harassment

If you saw the film *Disclosure,* then you probably know quite a lot about sexual harassment – when Demi Moore harassed her employee, played by Michael Douglas! Both men and women can encounter sexual and racial harassment. The degree of severity can vary, however. There is an obvious difference between a sexist or racist joke, which, whilst being offensive, will not physically harm anyone, and a boss who makes a strong pass at an office junior, or a group of workers who deliberately ignore or taunt someone of another race for weeks on end.

Most large organisations today have a code of practice on harassment which is issued to all staff and clearly indicates a situation where a complaint should be made. There should always be the provision for employees to be able to complain to a senior member of staff other than their line manager – in case the manager is the cause of the complaint. All employees should be aware that if they are found guilty of harassment, they will face disciplinary action which could lead to their dismissal.

Organisations are having to be more aware of harassment. Complaints have steadily risen each year with more complaints about sexual harassment being made by men than ever before. Claims have also increased. A record settlement of £34,000 for racial harassment was awarded to a black London salesman in an out of court settlement by his former employer.

Health and safety legislation

Health and safety legislation in Britain is covered by a major Act of Parliament and several regulations, some of which were introduced as a result of EU directives.

The Act is the **Health and Safety at Work Act 1974 (HSWA),** which has now been updated by the **Workplace (Health, Safety and Welfare) Regulations 1992.**

In some textbooks, you may find reference to the Offices, Shops and Railway Premises Act (1963). However, as from January 1996 this Act has been subsumed into the HSWA and no longer applies. The HSWA is also known as an 'enabling' or 'umbrella' Act which means that Regulations can be introduced to update or modify it. This is what has happened with the 1992 Regulations.

The key points in relation to the Act and the Regulations are given in Figures 7.8 and 7.9.

It is important to note that HSWA, for the first time, introduced the concept of **employee responsibility** in the area of health and safety. Details of the Act must be displayed in prominent places in the organisation for all employees to read. Any employee or employer who is negligent under the Act can be prosecuted as a breach of a health and safety requirement is regarded as a criminal action.

Under the HSWA a new enforcement agency was created called the **Health and Safety Executive (HSE)** with its own Inspectorate and Advisory Service. The HSE is directly responsible to the Health and Safety Commission (HSC) which comprises advisory committees on a variety of subjects and industries. Their task is to reach agreement on proposals for new Regulations.

An inspector can visit any industrial premises without warning either to investigate an accident or a complaint or simply to inspect the premises and

---

The Health and Safety at Work Act 1974

1 Applies to all work premises. Anyone on the premises is covered by and has responsibilities under the Act – whether employees, supervisors, directors or visitors.

2 Requires all employers to
   - 'as far as is reasonably practicable' ensure the health, safety and welfare at work of their employees. This particularly relates to aspects such as
     - safe entry and exit routes
     - safe working environment
     - well-maintained, safe equipment
     - safe storage of articles and substances
     - provision of protective clothing
     - information on safety
     - appropriate training and supervision
   - prepare and continually update a written statement on the health and safety policy of the company and circulate this to all employees (if there are five or more of them)
   - allow for the appointment of safety representatives selected by a recognised trade union. Safety representatives must be allowed to investigate accidents or potential hazards, follow up employee complaints and have paid time off to carry out their duties.

3 Requires all employees to
   - take reasonable care of their own health and safety and that of others who may be affected by their activities
   - cooperate with the employer and anyone acting on his or her behalf to meet health and safety requirements.

Figure 7.8

Workplace (Health, Safety and Welfare) Regulations 1992

Most of the Regulations cover specific areas of health, safety and welfare to supplement general duties on employers who have to ensure the workplace is safe and without risks to health under the HSWA 1974.

Employers and others in control of workplaces are required to comply with a set of requirements covering

1 **Work environment,** ie
   - effective ventilation
   - reasonable temperature
   - adequate and emergency lighting
   - enough space
   - suitable workstations
   - protection from adverse weather for workstations outside a building.

2 **Safety,** ie
   - traffic routes for pedestrians and vehicles to circulate in a safe manner
   - properly constructed and maintained floors
   - safe windows and skylights
   - safely constructed doors, gates and escalators
   - safeguards to prevent people or objects falling from a height.

3 **Facilities,** ie
   - sufficient toilets and washing facilities
   - adequate supply of wholesome water
   - adequate seating
   - suitable accommodation for clothing
   - rest areas – including provision for pregnant women or nursing mothers
   - provision for non-smokers in rest areas
   - adequate facilities for people who eat at work.

4 **Housekeeping**, ie
   - proper maintenance of all workplaces, equipment and facilities
   - cleanliness of workplaces.

Figure 7.9

question the employees. Offices and shops are usually visited by an environmental health officer employed by the local authority. If the working practices observed are unsatisfactory, the inspector can issue an Improvement Notice requiring the employer to put matters right within a specified period. If working practices are such that they are endangering either the workers or the general public, then the inspector may issue a Prohibition Notice which compels the employer to stop operations immediately.

On receiving a Prohibition Notice the organisation has the right to appeal to an industrial tribunal. If the appeal is lost and the organisation fails to comply with the terms of the notice, then it can be fined or the owner imprisoned.

Figure 7.10 An office worker who has not studied health and safety legislation!

Additional Regulations

Other Regulations introduced since HSWA include the following.

• The **Reporting of Injuries, Diseases and Dangerous Occurrences Regulations (1995) (RIDDOR).** These Regulations compel organisations to notify the HSE if any accidents occur which cause serious or fatal injuries or lead to a lengthy period off work. In addition, the organisation must keep records of all notifiable injuries, dangerous occurrences and diseases.

• The **Control of Substances Hazardous to Health (1994) (COSHH).** These regulations cover the control of hazardous substances and require employers to take steps either to eliminate the substance or control its storage and use/provide protective clothing.

• The **Electricity at Work Regulations 1989.** These apply to the design, construction, use and maintenance of electrical systems and installations.

• The **Noise at Work Regulations 1989** which require employers to assess noise hazards in the workplace, reduce these where possible, keep employees informed of noise hazards and provide ear protectors.

In 1992, as a result of EU directives, six new Regulations were introduced.

- The Management of Health and Safety at Work Regulations.

- Workplace (Health, Safety and Welfare) Regulations.

- Display Screen Equipment Regulations.

- Provision and Use of Work Equipment Regulations.

- Personal Protective Equipment at Work Regulations.

- Manual Handling Operations Regulations.

One of these, the Workplace (Health, Safety and Welfare) Regulations you have met already (see Figure 7.9). Key requirements for all the other Regulations are given in Figure 7.11.

Associated Acts and Regulations

Other areas which link to health and safety and which are controlled by their own Regulations include the following.

- **Fire Precautions (Places of Work) Regulations 1995.** These regulations give the fire authority similar powers to the HSE in that it can issue Prohibition and Improvement Notices and prosecute companies which ignore these. Designated premises, such as offices, shops and factories, each require a fire certificate which shows a plan of the premises, the position of fire-resistant doors and fire extinguishers and break-glass alarms installed. There must also be a proper fire-alarm system and a protected means of escape.

- **Health and Safety (First Aid) Regulations 1981.** Under these regulations the number of first-aiders in an organisation should be determined depending upon the degree of risk. In low-risk situations the employer is seen to need one first-aider for every 50 employees during normal hours. This number increases in more hazardous situations, such as a chemical plant or an oil rig. Information is also given on the training and duties of different types of first-aider.

- **Health & Safety (Safety Signs & Signals) Regulations 1996.** These regulations state that safety signs must be displayed in certain shapes and colours. They are more precise than the Safety Signs Regulations 1980 which simply stated that signs should be
  - red for a prohibited action
  - blue for a mandatory (must do) action
  - yellow for a warning
  - green for a safe condition.

The 1996 Regulations give specific instructions on the design required and the percentage of the sign which must be coloured. They also include instructions applying to red fire-fighting equipment signs.

1992 Regulations

1   The Management of Health and Safety at Work Regulations

These are more commonly referred to as the **Management Regs.** Under these all employers must

- carry out risk assessments which assess signficiant risks both to employees and others affected by the business
- keep a record of the assessment and the measures which have been identified to control the risk (if there are more than five employees)
- appoint competent people to help to implement the health and safety arrangements
- make arrangements to plan, organise, control, maintain and review health and safety arrangements
- set up emergency procedures to deal with situations of serious or imminent danger
- provide full information and training to all employees plus details on any risks involved in their work.

2   Workplace (Health, Safety and Welfare) Regulations (see page 306)

3   Display Screen Equipment Regulations

These apply to all employees who regularly use display screen equipment (DSE) as a significant part of their work. They relate to the furniture used in relation to a VDU (called a workstation) as well as the equipment.

Employers must

- assess all workstations for health and safety risks and lower the risks as much as possible
- plan work activities to incorporate rest breaks at regular intervals
- arrange and pay for eye tests and pay for spectacles or lenses if these are prescribed specifically for VDU work
- provide health and safety training for DSE users and retrain if the workstation is changed or modified
- provide DSE users with information on all aspects of health and safety which apply to them and measures being taken to reduce risks to their health.

4   Provision and Use of Work Equipment Regulations

The term 'work equipment' relates to any type of machine, appliance, apparatus or tools used at work. In an office these include photocopiers, fax machines and even staplers.

The employer must ensure that

- all equipment is suitable for the task and keep it well-maintained
- take into account working conditions and potential hazards when selecting new equipment
- issue appropriate information, instructions and training on its use
- restrict access when necessary.

5   Personal Protective Equipment at Work Regulations

These relate to the provision of protective clothing and equipment when risks cannot be eliminated. Obvious examples are ear muffs, safety helmets, safety shoes and safety goggles.

It will be up to employers to ensure that personal protective equipment is provided without charge, is suitable and fits properly, is maintained in good condition, stored safely and that information is provided on its use.

6   Manual Handling Operations Regulations

These require employers to

- avoid any manual handling operations in which employees could be injured (eg by using an automated or mechanised process)
- assess and reduce the risk of injury as much as possible
- provide employees with information on specific loads which will help them avoid risk.

Figure 7.11

Health and safety and company policies

One of the requirements of the Health and Safety at Work Act is that employers with more than five employees should draw up and implement a safety policy. This must include

- a statement of overall intent which includes an acceptance by management of its responsibility to apply and enforce current and future safety legislation

- an outline of the organisation structure which comprises
  - the names, job titles and safety functions of the personnel involved
  - the chain of responsibility from top to bottom
  - the role of the supervisors
  - the functions of the safety adviser, occupational health personnel (if any), the safety representatives and the safety committee(s)

- the arrangements for ensuring that the policy is being implemented, eg
  - the training and instruction given
  - the company rules for safe systems of work
  - emergency arrangements (fire, first aid, etc.)
  - accident reporting and investigation
  - identification of risk areas

- the signature of a senior manager.

The statement must be revised as appropriate, eg when new legislation or technology is introduced or when personnel changes occur. Such revisions must be made clear to all employees.

Safety representatives and safety committees

Many organisations have a **safety committee** which comprises a group of both management and employee representatives. The committee will form the basis of the company's monitoring system as it is part of its responsibility to check that legal and regulatory requirements are being followed and to alert management to any working conditions which do not conform to these requirements or which breach the company's stated codes of practice.

In addition, the committee must

- monitor local accident trends as shown by statistics and recommend preventative action

- consider reports of selected accidents and promote action to prevent recurrence

- consider suggestions and reports on safety matters and make recommendations to management

- promote local safety publicity and organise safety competitions and incentive schemes

- promote local applications of accident prevention techniques.

If no committee is in force, then these duties may be undertaken by a safety officer.

The Safety Representatives and Safety Committees Regulations 1978 give a legal right to trade unions to appoint safety representatives in the workplace provided that the union is recognised by the employer for negotiations. The representatives are elected by union members and not the employer. The number of representatives varies from one workplace to another, depending on the size of organisation, type of work carried out, potential hazards, etc.

A **safety representative's** duties include

- investigating potential hazards and dangerous occurrences at the workplace and examining the causes of any accidents

- investigating complaints by any employee relating to that employee's health, safety and welfare at work

- making representations to the employer on matters arising out of the point above and also on general matters affecting health safety and welfare

- carrying out inspections at least every three months

- representing the employees in consultations at the workplace with HSE inspectors or any other enforcing body

- receiving information from those inspectors

- attending meetings of safety committees.

Safety representatives must also be consulted 'in good time' by the employer in regard to

- the introduction of any measure at the workplace which may substantially affect the health and safety of employees

- the arrangements the employer makes for appointing competent persons to assist it in providing the measures necessary to protect the workforce

- any health and safety information the employer is required to provide for employees

- the planning and organisation of any health and safety training which must be provided

- the introduction of new technologies in the workplace – particularly at the planning stage.

Codes of practice

Some employers institute their own **codes of practice** which are designed to inform all employees of the **procedures** to be followed in situations such as evacuations through fire or security alerts (eg bomb scares or gas leaks), illness or accident. Some even extend to the operation of certain types of machinery.

In the case of accident or illness, for instance, the code may contain details about

- how to contact a named first-aider

- where the nearest first-aid box or medical room is situated

- how to send for the doctor or ambulance in the case of major accidents or illnesses

- when an accident report should be completed in accordance with company policy.

A code of practice for a fire alarm or bomb scare may contain even more detailed provisions. An example of a code of practice is shown in Figure 7.12.

Waverley Electronics Ltd
Code of practice

FIRE PRECAUTIONS

1   Keep all fire exits clear in case of emergency.

2   Make sure that you know what to do should a fire break out, ie
- how to operate the fire alarm
- how to use fire-fighting equipment if required to do so
- where to assemble outside the building
- how to reach it.

3   Display a fire/evacuation procedure notice in every relevant area and ensure it is constantly updated.

4   Keep the fire doors closed at all times except where the Fire Brigade has given permission for the doors to be held open by an automatic device.

5   Do not smoke in any part of the building where there is a risk of fire.

6   Make sure that bulk quantities or large cans of highly flammable fluids are locked away in a well-ventilated storeroom or metal cabinet when not in use.

7   Make sure that all combustible materials such as paper and envelopes are put into metal waste bins and removed regularly.

8   Ensure regular maintenance and checking of fire alarms and fire extinguishers.

9   Arrange regular fire drills.

Figure 7.12 An employer-devised code of practice

Risk assessment

Since the Management of Health and Safety at Work Regulations came into effect, organisations now have to identify, assess and record potential risks or hazards in a specific way. 'Suitable and sufficient' **assessments of risks** have to be provided both to employees and to any other people who may be affected, such as contractors or visitors. This may mean that you are asked to

- analyse which of your work activities could entail a particular risk

- carry out an assessment of each of them giving details of
  - the activity
  - the possible hazard
  - the control measures that are in place, eg protective clothing
  - the level of risk, ie insignificant/low/medium or high
  - possible remedial actions.

The full report will normally be submitted to the health and safety officer who may arrange for the provision of any training or special equipment based on the results of the assessment. Normally a reassessment will be carried out at a future date to see if the risk has been minimised.

Accidents

Organisations are required by law to record accidents. Usually safety representatives, appointed through the union, will investigate them and make appropriate recommendations to management. All employers with more than 10 workers must keep an accident book and records must be kept for at least three years. Normally organisations do not just record actual accidents which occur but also 'near misses', as these also indicate areas where improvements can be made.

Employees, too, have a responsibility. Unless they report accidents, they may find that they are not allowed to claim any statutory benefits to which they would otherwise be entitled. Usually the main details are recorded on an **accident report form** which is designed to include the main information, ie

- the full name and address of the injured person

- the date and time the accident occurred

- the place it occurred

- the cause and nature of the injury.

Most forms extend beyond these requirements and also include details of first-aid or medical treatment received and the names of any witnesses. Any person reporting the accident on another person's behalf *must* give his or her full name, address and occupation. Serious accidents must be reported to the HSE under the requirements of RIDDOR (see page 305).

In addition to the reporting of accidents an investigation may take place into what actually happened. It is important that nothing is moved or changed until this investigation takes place.

Accident monitoring relates to regular examination of the type and frequency of accidents to

- compare accident rates in the organisation with national statistics

- identify areas of particular concern

- identify any improvement or deterioration in standards

- identify any areas of change which may affect statistics (eg the introduction of a new item of equipment or method of working)

- check that any recommended action has been taken.

Health and safety and employee responsibilities

The 1974 Health and Safety at Work Act clearly indicates that there is a joint responsibility in this area by both employers and employees. Unless staff cooperate with their employer, then they could find that they are liable to prosecution!

Quite apart from not taking deliberate actions which would infringe health and safety policies (the most common is wedging open fire doors!), it also means that staff must follow standard procedures and also cooperate with any new initiatives. You should remember that 'employee responsibility' does not apply only to the Health and Safety at Work Act – it also applies to all the associated Regulations as well.

Therefore staff have a responsibility in each of the following areas.

- Reporting accidents.

- Wearing protective clothing.

- Operating equipment and machinery according to instructions.

- Reporting hazards and potential hazards.

- Following evacuation procedures.

- Undertaking any required safety courses.

As an administrator or assistant administrator, you are more likely to be involved in certain aspects of health and safety than others. This also means you should set a good example to the rest of the staff – particularly any junior employees! This means, for instance, *always* leaving your office promptly during a fire drill, regardless of how busy you are, and *never* using the lift or stopping to pack up your belongings!

Your additional responsibilities in this area may well include

- the recording and reporting of accidents

- carrying out risk assessment and identifying hazards

- relating health and safety regulations to
  - the layout of offices
  - good housekeeping practices
  - the purchase and maintenance of machinery, equipment and furniture
  - the operation of information technology equipment

- recommending improvements in working conditions

- identifying health and safety training needs

- being the key person to whom people can turn in an emergency!

Health and Safety Regulations in the office

As you will see in chapter 8, the layout and design of offices is important to productivity. However, it is also critical in relation to health and safety. Trailing wires, boxes in walkways and aisles, unfiled papers and overfull waste bins all represent safety hazards. The situation may be even more critical in an open-plan office where the actions of a few are felt by many.

Administrators also need to be aware of the hazard of **noise** as well as untidiness. Acoustic screens are commonplace in open-plan offices to minimise the spread of conversation. Noisy equipment should be kept out of any main working areas.

Basic good practice is to ensure that

- walk-through areas are kept clear

- nothing is stacked or placed to restrict exits

- flooring is non-slip

- sufficient storage space is provided for papers, files and reference books

- suitable lighting and blinds are provided

- any dangerous or flammable substances are stored in a separate area

- safety stools are provided for access to high shelves

- furniture and desks are ergonomically designed and at the right height, and allow for **wire management** so that all cables are safely stored

- adjustable chairs are provided which give proper back support

- all furniture, fittings and equipment are regularly monitored and maintained.

Minimum requirements of a workstation

Display screen – well-defined characters of adequate size; stable images; easily adjustable brightness and contrast; easily tilting and swivelling screen; no reflective glare

Keyboard – tiltable and separate from the screen; sufficient space in front of keyboard; matt surface; easy to use; adequately and contrasted symbols on keys

Work surface – sufficiently large and low reflecting surface; flexible arrangement of equipment; adequate space

Work chair – stable, allowing user easy movement and comfortable position; adjustable height (seat); adjustable height and tilt; foot rests available on request

Space – sufficient to allow operator to change positions

Lighting – satisfactory lighting conditions; appropriate contrast between screen and background; prevention of glare through positioning of artificial lighting

Reflections – positioning to prevent sources of light, such as windows, from causing distracting reflections on the screen

Noise – must not cause distraction of attention or disturbance of speech

Heat – must not produce excess heat causing discomfort

Radiation – reduced to negligible levels in respect of user's safety

Humidity – establishment and maintenance of an adequate level

Software and systems – software must be suitable for the task, easy to use and adaptable to the level of user's knowledge, principles of software ergonomics must be applied

---

Figure 7.13

In some cases, equipment requirements are specified by law. The Display Screen Equipment Regulations 1992 cover the provision of **workstations** which include the display screen, keyboard, desk and chair, software and systems used by operators *in addition to* environmental factors such as lighting, noise and humidity (see Figure 7.11). The minimum requirements of a workstation are shown in Figure 7.13.

Concerns relating to VDU work include **stress, repetitive strain injury (RSI)** and **eye strain.** To date there is no scientific evidence that VDU work is hazardous for pregnant women, although screens are available to reduce VDU emissions and may be used for reassurance, if nothing else.

Stress may be caused if an operator is under constant pressure to produce accurate work – and it is for this reason that regular rest breaks are required by law.

RSI relates to an injury caused by constantly making repetitive or awkward movements. Tenosynovitis refers to the inflammation of the tendon sheaths in the hand, wrist and arms and is an officially recognised industrial disease for which sufferers can claim statutory benefits if they have medical support for their case. They can also claim negligence against their employer, especially if no improvements have been made after their complaint.

The Regulations provide for adequate health and safety training to be given to all VDU operators to help to minimise this risk.

Eye strain can occur from

- a screen which is too bright or dark, is showing a reflection, is flickering or which has poor definition characters

- the keyboard, if keys are glossy or there are bright indicator lights

- copy on glossy or very white paper

- the windows themselves

- reflected glare from walls or ceiling.

Again the Regulations ensure that regular VDU users are provided, on request, with an appropriate eyesight test.

In addition, the employer is required to analyse all workstations to assess risks to health and safety and ensure that they meet minimum requirements.

Making recommendations
In a large organisation this may be easier, as there may be specific procedures in force for reviewing working areas, monitoring usage and making recommendations. In a small firm this may be less easy, particularly if you have a difficult boss who takes everything as personal criticism!

Changes in organisation structure, different work practices and procedures, legislation and new technology often mean that what was once a suitable layout with appropriate furniture, basic equipment and systems of working also needs to be changed.

Changes may be major or minor. A major change would be the inflow (or outflow) of several members of staff through relocation, different types of work carried out in an area or structural building alterations. A minor change might be the delivery of a new photocopier which is half the size of the old one and takes up less space.

Bearing in mind what you read about change earlier, it is obvious that staff will be more amenable if they are involved in the rearrangements and will often be able to make positive and useful suggestions about how the working area should be arranged. This is particularly the case if they are relocated staff who will be undertaking work which they have done before.

Your aim should be that at any given time

- all legal requirements are fulfilled

- space is used to the best possible advantage

- the appropriate 'services' are available, eg telephones, lighting, heating, power, etc.

- movement between areas is easy

- the area is designed to facilitate the flow of work

- noise is kept to a minimum

- the office area looks attractive and welcoming.

A useful first stage is to draw a plan (preferably to scale!) and then to work out how everything could be arranged and to list any key items which are required. Try to keep your list relatively short (by highlighting top priority items, for instance) so that you do not overwhelm your boss after a reorganisation which was originally meant to be saving costs!

Health and safety training

New legislation, change or new staff appointments can also mean that training or retraining is required on health and safety issues. Revised fire regulations or new evacuation procedures, for instance, should not just be posted on the main notice-board in the hope that someone will read them. Proper training is required for *all* staff.

Newly installed equipment may require more specific training to take place for those who will be involved in its operation. Given that you would not want a break-down to occur two days after its installation, it is useful also to design a related procedure which prevents untrained staff from using it. Any procedures which have been designed to improve the organisation's health and safety record must also be conveyed to all staff with those responsible for their implementation correctly trained on how to complete documentation and monitor effectiveness (see also chapter 8).

Dealing with emergencies

Even in an organisation which has excellent planning, emergencies can occur. It goes without saying that anyone employed in administration or secretarial work of any kind should be the *last* to panic, not the first!

The whole range of possible emergencies which may occur are far too long to list in the space available here. Suffice it to say they include

- employees and visitors having a serious accident or major health problem whilst they are on the premises

- emergency evacuations for any reason

- widespread power failure or breakdown of essential equipment (particularly at critical times)

- security alerts – from violent visitors to those who have wandered into secure areas; from theft to lost children.

Obviously the type of emergency with which you are involved will depend upon the business of the organisation. For those which can be foreseen, standard crisis procedures should be drawn up which are known by all staff. A theme park, for instance, would have a procedure for dealing with lost children, reported thefts, power failure and evacuations – as well as medical emergencies. If you work in a small organisation, it is worthwhile thinking about this area and perhaps using this exercise – and what you will learn in the next chapter – to start designing some procedures of your own!

Discussion point

1   As a group, discuss all the different types of courses linked to health and safety that you might attend. You might find it useful to look back at the areas covered by the legislation and also at the companion book to this, *Administration Procedures for Secretarial Students,* which gives further details of the responsibilities of administrators in this area.

2   As a group, discuss the best way of handling each of the above emergencies, assuming there is no standard procedure in force in your organisation.

Data protection legislation

You already know that the installation and operation of information technology equipment in an office is subject to health and safety legislation. What you may not have considered, however, is the implication of the data held on employees and customers on computers.

You would not, however, be very pleased to find that your personal details are common knowledge within the organisation because anyone can access the personnel files! You could reasonably expect that the organisation would take precautions to make certain that any sensitive information is protected in some way, never made public and that unnecessary personal details (eg about your personal relationships!) are not kept at all.

Such requirements are covered by the **Data Protection Act 1984** (see Figure 7.14) and it would therefore be an offence if your employer broke these provisions in any way. Indeed, as you will note from the requirements of the Act, it is even an offence for your employer to keep information about you on computer without your knowledge. However, keeping paper records is *not* covered by the Act.

Finally, you should bear in mind that, yet again, employees also have responsibilities in this area. Those working on personnel files must be aware

---

The Data Protection Act 1984

The Act requires employers using a computerised data system to register as data users. They must state

- what information is being stored on computer
- why it is stored in such a way
- how and from where they have obtained it
- to whom it will be disclosed.

The Data Protection Registrar must then try to ensure that personal data

- is obtained and processed fairly and lawfully
- is held only for one or more specified and lawful purposes
- is adequate, relevant and not excessive
- is not kept for longer than necessary
- is stored in a way which prevents unauthorised access of accidental loss or destruction.

Additional safeguards are required in respect of personnel data covering

- racial origin
- political opinions or religious or other beliefs
- physical or mental health or sexual life
- criminal convictions.

Note: Employees have a **right of access** to all computerised information held about them and may claim compensation for damage and distress if the information is inaccurate.

Exemptions
The provisions of the Act do not apply to data held for

- the purposes of national security
- the detection or prevention of crime
- calculating payroll or for keeping accounts
- household affairs or recreational purposes
- the subsequent preparation of text (such as documents held in a word processor)
- the purposes of recording the 'intention' of the data user.

Figure 7.14

- of the terms of the Act

- of the confidential nature of the information they are handling

- that they are liable for prosecution under the Act if they allow such information to be made public. This could be caused by leaving a disk out on a desk by mistake instead of locking it away, issuing a password to an unauthorised user or not keeping confidential computer print-outs in a secure place.

For these reasons there are usually standard procedures to be followed by staff involved in handling confidential or sensitive information. In addition, the computer system will usually incorporate a series of security codes or passwords to which only authorised users have access. These must never be written down and there must be a set procedure for the reissue of passwords to authorised users who have forgotten one quite genuinely!

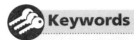

Keywords

Important keywords and abbreviations from this chapter are given below. Check that you know exactly what is meant by each one.

appraisal interviews	job specification
basic change	motivation
codes of practice	physical environment
conflict	proactive change
constructive dismissal	qualifying rights
contract of employment	reactive change
COSHH	racial discrimination
data protection	racial harassment
disciplinary procedures	redundancy
discrimination	resistance to change
equal opportunities	RIDDOR
ergonomics	risk assessment
fundamental change	safety committee
grievance procedures	safety representative
HSE	sexual discrimination
HSWA	sexual harassment
hygiene factors	skills audit
induction	style of management
job content	summary dismissal
job description	welfare
job design	working conditions
job enlargement	workstation
job enrichment	victimisation

Examination practice

Short-answer questions

1 Identify four employee needs which should be met for job satisfaction and motivation to be achieved.

2 Outline two pieces of legislation designed to protect the individual at work.

3 Identify four of the responsibilities of the employer as outlined by the Health and Safety at Work Act.

4 Suggest how staff can best identify their own training needs.

5 Your boss is organising a training session on VDUs. State four items which should be included.

6 Identify three benefits to the organisation of offering training to employees.

7 Your office needs a trainee administrator. Identify four sources of recruitment you could use.

8 Identify six of the items you would expect to be included in your contract of employment.

9 State four ways in which a company restructure could affect the organisation of an office.

10 Identify four ways in which management style can affect motivation.

Definition questions

1 Explain clearly the difference between each of the following terms.
   a summary dismissal and constructive dismissal
   b job enrichment and job enlargement
   c sexual discrimination and sexual harassment
   d grievance procedures and disciplinary procedures

2 Write clear notes to explain each of the following terms.
   a ergonomics
   b appraisal systems
   c motivation
   d job design

Essay questions

1 Your organisation is about to introduce appraisal systems for the first time. However, your boss has received conflicting reports about their effectiveness. Identify the key points which must be borne in

mind in order for the appraisal scheme to motivate employees and improve organisational efficiency.

2   Identify the benefits to both organisations and the staff within them of an effective training policy. In your answer, clearly differentiate between types of training and levels of training.

3   The objective of recruitment is to provide the best possible new employee in the most cost-effective way. How can success in this area best be achieved?

4   Analyse the key points which should be included for new supervisors on a training programme on motivation. Give reasons for each of the points you select.

5   Equal opportunities policies have been criticised for being no more than 'meaningless pieces of paper' in many organisations. Explain what you think is meant by that statement and state what actions a company might take to demonstrate it is committed to equal opportunities.

6   **a**   Identify the key features of an induction programme.
    b   Explain the benefits of induction to both new employees and the organisation.

Case study

The management of Wolstenholme Electronics is currently planning a major restructure of the company which will result in a flatter organisation structure and several redundancies. It is also intending to introduce new technology in several areas to reduce costs and improve efficiency. Your boss, Roshani Bhamara, is the human resources manager and is concerned about the effects upon staff morale and motivation.

a   What main points must the management bear in mind when planning the change to reduce stress and anxiety amongst employees?

b   What is the likely effect on the managers who will remain in the company after the restructure?

c   How may training assist to retain staff motivation and improve efficiency?

d   In the negotiation with the unions, what suggestions are likely to be made to minimise the shock of the redundancies?

e   Give examples of the legislation which must be considered by the Human Resources section in relation to the introduction of new technology and the welfare of employees.

The administration of business

● Introduction

This chapter concentrates on the administrative function and examines this in greater detail than the overview given in chapter 6. After all, if you are going to work in administration, then this will be the key function with which you will be involved! The role of administrative staff is also discussed together with their relationship to the managers of the organisation.

A large proportion of an administrator's job is concerned with information and communication, and responsibilities in this area are discussed in the first part of the chapter. The developing, monitoring and maintaining of systems and procedures are crucial if objectives are to be achieved. The difference between these is discussed with examples of an administrator's role.

Finally, the chapter concentrates on the way in which administrators can contribute to organisational efficiency through the way in which they plan work, manage their staff, coordinate activities and, through checks and controls, ensure that work is carried out according to plan.

All these areas are also covered from a practical perspective in a companion book – *Administrative Procedures for Advanced Secretarial Students*. This chapter is concerned with the theory that lies behind these responsibilities.

● The administrative function

What do administrators do? What is the difference between secretarial and PA work and administration? And is work in these areas increasing or decreasing?

Before we can answer any of these questions it is important to look at the role of all these individuals in more detail and then to examine how staff involved in administration fit into the organisation.

Administration – in any form – is concerned with the following duties.

- Providing **office or administrative services** which are a necessary prerequisite of any organisation.

- **Coordinating** the administrative work of the section with that being undertaken elsewhere in the organisation.

- Organising the **resources** required to undertake administrative tasks.

- Facilitating the **flow of information and work** through the office.

- **Supplying and communicating information,** as required, to assist managers to make informed and accurate decisions.

- Supporting managers by **planning, monitoring and controlling** work – so that outcomes are achieved. This may require the devising, monitoring and controlling of **systems** and **procedures** which relate to administrative duties.

- **Setting standards** to monitor the output and quality of the work produced.

The main difference between administrative and secretarial work is one of scope. Traditionally, a secretary worked for one, or possibly, two managers exclusively – and undertook very similar duties to those above, but in a more specific way. For instance, a main administrative function is to deal with visitors to the organisation and to handle incoming telephone calls. Secretaries would do this, but only for the visitors to their own managers and telephone calls routed to their office. At PA level the requirements are more exacting – efficient office services are taken for granted and there is a greater requirement for a PA to be the boss's indispensable aide who can anticipate needs accurately and is also blessed with a good measure of PR skills. Therefore, at this level, the *depth* of required knowledge and expertise increases.

Over the past few years, many organisations have been replacing secretaries with administrators or administrative assistants. This has had the result, generally, of widening the secretarial or clerical job role and, in many cases, given staff in these areas more responsibility. A top administrator is, however, expected to operate with the breadth of vision of a PA, but usually on a broader front – organising the work of a whole section or department rather than that of one senior manager.

This change has been caused by two main factors, which have interacted to change the balance – decreasing the secretarial requirement and increasing the administrative workload of most organisations.

- An increase in **computerisation** which has led to
  - an increase in the amount of information which can be processed and retrieved
  - the ability of executives to draft their own documents and send electronic mail messages (e-mails) using a desk-top PC (all tasks once performed by a secretary).

- A concerted drive to improve **profitability** by increasing sales and reducing costs which has resulted in
  - fewer managers who can afford the luxury of a personal secretary
  - broader job roles for most staff
  - an increase in systems and procedures to achieve **objectives** or **targets** (all of which must be carefully monitored)
  - a greater focus on **customer service** by all staff.

Rewards for customer-oriented staff

Research has shown that many organisations are investing money and effort into creating customer-driven organisations. Examples include sophisticated information technology databases which give full information on all customers across the organisation, multimedia applications where graphics showing any product can be displayed on screen by all staff, and rewards for staff. For example, AA Patrolmen of the Year win a luxury two-week holiday and have a special logo emblazoned on their patrol vehicles. At Unipart, the car parts group, gold pins are given to individuals and teams who provide outstanding customer service – taught on courses held in the in-house

university which was established in 1993 at a cost of £2.5 million.

Unisys, the information group, presents achievement awards valued at up to £2,500 for initiatives to improve quality and service. Unisys's Chief Executive George Cox is strongly committed to the concept of good customer service. He is aiming to create 'the kind of company where customers can't dial a wrong number. Where anyone they contact will take ownership of the problem and deal with it'.

McDonald's takes a similar view – staff are expected to deal with unhappy customers without referring to a manager every time.

Discussion point

Obtain a local or national paper or news sheet which advertises a wide range of jobs. Select four jobs that relate to administrative or secretarial work. Compare the duties shown and the qualifications specified in each advert.

As a group, make a list of the main requirements of employers for *both* types of job.

The organisational infrastructure

A key role of the administrative function is to coordinate work *across* the whole of the organisation. Large organisations, which employ departmental administrators, will expect them to liaise frequently both formally (eg a weekly meeting) and informally (eg a personal telephone call). This is because they have the remit to ensure that the *same* approach is being taken to similar work throughout the organisation, that the free exchange of information is facilitated and that people are moving in the same direction – rather than one department accidentally or deliberately obstructing the efforts of another!

For this reason, it is likely that systems and procedures (see page 337) have either been devised centrally and/or that good practice is shared with other sections. Indeed, the coordinating role of administrators cannot be over-emphasised (see page 357).

The term **infrastructure** refers to the internal structure of the organisation (Figure 8.1) and the relationships which exist between different sections and different personnel. As you know from earlier chapters, these can be divided into

*   **the formal structure,** as shown in the organisation chart – if this is hierarchical it may give the impression, for instance, that there are five distinct departments and information is passed from top to bottom (and back again)

*   **the lateral structure,** where meetings are held and information exchanged between people at the same level in different sections

*   **the informal structure,** which means that
    *   information can cross the organisation through the grapevine quicker than any other route (see page 188)
    *   messages can be reinterpreted as information is passed around, according to the viewpoint of those receiving and passing on the information.

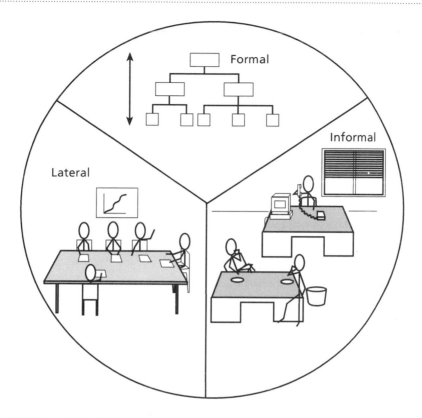

Figure 8.1 Organisational infrastructure

The larger the organisation, the more likely is it that administrators will have the task of **verifying** (ie checking) conflicting information from different sources and through different routes to find out which version is the definitive one!

Discussion point

Look back at the information given in chapter 6 on the interaction of different functions in an organisation. Also review chapter 5, pages 186–189, which discussed the structure of organisations and formal and informal communications.

1   As a group, identify the differences and similarities in the work carried out by administrative staff working in Marketing, Finance, Human Resources and Production.

2   To what degree do you think the administrative role would be different in a small organisation or one with a flat structure?

Office or administrative services

A key requirement of the administrative function is the provision of office or administrative services. This may be **centralised** (if Administration is a separate section) or **decentralised** (if Administration is a function of each section or department).

Office or administrative services include

- dealing with visitors and telephone calls
- recording information concisely and accurately
- reprographics
- mail or post duties
- production of documents for internal and external use
- transmission of fax and e-mail messages
- the storage and retrieval of records and documentation – both paper-based systems and electronically
- purchasing of consumables and stock-control systems
- operation of the petty cash system
- arranging meetings and interviews.

Other duties for certain administrative staff may include

- responding to correspondence
- making and monitoring financial payments
- ordering equipment
- arranging travel and accommodation
- arranging events (eg seminars and conferences)
- making appointments
- researching information
- monitoring and controlling financial systems.

Detailed information on all the main office service and administrative functions is given in the companion book to this. In this chapter, we are concerned with examining how this range of duties can be coordinated to promote the effective and efficient operation of the organisation.

Organisational skills

No administrator can do all these tasks effectively on his or her own, unless the firm is very small and the workload in each area is minimal. The job of

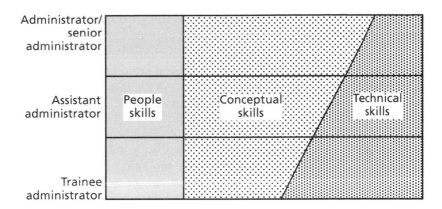

Figure 8.2 Levels of skill required by administrators

an administrator, therefore, is to **organise** the work so that all the services are provided to the required standard at all times. This is in addition to ensuring that the quality of information given to managers is first class and available promptly. The degree to which all this is achieved, in a atmosphere of calm efficiency, is highly dependent upon the organisational and personal skills of the administrator!

The first point to remember is that as administrators progress up the ladder their skills also need to change (Figure 8.2) – this is similar to the way in which managers need to develop new skills at different levels (see page 142). Assume an organisation employs three levels of administrator – **trainee administrators, administrative assistants** and **administrators.** How will the duties change and skills differ at each level?

- As a trainee administrator, there will be a high concentration on learning the skills required to provide specific office services. As one skill is learned, then another is introduced and so on. Trainees may receive both on-the-job and off-the-job training to help to improve their skills. The main focus, therefore, is on the **technical** aspects of the job. People skills are also important because all administrative staff deal with a variety of internal and external visitors every day. However, there is only a small requirement, at this level, for **conceptual skills** which enable the administrator to visualise the entire throughput of work and what is required by managers.

- For an administrative assistant, the level of skills should be high so that advice can be given to staff involved in delivering office services as well as some personal involvement in this area, especially when complex or very urgent jobs are received. People skills will be even more important – especially if difficult situations have to be handled, such as conflicting instructions or disagreements between staff. The job will entail greater development of conceptual skills so that the assistant starts to take a more global view and makes decisions with the good of the whole section in mind, rather than one particular part. There will also be a need to develop the skill of looking ahead, so that the workflow can be managed as smoothly as possible, despite the peaks and troughs which inevitably occur. Being able to plan and organise become far more important.

- At administrator or senior administrator level, technical skills are taken for granted. Good administrators should understand the work being carried out by each person in their team and be able to undertake more difficult aspects of almost any job. Good people skills are vital, as the administrator will need to deal with a wide variety of people at different levels in different situations. Conceptual skills become essential – not just in relation to planning and organising the work but also in relation to developing reliable methods of undertaking and monitoring the work and taking prompt remedial action if things are going wrong. As a general rule, the better the administrator the fewer the emergencies which occur. Good administrators are almost always two jumps ahead of everyone else in anticipating their needs and checking what is happening without being asked.

Organising resources

Resources refers to the physical items required and used by an organisation. No administrative office, for instance, can operate without paper or without staff! The resources required usually include

- staff members
- staff skills and abilities
- space
- equipment
- consumables
- time.

Resourcing is a crucial area in all organisations, mainly because

- resources cost money
- resources are (therefore) usually in scarce supply!

There are several important aspects in relation to resources. They need

- acquiring
- allocating
- organising
- using efficiently and effectively.

The acquisition of resources

Until you are employed at senior level, you may not be involved with acquiring resources, apart from basic needs such as stationery. However, it is worth knowing now that you will be expected to make out a justifiable case for any resources you need – often with details of the proposed costs and benefits (see page 344). The more expensive the resources, the more convincing you will need to be. A request for three additional pairs of scissors is hardly likely to need the same amount of research and information to substantiate your claim as a request for a new photocopier, six additional PCs and an extra member of staff!

The allocation of resources

The allocation of resources is often determined centrally or at senior management level. Whereas you will only have the interests of your own area or office at heart, managers will be receiving numerous requests for resources from all parts of the organisation. Given that only a proportion of these requests may be capable of being granted for financial reasons, some difficult decisions have to be made by managers so that

- resources are allocated to the areas in greatest need

- the allocation is seen to be fair, ie the same areas do not benefit every time.

Again, administrators will be expected to assist their own line managers to present rational and objective cases to win their share, based on financial costs and projected benefits.

Incidentally, if you, as an administrator, are responsible for the allocation of resources between your own staff, then you, too, should bear in mind the principles of 'need' and 'fairness'.

The organisation of resources

The task of the administrator is to organise the available resources in such a way that output is maximised, bearing in mind the needs of staff, the needs of customers (internal and external) and both the short-term and long-term objectives of the section. Therefore, although it might seem most effective to keep the junior administrator photocopying all day, it will do little for his or her motivation and future development! In the long term, therefore, it is better to encourage a diversity of skills amongst staff as this will enable a greater degree of efficiency to be achieved in the long run.

One of the most difficult resources to organise – yet without doubt the most precious – is **time.** Time is the one resource which is totally irreplaceable. **Time management skills** have long been the subject of many specialist courses and are covered in detail in the companion book to this. However, later in this chapter you will find information on **planning and scheduling** which is useful for time management skills. Thorough planning, so that you know exactly what you are going to do, when and how, can save hours and hours later. There is nothing worse than to have to do a job twice because you were not clear about the instructions or what was required the first time round! The other key factor, of course, is to minimise time wasted on unnecessary activities – such as having to plough through piles of paper because nobody has filed anything for three weeks, or chatting to other people when you should be working!

The working area, its layout and the optimum use of space are other resources which are often taken for granted. Walking down a long corridor every time you want to send a fax wastes time – how much simpler to move the fax machine nearer to where everyone needs it.

Office layout and workflow are dealt with in more detail on page 355.

Efficiency and effectiveness

You may remember from your earlier reading that **efficiency** is concerned with **doing things right** and **effectiveness** with **doing the right thing.** Both these concepts are useful to remember in relation to resources.

Efficiency saves money – and will prolong the life of your capital equipment and minimise the cost of consumables. Doing things right therefore means

- making sure that staff only use equipment they are trained to use and can understand
- there are clear procedures laid down for dealing with faults and arranging repairs
- ensuring that staff realise the cost of resources and the importance of preventing wastage.

The member of staff who cannot photocopy without wasting paper or create any document without several wasted copies is costly both in relation to consumables and time! Doing the right thing *first time* will always help to maximise resources.

Effectiveness relates to what is done, when and how. Bad planning and poor organisational skills are costly, both in terms of staff motivation and the actual cost of providing resources. Work scheduling can be carried out to maximise the use of shared resources. Good scheduling can improve the throughput of work (see page 367). A cooperative and positive attitude amongst staff can work wonders when the pressure is on.

If necessary, administrators must appeal for additional training if staff are lacking in the skills that they need to do their job properly. The ability to undertake work both efficiently and effectively is essential. Finally, care and regular maintenance can extend the 'life' of physical resources – just as care and consideration of people's needs can increase the willingness and cooperation of human resources!

The cost of administration

If you think that resourcing administration is easy or cheap, then look at the following figures – all quoted in 1995.

- The Unemployment Unit of the Department for Education and Employment reported that the cost of administering all the benefits for which it was responsible would be over £1 billion!

- National Lottery money was awarded to Norwich central library after it burnt down in 1992. The library is to incorporate a computer centre and high-technology museum, and £7.5 million has been designated for administration and contingency costs!

- The British Chess Federation has allocated £51,000 out of its budget to send British players overseas and £68,000 on running domestic tournaments. Yet it estimates it needs £78,500 on office administration.

● Information flows

Administrators are largely involved with the **flow of information** through an office or department and it is the speed, quantity and complexity of this information which can make the job easy or difficult. Despite this, managers will expect answers to their questions as and when (or preferably even before!) they have asked them. Key skills for administrators therefore include

- **prioritising,** so that the most urgent and important tasks always take preference

- being able to identify important information quickly

- differentiating between vital/urgent or specific information and requests and those which are more general

- being able to obtain maximum cooperation from other people to make progress quickly

- interpreting information correctly in the context in which it is meant

- using their own **initiative** to solve potential problems

- seeing the relationship between different pieces of information which may interact to give a different picture

- **communicating** information accurately and rapidly to those who need it.

Discussion point

It is easier to see how these factors can come together by looking at a particular example. Read the case study below and then, as a group, decide your answers to the questions which follow.

Louise, the senior administrator in the Marketing office, is on a week's leave. Her assistant, Sarah, has therefore been given the responsibility of ensuring that everything runs smoothly.

On Monday morning the marketing director Martin Lewis asks Sarah to complete the spreadsheet containing the sales targets which Louise had started the week before. This has been compiled from regional information forecasting sales over the next 12 months and is to be presented at the board meeting at 10 am on Wednesday.

On Tuesday, which is a frantically busy day anyway, Martin hands Sarah a detailed report from the south-west representative with a scribbled note attached from the area manager saying that some of the information contained in the report should 'inform' the targets. Martin asks Sarah to sort it out, though she struggles to make much sense of the instruction and cannot read some of the writing.

Just before 5 pm Sarah receives an urgent telephone call from the finance administrator asking her to make sure the spreadsheet also includes a column which shows the percentage difference between target and actual sales for the last 12 months for each product and to update the financial summary accordingly. Sarah stays late to add the additional column, although she is worried about the formula she has entered and can't find the financial summary.

The following morning, she overhears a member of the Sales team talking on the phone to Production about how production of one line has had to be stopped because of a suspected serious design fault. Sarah assumes Martin Lewis must know about this and returns to her own office to print the report for the meeting.

As the last page is nearing completion and the deadline is closing, one of the sales managers, who has seen a draft version of the spreadsheet, rings to say she thinks some of the figures on the second page have been transposed. Sarah makes it clear she is annoyed at being interrupted and being given yet another set of instructions in relation to the spreadsheet and frantically tries to check down the page.

No sooner has she started than Martin Lewis enters her office, demanding the spreadsheet immediately or he will be late for the meeting. Sarah hands it over.

1   Make a list of all the occasions on which you think Sarah made an error of judgement.

2   Now suggest, in each case, what Sarah *should* have done.

3   As a group, consider the implications of Sarah's actions in relation to
    a   the area manager she spoke to on the telephone
    b   the marketing director who is presenting the spreadsheet at the board meeting
    c   the directors of the organisation who are issued with the spreadsheet
    d   the Marketing team, who will have to meet the targets which have been entered.

4   On several occasions, Sarah made assumptions rather than checking to make certain. Discuss with your tutor the dangers of making assumptions, particularly in relation to administrative work, and the importance of detail.

5   Sarah's problems mainly stemmed from her inability to control and process the flow of information she was receiving. What additional skills do you think she needs to develop in this area before she can cope with the administrator's job?

Information and communication aspects

The problem for any administrator – as for Sarah – is that information flowing into an office cannot always be controlled. A great deal of information can arrive very quickly, some of it detailed, some of it unclear and some of it at the last minute. All of this needs **processing** *correctly,* in one way or another before it is communicated onwards and/or stored for future reference.

Communication can be considered from two different aspects, both of which affect administrative staff.

* The **types and systems of communication** in common use in the organisation, eg paper-based (from hand-written messages to bound reports), computerised (from e-mail messages to financial information) or a mixture of both.

* The **communication process** – this includes the sources of communication and information, the way in which information is handled, processed, stored and retrieved.

The ability to access, understand and prioritise incoming information is obviously essential. Being able to draft and write concise and clear communications yourself and use any computerised systems to the full are other vital skills, which are dealt with in the companion book. Another key attribute that is covered is being able to select the most appropriate type of communication for each particular set of circumstances.

In this book we are more concerned with the administrator's role in relation to the communication process. Managing this process is one of the main reasons why organisations introduce systems and procedures for people to follow. A good system includes control mechanisms to minimise problems and ensure the quality of the output. This means that all communication is accurate, valid, complete and up to date. Good administrators should never hamper communication but should *assist* and *promote* the process by

- identifying the best sources of information

- extracting the most relevant and/or the most urgent information

- making certain that storage and retrieval systems operate efficiently

- checking that recording systems always contain up-to-date and complete information

- checking that the details are correct

- monitoring the communication process, identifying faults or problems and taking remedial action, eg chasing up overdue information (without being asked!), clarifying missing or incomplete details, reporting potentially serious difficulties to their line managers

- passing on information accurately and promptly and in a form whereby it will be easily understood.

This also means passing on information objectively and dispassionately – *not* with personal opinions included, unless these are specifically requested!

The quality of information is important because it is on this that managerial decisions are based. Misguided, inaccurate or out-of-date information will therefore make it difficult, if not impossible, for managers to do their job effectively and can have tremendous implications on numerous aspects of the organisation. Imagine one simple example. The directors are considering staffing cuts following a fall in revenue from sales. What they do not know is that on the revenue print-out two pages of data were keyed in wrongly. This shows a shortfall of £50,000 in income. Based on this information several members of part-time or casual staff are laid off. Not only have these people lost their jobs unnecessarily, but when the mistake is discovered, someone may have the task of having to refill their positions and organise any training required!

Not all information errors have such calamitous results, but many have that sort of potential. Managers have many decisions to make in the course of a day. Some of these decisions may be fairly basic and fundamental, others will be more far-reaching and have implications for a large number of people. Managers will rely on information which has been received from a variety of sources and assembled by their administrator – from the files, messages taken, incoming documents and even informal discussions. If key decisions are based on inaccurate information, then the results can range from considerable inconvenience to disaster. The best administrators know which areas are the most significant in relation to managerial decision-making. In any of these areas they check the details extremely carefully, watch out for information which may change the situation and never make assumptions or jump to conclusions.

Systems and procedures

Systems and procedures have been mentioned several times in the last section. Whilst you may have some vague notion about what these terms mean, it is important that you fully understand them as in most organisations they are the basis on which most administrative functions are organised.

What is a system?

Technically, a system is something which receives **inputs** from certain sources and, through a series of activities or processes, converts these to **outputs** to meet a particular objective or **goal.** A system should also provide **feedback** on the results and allow for the activities to be monitored and controlled.

That may seem very complicated, but it can be explained very easily – because you are surrounded by systems that you use every day! In fact, the term 'systems' was derived from engineering but now the use has spread to any type of 'system' which needs controlling.

Consider the example of a hairdryer. This can be seen as a system (see Figure 8.3). Firstly, what do we call the system? A hairdryer can be defined as 'a system to heat cold air'. The inputs are two-fold – cold air and you setting the controls to make it work. In a systems diagram the switch would be an **actuator** – it activates the system. The process is designed to heat the air so that the output is warm air. Inside the hairdryer is a control or **sensor** – linked to a thermostat – to check the heating element is working and that the air is not too hot or too cold. Both you and the thermostat receive feedback and act as a **comparator** – the thermostat will shut down the hairdryer if the sensor shows the temperature is too high; you will turn off the hairdryer if you smell burning, for example. You can test the heat throughout the operation and adjust the controls so that you will reach your goal of having dry hair.

Now apply the same theory to your class. Assume your class is 'a system to get you through the examination'. What are the inputs? Obviously you are,

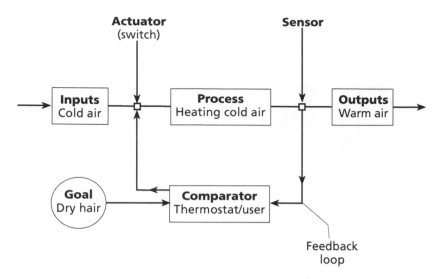

Figure 8.3 Example of a system

plus your tutor, plus this book, any other materials or information you receive and the time it takes to teach you (ie the required resources – see also page 330). The process is your class tuition and homework activities. The output is (hopefully) successful students! The sensor is anything used to monitor your attendance and progress. Feedback to your tutor (the comparator) is given when any of these activities are set and marked and during oral questioning in class. The tutor can then try to adjust the inputs as required. The aim is to reach the goal of all students passing the examination. Now look at Figure 8.4.

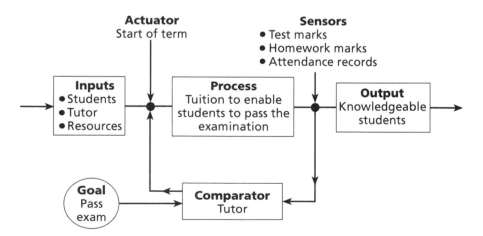

Figure 8.4 'A system to get you through the examination'

What are procedures?

Procedures are *part* of a system which are designed to support the system and help it to operate. You follow a procedure when you adjust the controls on your hairdryer if it is too hot or too cold. In class, your tutor will follow certain procedures, eg for collecting homework. Procedures mean that you do not have to keep asking what to do – the system works because you are familiar with its components and know the part you have to play. In certain cases you will follow the procedure almost automatically – as in the case of the hairdryer.

The key points about having procedures are that

- they can be done almost automatically

- everyone does the same thing

- quality can be maintained.

Again, you are involved with systems and procedures every day, eg

- If you are a driver, then you follow the procedures laid down in the *Highway Code* – which are all part of a system to keep traffic flowing safely.

- You follow a procedure when you evacuate a building during a fire alarm, which is part of the safety and security system of the organisation.

- You follow a procedure when you buy a ticket in a 'pay and display' car park – which is all part of a system for keeping cars off the street at minimum cost to the car-park owners.

There are many more examples, but by now, hopefully, you have understood the link between systems and procedures, and why they are both so important.

 Discussion point

The next stage is to link systems and procedures to administrative work. An obvious example is a paper-based filing system. Before we develop this example, see if you can

a   find a suitable name for this system (ie what is the system trying to achieve?)

b   name the inputs

c   decide the outputs

d   define the goal you are trying to achieve

e   decide what the comparator will be and how feedback will work.

Finally, can you draw a diagram to illustrate this?

Applying systems and procedures to administrative work

You may have found the previous exercise a little difficult, but at least it should have concentrated your mind on how a system is supposed to function. Your difficulty may have come from the fact that the *user* of the system is the final comparator – a paper-based filing system is not like a hairdryer. Unfortunately, there is no component inside it to check everything is in order! The number of complaints about delayed papers and misfiled documents (or the lack of them) gives feedback on whether the system is working. So, too, does the time taken to find the papers.

At any stage, if the goal is not being achieved, the system can be examined to find out why. It may be that the system is faulty in some way, eg

- It is trying to achieve too many goals or objectives (it is always better to design a system with one clear goal in mind).

- There is no comparator (if files are archived and stored in the basement for years and never touched, no one would know whether the system worked or not!).

- The comparator does not provide feedback (ie a user who cannot find a paper simply goes away again without saying anything).

- The feedback does not relate to the goal. If the user remarked that you had 20 files in one drawer and 60 in another, then this might be useful information, but is not vital to achieving the goal.

- The goal is unrealistic in relation to the inputs. If you received 100 documents every minute, you could hardly expect to reach a goal of filing everything accurately in five minutes flat!

At the level at which you will first operate in an organisation you would not be expected to be able to design complex systems. Indeed this is a difficult task even for some very senior administrative staff. What you will be expected to do, however, is to use procedures and, in some cases, develop these to support the system.

Basic procedures

If you were the sole user of a small filing system, you would probably file documents almost automatically. If you were in charge of a filing system which everyone used, then you would need to introduce some type of formalised procedures so that everyone knew what to do and did not keep asking you. This is the only way that you could ensure that everyone did the job correctly so that quality would be maintained. These procedures may be as basic as having managers who have finished with papers tick them in one corner to indicate they should be filed. However, this procedure will prevent current documents being filed by mistake so it will help to control the inputs.

Equally, you may have a procedure whereby everyone who removes a file must sign for it. This will help both to control the outputs and to act as a comparator – any users can easily check that the file they want is available. However, you would need to monitor or check that this procedure is being followed. Otherwise you may find people ignore it and the system starts to fall apart. Why people may be tempted to ignore it can vary – it may be too complicated, too time-consuming or appear pointless to them – in which case the procedure may need to be refined to allow for this.

Devising a procedure

The procedure above is very basic and would take very little time to instigate. Imagine, however, that you have to devise a more complex procedure to support a more involved system.

Your organisation is putting security systems in place because there have been several thefts on the premises in recent weeks. You have been given the task of designing a procedure for checking the authenticity of any visitors to the premises, making sure that they are accompanied during their stay and checking that they have left at the end of the day. At the same time you have the problem that there are three junior staff in the office who have to follow the procedure and deal with a variety of visitors, some of whom are important but who may not have an appointment. How will you control this to ensure that junior staff follow the system? At this point you have to work out what procedure to introduce for the junior staff.

Start by considering the following.

- What is the procedure designed to achieve, ie what are its objectives?

- How can its effectiveness be measured?

- What other effects might its implementation have?

- Who are the users – and what will they need to know?

- Are there any organisational policies or regulations you must bear in mind?

- What format would be the most appropriate for users?

- What will be the costs and benefits of its implementation?

Designing a procedure

There are several formats you can use to display a procedure. You could choose to document it using a step-by-step approach which will act as a checklist for users. However, if there will be several feedback loops at various points, or alternative actions to take, then it is more usual to summarise this in a **flow chart.** The advantages of using this method are that

- the chart sets out the procedure in a logical order

- it helps users to understand the points at which options are available or at which checks should be made

- it shows the alternative actions which can or must be taken in the event of different results

- it enables feedback loops to be included.

The aim of a flow chart is that no matter which route you take, you get to the end!

Start by dividing the proposed procedure into simple steps. Then think about whether you need feedback loops at any points and how to illustrate this. Keep your chart *simple* – you can always attach explanatory notes for first-time users.

Worked example

In the example above, for a reception procedure, you need to think of what you could do to monitor that all visitors are bona fide when they are on the premises. The obvious idea is passes or badges, issued to visitors as they arrive. The second thing you have to consider is how you will check that all the visitors have left at the end of the day. Again the obvious suggestion is that they return their passes or badges which can be checked against those issued. Finally, you have to ensure that visitors are collected promptly and accompanied whilst on the premises.

You can now sketch out your procedure which is what would happen if all goes well. Always use a pencil! Start by doing a simple list (you may have to do this a few times before you get everything in the right order), then draw rectangular boxes around each item to show it is a part of the process and link them with flow lines.

The next stage is to consider what could go wrong – and what you would want the junior to do in each case. This is when you can start inserting YES/NO options – which are usually put inside a diamond shape to indicate a decision has to be made. You will find it easier if you keep negative actions to one side, and the successful procedure in the middle. At each point where an alternative is introduced you have to develop a little sub-routine to take you back on track again. Finally, link the whole thing with flow lines – and make sure you show all the arrows which indicate the direction to follow.

The key thing to remember is not to miss out an essential stage in the procedure. Figure 8.5 gives an idea of how the finished version might look.

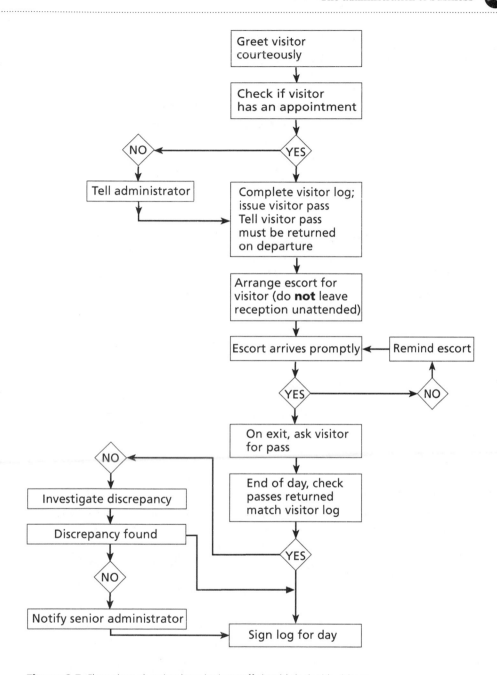

Figure 8.5 Flow chart showing how junior staff should deal with visitors

Discussion point

It can be very difficult to draw a flow chart showing a sequence of events for even very simple procedures. Try it now by drawing one to show someone the recommended procedure for making a cup of tea. Imagine you have a jug kettle which switches itself off as soon as it boils – but you need the water freshly boiling to make the tea. This should give you the opportunity to build in a feedback loop! Compare your attempts with other members of your group.

Developing procedures

Once you have devised a procedure it is sensible to test it on someone else and obtain feedback. Ideally, this should be someone who would be using the procedure. You can then obtain their views on whether it makes sense or not – and modify it accordingly. Remember that the objective should be borne in mind at all times – do not over-elaborate your procedure with routines which would not help to achieve this.

Costs and benefits

An important aspect of the procedure is the **benefits** it will bring and the likely **costs** which will be incurred. It is hopeless suggesting a procedure which will accrue little or no benefit and cost a fortune! Quite obviously, the emphasis should be the other way round.

Imagine, for a moment, that your procedure to increase security in relation to visitors had included the building of a gate-house, the installation of an automatic barrier and the employment of a full-time security person. If the thefts had involved classified information and dozens of visitors a day were arriving at a large-scale but highly secret defence establishment, then your suggestions might have been implemented! In most places, however, management would have looked aghast at the cost implications in relation to the potential benefits.

For this reason, many systems and procedures are subjected to a **feasibility study.** This is carried out to see

- which type of systems or procedures would be applicable, bearing in mind the objective and the needs of the users

- the resources which would be required to devise and implement the system or procedure

- whether the benefits would outweigh the costs (or vice versa)

- the likely time scale for the introduction of the recommended system or procedure.

For example, if you worked for a hotel which had foreign visitors and which wanted to improve customer care, and you suggested a procedure to teach everyone Spanish privately in a week, you would probably fail on every single count!

Considering costs

When you are thinking about costs, remember that

- a cost is always negative

- costs may be financial or social

- costs usually mean the purchase or increased use of materials, equipment, labour or capital

- a cost can usually be quantified or calculated.

If, for instance, as part of your security procedure you had wanted the receptionist to stay late for 30 minutes each night to check the visitor passes, then there would have been the financial cost of the receptionist's overtime *plus* the social cost to the receptionist of working longer hours.

Considering benefits

When you are considering benefits remember that

- a benefit is always positive

- benefits may be financial or social

- social benefits may be very difficult to calculate or quantify

- financial benefits usually imply the more effective use of materials, equipment, labour or capital or **savings** in any of these areas.

Making a recommendation

The difficulties of making a recommendation after a feasibility study has been carried out are usually

- lack of clear information on which to base a recommendation

- lack of clarity about the objective or goal to be achieved

- multiple goals which cannot be achieved by introducing just one system or procedure

- creators refusing to accept clear evidence that their idea is unlikely to work – or would cost too much to implement!

As an example, imagine that you have been put in charge of stationery stock control. There is no clear system, the stock is chaotic, supplies are frequently running out and damaged stock levels are high. You have been told to recommend a system which would work.

You have recently seen demonstrated a few superb computerised stock-control packages which would almost do the job for you – and you long to have one! The only problem is that you do not normally use a computer for much of the day so the costs would involve the purchase of both the hardware and the software. How objective would you be in your recommendations and linking the benefit to the cost? There is obviously a difference if you work for a small organisation which has only a tiny amount of stationery to control rather than a large office with a centralised stationery supply! And how would you choose between each package, or different computers for that matter?

Because of these problems many people who undertake a feasibility study offer their boss more than one alternative – accurately outlined – and let him or her make the decision about which one to implement.

Japanese feasibility studies

The degree of accuracy required by the Japanese when submitting feasibility studies is far greater than that usually required in Britain – so much so that those who work for them can sometimes suffer a culture shock. Martin Chambers won an award as Young Project Manager of the Year after overseeing the building of a £9.5 million photocopier-toner cartridge plant in Telford – built on behalf of Japanese clients. He was not allowed to include any 'contingency' sums in his costings – issues such as inflation and possible enhancements had to be costed in at the outset. The case had to be properly researched, argued and justified. The time scale for implementation had to be measured in hours, rather than days or weeks. Only when value for money had been clearly demonstrated were discussions held about minor adjustments. The project came in on time and within budget – one of the reasons why Martin Chambers won his award!

Discussion point

As a group, decide on the likely costs and benefits that would accrue from introducing a computerised filing system which would enable all documents to be electronically scanned and retained on computer.

The companion book, *Administrative Procedures for Advanced Secretarial Students,* includes details on this type of filing system.

Monitoring and revising systems and procedures

Now that you have a basic understanding of systems and procedures, it is important to see how these can be monitored and may have to be revised.

You have already seen that some systems have a comparator which provides automatic monitoring – as with the thermostat in a hairdryer. If the system goes wrong (ie the thermostat breaks), then it is immediately obvious because the output changes and the goal cannot be achieved. Unfortunately, with many procedures involving people there is no automatic monitoring – so this then becomes the job of administrative staff. Monitoring simply means regularly checking that the goal is being achieved.

Monitoring procedures is the same – checking that the objective is being achieved. If feedback from users indicates that there are problems, then it is very likely the procedure will need revising.

A **systems audit** may be carried out at regular intervals to check that the systems in use are

- appropriate
- still achieving their goal.

This involves *checking* on the systems in use to see which are satisfactory, where there are omissions and where systems need updating or modifying. The check can be made by talking to staff who use the system or evaluating the outputs against the goal. The results will be analysed by specialists who may then suggest

- the introduction of a new system
- the modification or replacement of an existing system.

It is usually the case that staff become very inventive at circumventing systems and procedures that they do not like or think are useless! Systems people may find, for instance, that whereas there is supposed to be a procedure in force for all staff to log in at reception each morning, they may find that staff ignore this, particularly if there have never been any repercussions! This points to the fact that

- the procedure should be abolished – because the reason for it has gone or never really existed in the first place, or
- the procedure should be updated (eg by swiping an ID card through a computer system), or
- faults in the procedure must be rectified (eg if staff did not log in because the receptionist was not always on duty).

Administrative staff have a role to play in influencing this process. They are in the best position to collect data and information to back up their argument as to why a particular system or procedure may need changing – and to make suggestions as to the type of system or procedure that would be more effective.

Information can be obtained by listening to feedback from staff on existing procedures and thinking about ways in which improvements can be made. Administrators will also know those parts of a system or procedure which staff find confusing or difficult to follow – as well as those which they actively avoid! The role of senior administrators is therefore to be proactive about making changes, rather than have these forced upon them.

The same applies to procedures. It is wasting everyone's time to have a procedure in use which serves no useful purpose. However, reviewing procedures does not have to be done by specialist staff. It is usually the role of administrative staff to listen to feedback on existing procedures and to examine ways in which they can be improved or modified. Equally, it is up to administrative staff to ascertain where new or modified procedures should be introduced, either because there is confusion amongst staff about what to do or because a new process or system has been introduced.

Discussion point

You work as an administrator in a small organisation which employs 30 staff. Few formalised systems and procedures are in operation although, as the business grows in size, the need for these is becoming more apparent. Your boss is concerned at the moment that people are taking personal leave almost at random and that there are no checks on their days off against their annual leave allowance.

He has asked you to devise a procedure to record and monitor staff leave.

1   Draw a flow chart which will show your suggested procedure.

2   Identify the costs and benefits involved.

3   Identify how you would monitor the procedure.

4   Suggest why the procedure might have to be revised
    a   when you have devised it
    b   two years later.

● Organising for efficiency

At the beginning of this chapter we examined the remit of an administrator and the problems inherent in the job. At that point you might have thought that operating efficiently and doing everything properly must be virtually impossible! This is simply not true, as is evidenced by the thousands of administrative staff working happily – and efficiently – every day.

They achieve this level of expertise because of the way in which they approach their job in three key areas.

- Planning and implementation.
- Coordination.
- Monitoring and control.

Administrators who get these factors right usually find that the rest falls into place fairly easily. For that reason we will examine each of them separately.

Planning

Planning is the first stage in the administrative process. Quite simply, unless you know where you are going, you will never know if you have arrived! Planning, therefore, is essential for objectives to be achieved and is a prerequisite to being able to organise anything or control anything.

Planning involves several stages.

1 Assessing where you are now.

2 Assessing what the future will hold.

3 Setting goals for the future.

4 Obtaining information relating to these goals.

5 Considering alternative courses of action to reach the goals.

6 Deciding the most suitable action to take.

7 Commencing chosen course of action.

8 Setting interim goals.

9 Monitoring progress.

You will have done the above many times in your personal life. Imagine you decide to go on holiday with two friends next summer. You have already achieved stages 1–3 above. The next stage is to obtain information on the holiday and decide which is the one you most like and can afford. Perhaps you are short of money. Deciding how to obtain this is all part of stage 5. Stage 6, therefore, might involve deciding to obtain a Saturday job. There

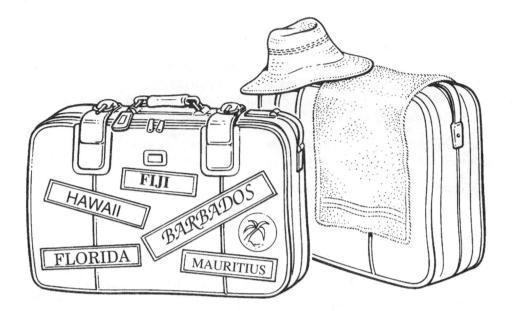

will be other actions involved – you will have to book the holiday and pay a deposit. These relate to stage 7. Working out how much you should have saved each month links to stage 8 and checking your bank account qualifies for stage 9!

The better your plans, the more likely you are to achieve your goal and the less likely you are to receive nasty shocks. Life as an administrator should certainly not be one continuous surprise!

The principles of planning
There are certain principles of planning which lead to a good plan – one that works – as opposed to a poor one, which doesn't!

- Your plans should link to those of the department – they should not be conceived in isolation.

- Plans should be realistic and take account of available resources.

- Plans should identify a result or an outcome.

- Plans should have a clear time scale for completion.

- Plans should be flexible – to take account of changes.

- Progress should be measurable – so that you can clearly see what you have achieved, whether you are on target and what still needs to be done.

Types of plans
Plans can be divided into those which are long-term (usually a year or more), medium term (3–12 months) and short term (up to 3 months). Short-

term plans are always the easiest to devise – although sticking to schedule may not be that easy. Long-term plans need more consideration and there is a danger that with a long time scale things may be forgotten about. It is for that reason that planning aids are involved.

Strategies for planning

'How to plan' may be second nature to someone who is naturally well organised. For those who are less so or who are not naturally methodical, it can be a more difficult task. If this applies to you, below are several steps which should help.

1 Make sure you clearly understand what you have to do, ie your objective(s).

2 Break down this objective into the tasks it contains. For instance, if you are planning a sales conference, there would be various jobs you have to do, eg
   - obtain quotations from hotels for required dates
   - ask your boss to agree which is the most suitable
   - make booking
   - invite participants
   - circulate information on hotel and facilities
   - arrange for documentation to be produced and ready for date
   - check with hotel all required facilities are available
   - take documentation to hotel.

3 Work out your plan of action *backwards* from the final date when everything must be ready. Allow time for checking key points (eg where you have to consult with your boss), for printing to be done and for letters to arrive.

4 Tick off actions completed so that you know at a glance where you are (see **checklists** below).

5 Monitor your plan or make checks regularly to ensure that everything is going to schedule.

6 Keep all the papers, and the checklist, safely in one clearly labelled file, so that all your information is easy to find.

7 If other people are involved in the planning process, make sure they know what they have to do and monitor *their* adherence to deadline dates as well as your own (see coordination on page 357).

Methods of planning and aids to planning

One of the most fundamental aids to planning is a list! A shopping list is a plan of what to buy. You can even tick off items one by one as you get them. Many top administrators rely on their list of 'jobs to do' and are distraught if they lose sight of their notepad for more than five minutes!

Written lists are ideal for very short-term planning but are less useful for anything longer than a few days, especially if you are constantly crossing-out some items and adding others. After a week the list would be unreadable! A scribbled, written list is also hardly the document to provide to your boss who wants to produce a schedule for the next sales conference! Neither is such a list suitable for permanent use, as a reminder of the things which must be done regularly. For that reason a variety of other aids and methods are used.

Checklists

A checklist is simply a more formal list which details action to be taken to complete a job. Checklists are useful for jobs which are done at regular intervals as the old list serves as an aide memoire the next time the task comes up. An example would be a checklist for arranging interviews. In this case, all the steps to be undertaken are listed, one under the other, and the checklist kept in a central file. Anyone who is involved in arranging interviews can then use the checklist for guidance.

Action plans

These are more likely to be devised for one-off jobs which may involve several people. The plan usually indicates who is responsible for each 'action' to be taken and the date when each action must be completed. This means that people are made responsible for their part in following the plan and are accountable for the results they achieve. A simple **action plan** is illustrated in Figure 8.6 – note that it is always easier to follow if the actions are listed in date order.

PENMERE ANIMAL SANCTUARY

CHECKLIST FOR VICTORIAN CHARITY STALL ON 29 JUNE

Action	By	Date
Reserve stall and pay deposit	M Jones	1/6
Hire costumes	L Barnes	6/6
Arrange stall decoration and trimmings	T White	15/6
Obtain tombola prizes	All	17/6
Organise tombola	M Jones	20/6
Organise apple-bobbing	L Barnes	21/6

Figure 8.6 A simple action plan

Scheduling

You follow a complex schedule every day when you follow your timetable! A schedule is a plan which many people can follow over quite a long period. It shows what everyone should be doing and when.

In industry, production schedules are formulated as a result of production planning. These show which products will be made, when and who will be responsible for the operation.

Planning charts and boards

These are usually used for long-term plans, to remind people when action must be taken. Planning charts are usually clearly visible on walls of Marketing and Production offices to remind people of major events, actions to take and routine activities. You will see illustrations of them in any office supplies catalogue.

Diaries and electronic systems

Everyone in business uses a diary as their personal planner of events. Some simply write appointments in them, others use the remaining space to remind them of jobs to do. Today many business people use electronic diaries. The diary facility on a networked PC has the advantage that it can be accessed by all system users so that mutually convenient appointments can easily be arranged.

'Bring forward' systems

These are reminder systems which prompt the user that an action must be taken on a particular day. A variety of different systems can be employed – from entering actions in a diary to completing index cards. Again, some electronic diary systems allow for 'bring forward' entries.

You should note that planning aids are discussed in more detail in the companion book *Administrative Procedures for Advanced Secretarial Students.*

 Discussion point

You have just attended a marketing meeting where your boss was discussing

a   the annual sales seminar which is to be held in six months' time
b   a business trip that she is making next week
c   an advertising campaign in which everyone is involved over the next two months.

As a group, decide which methods or aids you would use to ensure that all the actions being taken are carefully noted.

Planning and implementation

There is a well-known saying, 'The best laid plans of mice and men ...', meaning that things can – and will – go wrong with even the best of plans.

Plans may not be met because

- they were unrealistic

- no one bothered to check if things were being done to schedule

- the office is too disorganised to get very much done at all

- nobody knew what anyone else was doing

- several people were given jobs to do outside their own area with no help or guidance

- outside forces intervened.

In the example in the discussion point above, the business trip may have to be changed at the last minute, two people involved in the advertising campaign may be off sick and the hotel in which you normally hold your sales seminars may burn down a week beforehand!

None of these factors is under your control – so you just have to grit your teeth and make new arrangements – revising your plans to match the new events.

However, apart from 'outside forces', other areas *are* under the control of an administrator. Checking and controlling that plans are going to schedule is discussed on page 367. However, a critical area is the office organisation or the **workflow.** If bottlenecks occur and plans break down, then you are likely to be held responsible.

Efficient workflow

This simply means that jobs which are scheduled to be done at a certain time are completed according to plan. If they are not, then there should be a very good reason. If everyone goes down with flu or an urgent, unexpected job arrives and everyone has to lend a hand, then these may be valid reasons for something else being delayed – and schedules will have to be adjusted accordingly.

Work not being completed because people couldn't be bothered, because they did not know what they were doing or because the workplace is disorganised are not acceptable! Factors which affect efficiency, therefore, include

- the number of staff

- the quantity of work

- the motivation of staff

- communication within the organisation in general and the department in particular

- the ability of staff to do the jobs they have been given

- the effectiveness and suitability of the systems and procedures in place

- the attitude and style of management

- the physical organisation of the workplace

- the resources available.

Most of these areas have been discussed in previous chapters – others are obvious. One aspect, however, which deserves special consideration is the effect of the physical organisation of the workplace and its effect on workflow – again, because that is part of the administrator's remit.

Maximising workflow

Workflow through an office is maximised when the layout has been designed so that

- space is used to the best possible advantage

- there are appropriate 'services' close at hand, eg telephones, lighting, heating, power

- sufficient resources are available within close range, eg photocopier

- movement between areas is easy

- everything is neatly stored and easy to find

- the layout takes into consideration the usual 'flow of work' through the area and minimises 'walking time' and 'wasted time'.

Do bear in mind that health and safety considerations are also essential (see page 303). Remember, too, that 'space' in an office is required for

- the people employed and the work they are currently doing

- the equipment necessary to assist that work

- storage for incoming and completed work, consumables and any other supporting material and files.

Given these requirements, it is no use ordering the most expensive desk in a catalogue because it looks great if it will not fit in the space available! You are buying **functional** furniture which has a specific purpose. The objective is more important than its looks! Bear in mind, also, that furniture should be bought with **ergonomic** principles in mind (see page 267) and nothing in the area should contravene health and safety regulations (eg a photocopier jammed up against the wall and blocking the air vents).

Planning at BSI

The British Standards Institution (BSI) managed to refurbish a 1960s office block in West London in 56 weeks – within budget and on schedule! Throughout the project staff were kept informed of progress and involved in decisions on the new office layout. The interior designers set up a pilot office with four different layouts, furniture ranges and colour schemes. The office was used by one department for several months to assess and report back on working conditions.

At the time of the move each member of staff received a welcome pack giving information on safety, security, first aid, parking and the computer systems. Also included in the pack were a local map, the first day's menu in the staff restaurant and a questionnaire.

Day-to-day work on maintenance, cleaning, security, catering and waste has been contracted out. The facilities manager is responsible for reception, conferences, reprographics and messengers. This means coping with national and international conferences, about 40,000 visitors a year, 5,000 committee meetings and 700 staff!

Discussion point

1   Look at Figure 8.7. Although the photocopier is not up against the wall, this reception office is certainly not laid out with workflow in mind! As a group, how many problems can you identify, and how would you reorganise the area?

2   Discuss how each of the following situations would affect workflow through an office.
   a   The photocopier is down a long corridor, at the other end of the building from the fax machine.
   b   Alex's desk is such a tip nobody can find anything on it.
   c   The filing hasn't been done for three weeks.
   d   The administrator's office is a considerable distance from the main administration office where her staff work.
   e   There is only one telephone which is situated on the far desk in a large office.
   f   Shelagh is responsible for checking all invoices received and Winston has the job of entering them on the computer system once she has done this – yet their desks are at the opposite ends of a large open-plan office.

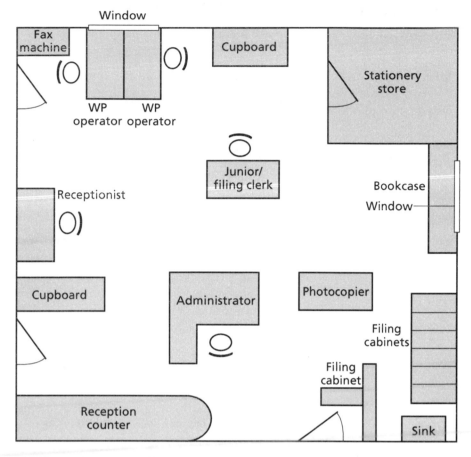

Figure 8.7 Plan of a reception office

● Coordination

Coordination relates to the skills of uniting the efforts of different people to get work done in the most effective way. Within an organisation everything is dependent upon everything else – Production depends upon Sales to give clear information about orders, Sales relies upon Production to make the goods, everyone relies upon Finance to obtain payment for orders so that the organisation stays in business. Within an office the same thing occurs – people who are part of a team rely on each other to do a specific part of a job. Those who do not fulfil their responsibilities, or make a mess of them, not only let themselves down but everyone else as well.

The role of administrators is to coordinate the efforts of their team so that everyone is pulling in the same direction and all the activities link together within the agreed time scale. Therefore coordination must also be planned – it does not happen on its own.

Coordination mechanisms

Within every organisation there are formal mechanisms to ensure that coordination exists.

• Meetings will be held – from the board of directors to departmental meetings. There may be steering group meetings to pursue a particular outcome or ad hoc meetings for a specific purpose.

• Liaison roles may be held by certain people in the organisation. Their job is to liaise with other people and to ensure there is good communication between them.

• A task force is a group formed to solve a problem or pursue a particular issue.

• The formal structure allows for departmental communication and shows which person has responsibility for which area. Usually there are some formal arrangements for reporting from one level to another – your boss may produce a report for senior management at regular intervals. This, together with reports received from other managers, helps senior staff to coordinate departmental approaches.

• Certain members of staff are given an official coordination role and this is shown by their job title, eg sales office coordinator.

Planning coordination

Effective coordination can be very difficult to achieve. It is rather like throwing several balls in the air at one time with a plan that they all land in the right place at the right time! It is more likely to be achieved if

• everyone knows exactly what they are supposed to be doing – if a complex job is involved, instructions and information should be in writing

• everyone is working towards the same objective – and it should be clear what this is

• people's job descriptions make it clear which areas they are expected to work in, and they know their responsibilities in this regard

• an administrator expected to delegate work to a team, or coordinate work within a department, has the clear authority to do this – so that people know it is part of their job to comply

• staff dealing with a new task or responsibility are given suitable training and guidance and know who will give them additional assistance, if required

• the administrator has a method of controlling output and checking that work is being done according to plan (see page 362)

- communication is effective and accurate – both formal and informal

- as much direct contact as is necessary is encouraged between the person responsible for coordination and those in the team.

Team working

As an administrator, your main role in relation to coordination will be concerned with the team of people in your office or department. Many jobs require the efforts of more than one individual for everything to be done on time. This may mean that you have the responsibility of delegating tasks to junior staff in order to get the work done. Obviously, you then need their cooperation to do the job not only on time but also to the best of their ability – and to inform you if there are any problems.

What is a team? The easy model is a sports team. This is a **group of people who are all working towards the same goal.** The coordinator is the 'captain' who gives feedback on performance, acts as the motivator or leader by giving encouragement, clarifies any queries and constantly monitors team performance, making adjustments where necessary. This may be a minor adjustment such as asking one person to support another or more major, such as the substitution of a player!

Teams work better – and motivation is greater – when the participants are actively involved in plans which relate to them. You would hardly find a football manager and coach deciding how to play a game without the team being present! They can then make suggestions on the best way to do a job, what is possible and what is not. They can also suggest a realistic time scale for completing a job bearing in mind the other work with which they are involved.

Therefore, if action plans are being drawn up, this is better undertaken at a planning meeting so that people know what to expect. They also need to be clear on the degree of scope that they have to do the work on their own, and the aspects they must check where necessary. In other words the rules of **delegation** apply. This is important because if you have been given the task of reporting back to your boss and overseeing the task, then you are the one who is accountable for its success – not your team. Your boss will not expect you to blame other people if things go wrong – the responsibility is yours!

Strategies for team work

- Make sure participants understand the benefits they will personally gain from working as a member of a team – help and support, exchange of ideas, ease of meeting joint targets, specialisation of individual strengths and abilities.

- Make certain that all members of the team are well informed about their responsibilities.

- Encourage formal and informal communication amongst the team.

- Engender a team spirit by focusing on the group goal, rather than individual objectives.

- Encourage loyalty within the team (and set the example by always protecting your team).

- Encourage group decision-making about team efforts and goals.

- Make the work as interesting, challenging and demanding as possible.

- Foster team morale, rather than individual morale.

- Play to individual strengths and assist individual members to achieve their personal aims, providing this does not encroach on the morale or goal of the group.

The Belbin findings

A management writer, Dr Meredith Belbin, argued that an individual can never be perfect but a team can. He meant that, given the right mix, a team can collectively have a variety of qualities which result in more 'strengths' than can ever be found in one person. Belbin considered there were eight team roles and to each he ascribed typical features, positive qualities and allowable weaknesses. Sometimes, of course, people can carry out more than one role depending upon their individual personality trait. The important point is that all the key roles must be carried out adequately by at least one member of the team. To be effective, the team must get on well together, support each other and be able to rely on one another to get the job done. This means sometimes filling roles which may not be their first preference but which are 'missing' in the team – or being prepared to assist in making up the deficit.

A simplified version of Belbin's summary of team roles is shown in Figure 8.8.

Type	Personality	Contribution to team
Coordinator	Calm, self-confident and in control	Treats suggestions objectively, on merit and without prejudice. Good communicator
Shaper	Extrovert and dynamic	Self-starting, welcomes challenges, ideas person. May be impatient or restless
Plant	Creative, intelligent and original	Visionary but may be poor on details
Monitor-evaluator	Introvert, analytical and dispassionate	Objective judge but may upset others
Implementer	Stable, reliable and sensible	Good organiser who will see jobs through but may be inflexible
Resource investigator	Enthusiastic, sociable and positive	Good at networking with others and reacting to a challenge. May be easily bored
Team worker	Sensitive, good people skills, stable	Good at supporting others and helping to retain harmony. May be indecisive at critical times
Completer/ finisher	Introvert, anxious and conscientious	The perfectionist in the team but a worrier. May get immersed in the detail

Figure 8.8 Belbin's team roles

Discussion point

1   Look around your own group or class and decide which is your own preferred role and which is preferred by your colleagues. Then see if your findings agree! Now decide how good a team you are!!

2   Turn back to page 182 and reread the section on delegation, accountability and responsibility.

Then decide, as a group, how you would cope with the following situations.

a   A member of staff who will not follow instructions – and therefore constantly does the wrong thing.

b   A colleague who is one of your closest friends, but constantly puts off doing jobs she does not like doing, in the hope that you will 'rescue' her and do it yourself.

c   A member of staff who does not see why he should follow your instructions.

d   Someone who will never tell you when things are going wrong – with the result that you have been in trouble three times recently trying to sort out the resulting problems.

e   A colleague who goes over your head whenever anything goes wrong and reports the problem directly to your boss – without even telling you or giving you the opportunity to put things right.

Monitoring and control

Before you can check that anything is being done according to plan, it is essential that you understand exactly what you are expected to achieve. The objective must therefore be clear. You then have three aspects of the job to consider.

- The quantity to be produced. This is related to **productivity** or **output.**

- The **quality** or standard required.

- The **time scale** in which the work must be done. This is where scheduling and time management are so important.

Productivity or output

Productivity or output is concerned with the amount of usable work being produced in a certain time scale. There are various factors which affect productivity, including

- the complexity of the job

- the level of accuracy or detail required

- the skill of the person undertaking the task

- the quantity of work to be done

- the number of interruptions.

You only need to think of producing a particular document on a word processor. It is an easy task to accomplish if the original document comprises two pages of typescript, the final document need only be a draft and the administrative assistant is left in peace to create it. It is quite a different matter if the draft consists of 23 pages, is handwritten, full of alterations and has to be produced perfectly for external presentation – especially if the person typing it is expected to answer the phone and look after reception at the same time!

Because of the variety of work in an office, it may seem an impossible job to have clear expectations of when you could reasonably expect a piece of work to be completed. For this reason, there are various ways in which work output can be assessed or measured. These are all designed to give guidance on rates of output.

Work measurement systems

Work measurement systems range from the very precise to the more general. Data input clerks, for instance, may be expected to carry out a minimum number of key strokes every day – and this can be 'counted' by the depressions they make on a keyboard and the information stored by computer. Word processor operators or audio typists may be expected to produce a minimum number of A4 pages each day, assuming that this is the only work they do. As you are probably aware, many text processing, typewriting and word processing examinations insist on a minimum level of output before you are awarded a pass.

In this way, both output and performance can easily be measured. Quite obviously, these are exact measures and are usually not suitable or appropriate for general office administrative staff who might undertake a broader range of duties.

More suitable ways of measuring work may include

- estimating appropriate output yourself
- asking subordinates to **estimate** their output
- completing **work completion sheets**
- **activity sampling**
- personal **observation.**

Estimating output

It is always easier to estimate output if you can do a job yourself. That way, you are less likely to be fooled by anyone else! If a new word processor operator told you that it would take all day to key in a five-page document, you would have every right to look astounded. You would also be sceptical of any claim to turn the whole thing around in 15 minutes! Your own experience, therefore, is very useful in assessing realistic output targets. However, you have to be careful to allow for other relevant factors, you may be more or less skilled than your colleague, who may have more interruptions than you and so on.

It is therefore sensible to estimate output *in discussion with* the people doing the work. Experience will tell you when people are giving you a reasoned argument that your own targets need adjusting – and when they are not! One factor you should always consider, however, is the amount of work a colleague has to do for other people. If you consult colleagues for a realistic deadline, you should both consider the pressures of other jobs they have to complete and when the work can sensibly be fitted into their work schedule.

Work completion sheets

In some offices, certain types of job are entered into a log book on receipt. A planned date/time for completion and then an actual date/time for completion is entered when the work is finished. Sometimes a work completion sheet is attached to the work which is then filled in and filed (Figure 8.9).

WORK COMPLETION SHEET

Urgent/non-urgent

Date submitted .... Job no. ....

Originator ....

Task description ....

....

....

....

....

....

No. of copies required ....

Draft quality YES/NO Final quality YES/NO

Date required ....

Task carried out by ....

Checked by ....

Date completed ....

Figure 8.9

Looking through these will tell you the usual rate of turnaround for this type of work. If office staff sign the log or the work completion sheets, then you can also analyse these to find out the output rates of different members of staff. You have every right to have certain expectations, for instance, that more senior or skilled staff can handle complex jobs more easily, and routine jobs more quickly, than junior or new staff. If the log tells a different story, then it is the responsibility of the administrator to investigate the situation to find out why this is the case.

Activity sampling

Activity sampling means making random inspections of what everyone is doing at regular intervals. This is obviously very difficult if you are trying to do your own job at the same time. The easiest way is to sample throughput or turnaround by looking at the amount of work outstanding and seeing how fast this is being cleared.

If there is regularly a backlog, then it is likely you will also hear about this from other sources – mainly people complaining that their work has not been completed on time. At this point you need to find out what 'lead time' was given (ie whether adequate notice of a job was given or it was handed into the office at the last minute on a busy day), the complexity of the job and whether the person giving the task had agreed a realistic deadline with the member of staff involved. The frequency of complaints is also important – and who made them. Regular moans about the administrative staff made by the most disorganised member of staff in a department is rather different from 10 complaints in a fortnight made by a very organised and efficient manager about one of your team!

Personal observation

You may think that observing people's performance is similar to 'spying' on them. However, if an administrator is trying to organise the office so that work is completed smoothly, then it is essential that he or she knows what is going on. If the office junior disappears with 10 pages of photocopying and returns in a hot, dishevelled state after half an hour, then he or she may have had a particularly unfortunate experience, with the photocopier breaking down, a queue forming, paper running out, etc. If this occurs every time any photocopying needs doing, then there is clearly a problem. The junior may not be capable of doing anything more than the most routine jobs – but may not wish to say anything for fear of looking silly. It is *your* job, if you are the administrator, to spot the problem, find out what is causing it and put it right!

Setting quality standards

Let us assume the same junior does the 10 pages of photocopying in just five minutes. However, the result is unusable with half the documents off the page, 50 spoiled pages and the photocopying area turned into a mess. Quite reasonably you may wish that he or she had taken 10 minutes and produced usable documents.

For this reason, output *on its own* is clearly insufficient. Work must be usable, ie it must be free of errors to the point where it does not have to be redone – otherwise, the costs of producing it are obviously increased because the time taken to do the job satisfactorily is virtually double.

Deciding upon the standard required is important. Some types of work do not have to be 100 per cent accurate, eg a document in the mail delivered to the wrong desk will usually be rerouted by the recipient. The only time a serious problem will occur is if the document is both urgent and very important, when more care needs to be taken.

Similarly, a draft internal report which has to go to the author for amendments need not be as accurate as a report for the board of directors or a letter to an important customer.

However, the danger with any errors in clerical or office work is

- their potential to cause serious problems

- their potential to damage the company image

- the frustration and exasperation they cause staff.

A piece of paper filed in the wrong place may not seem disastrous – until the managing director needs it in a hurry and you are the one given the job of finding it quickly! A letter to a customer with three mistakes may mean the customer considers that if the quality of your products is similar, then he or she would be as well going elsewhere. A spreadsheet with transposed figures can have endless repercussions, as you saw earlier in this chapter.

This potential for problems is why, in most administrative and text processing examinations, error tolerance is extremely low indeed.

You need to set similar high standards in any office in which you work – and, of course, your own work must be virtually faultless. Given, however, that we are all human beings and all make mistakes from time to time, no one can assume that they have done everything correctly, no matter how skilled or experienced. For that reason **checking** is absolutely vital.

The degree of checking or type of **proof reading** will depend upon the standards which have been set, eg

- **Important** or **complex** documents should be **checked word by word.** Figures, in particular, should be checked by two people, one doing the reading and the other the checking.

- **Internal** work should be **sampled** by the administrator and **feedback** from users noted. This applies to areas such as filing, mail delivery and photocopying.

- **Partial checking** is usually sufficient for routine internal clerical duties, such as flicking through index cards to check the headings have been completed, checking quickly down a telephone extension list that no one has been excluded.

Kaizen – the Japanese way

The Japanese have a philosophy of **kaizen** or continuous improvement. They argue that it is expensive to make corrections once something has been done. They are therefore strongly committed to checking everything whilst it is being produced so that faults do not occur.

The same is just as true of office work as it is of production work!

Scheduling

Scheduling in this context relates to the time scale within which work must be completed. Usually, in any administrative office, work can be divided into three categories.

1 Routine, everyday tasks, eg mail handling, photocopying, filing and routine document production.

2 Larger, more complex, tasks which are undertaken on a regular basis, eg preparation of monthly reports or accounts; organisation of trips, seminars, mailshots.

3 Complex 'one-off' jobs, eg organising hospitality for a special group of foreign visitors, involvement in an expensive advertising campaign, submission of documents for a detailed contract or bid.

The basic rules are that

- any complex jobs need to be carefully scheduled

- there should be a realistic action plan with clear areas of responsibility so that everyone knows who is doing what, and by when.

A well-organised office is one where each person knows the jobs for which he or she is responsible. This is usually easily sorted out, preferably with all the staff present, if the key areas of work undertaken by the office are listed. Generally,

- daily routine jobs can be shared by everyone

- regular routine jobs can be delegated to one particular person who takes responsibility for this area, with a 'back-up' person for assistance and cover during absence

- complex 'one-off' jobs should be planned between the team.

This approach usually appeals to staff as everyone prefers to be responsible for a 'whole job' rather than a series of unrelated tasks (see motivation and job design, chapter 7).

Each person should be clear on the deadlines that have to be met in their own area of responsibility. Wall planners can be used to highlight progress on all types of complex jobs but these can be invaluable for 'one-off' jobs which involve several people – given that everyone is undergoing a learning experience as they fulfil their obligations. A **Gantt** chart is a particular type of wall planner which shows the difference between planned outcome and actual outcome to date (Figure 8.10).

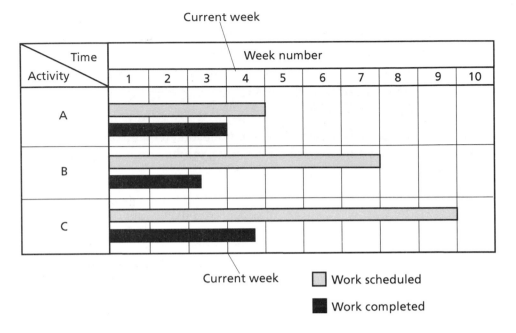

Figure 8.10 A Gantt chart

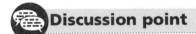

Discussion point

An administrative office in a college is responsible for undertaking the following jobs.

- Routine photocopying for staff.
- Internal mail collection and delivery.
- Preparation and posting of outgoing mail.
- Routine filing.
- Routine document production.
- Ordering goods.
- Dealing with telephone enquiries.
- Monitoring petty cash.
- Payment and recording of invoices.
- Monthly accommodation checks and report to buildings supervisor.
- Arranging interviews for new students.
- Arranging interviews for new staff.
- Preparing complex submissions for new courses.
- Recording register entries on computer.
- Staffing reception and dealing with visitors.
- Arranging hospitality for meetings and visitors.
- Making examination entries.
- Compiling statistics from examination results.
- Maintaining equipment, eg OHPs and videos.

There are six members of staff. Janet, the eldest member of the team, works part time, five mornings a week. All the rest work full time. Firoza is good at dealing with people and undertaking general work but has no eye for detail. Her keyboarding skills are average. Lisa is an excellent typist and loves working on computers, as does Sarah. Gillian, the longest serving member of the team, is the assistant administrator. In addition to her other work she is also involved in assisting with marketing duties and mail shots. The administrator, Rebecca, mainly undertakes PA duties for the head of the department.

Gillian and Rebecca want to sort out the work of the office so that everything runs more smoothly.

As a group, decide how you would delegate the work of the department so that you play to the team's strengths and, at the same time, have clear areas of responsibility in the office. (You may find it useful to look back at Belbin's work on teams on page 361 before you do this exercise!)

Organisation and methods

Organisation and methods (O & M) was designed to improve office systems. The American version 'work simplification' was defined as 'the organised use of common sense to find easier and better ways of doing work'. This is probably the easiest definition to understand. Quite simply, it is a technique for improving workflow and eliminating waste without reducing quality.

An O & M investigation may be undertaken on one aspect of office work or it may be much broader, and look at improving the systems and procedures in operation in an entire office. It is often useful when *change* has affected the type and quantity of work being undertaken in an office. In this case, new systems may be more appropriate than ones which have been used for years. A change of layout or the purchase of new equipment or software may be appropriate. External consultants may be hired to take an objective and dispassionate view of what is happening and then make their recommendations for improvements.

The key stages in an O & M investigation usually include

1 deciding on the objective of the assignment

2 planning the assignment

3 collecting information by studying records, forms, making personal observations, holding discussions with people doing the job and senior managers – sometimes questionnaires are used to obtain information

4 analysing the facts in terms of what is done, why it is done, when it is done, where it is done, who does it, and how the work is carried out

5 submitting recommendations for change.

An O & M example – forms control and design

One popular area for O & M study is **forms design.** Forms quickly go out of date. This means that they collect information that no one uses and *do not* collect the information that people now need. In some organisations it is possible that some people are completing forms which no one ever looks at again. **Forms control** is concerned with ensuring that

• the number of forms in circulation is kept to a minimum

• information is not duplicated by being requested on two different forms

• the form is designed with its purpose clearly in mind

• forms are standardised, so that they are easy to recognise

• forms are simplified, so that they are easy to complete and 'user friendly'.

Change affects all types of forms. No doubt when you started at college, you completed an enrolment form. If you ask your tutor, you will probably find that this form has been changed virtually every year to obtain different types of information. You can also check whether your college has any system of forms design in operation. If you have already been asked by three people to write out your qualifications to date on different forms, then you would be right to challenge the system!

Forms design is concerned with the layout of forms and the information they ask for. Some basic points are listed below.

• The purpose of the form – does the form ask for key information only? A clear title is usually essential – to focus everyone's mind!

• The users of the form – is the form itself and any instructions it contains easy to understand? Is the name of the organisation clearly shown? Are there distinct instructions on parts of the form which should *not* be completed?

• The order in which information is asked for. This should be logical (you would not expect to put your name at the end of the form, for example).

• Sufficient space available for entry of information.

• The style of print and wording, so that instructions for information are clear.

• The type of paper used – for instance, whether multiple copies are required and if so, how many.

• Correction of errors – whether this is easy or difficult.

- Extracting information – whether information is consistently given in a format which can easily be utilised (for instance, clear instructions on how to write your date of birth).

- Cost of producing the form – this relates to the size of the form, quality of paper and number of copies.

- Form handling and filing – different colours can be used to assist distribution of copies, code numbers for filing should be clearly visible, etc.

The basic rule is that the form should look neat, simple and be easy to read and understand.

Usually, a trial run is useful to identify any ambiguities or problems. These may be identified both by people who will fill in the form and those responsible for extracting and analysing the information it contains. The increased use of computers has meant that the format in which information is presented has had to become very standardised. For that reason code numbers are often allocated to certain options (eg ethnic origin questions). Having a trial run can enable people to check that all the possible options have been covered by any coding system in operation.

 Discussion point

1 As a group, obtain four different forms – these can be either from your college (such as an application or enrolment form) or from outside (eg a job application form, driving licence form or passport application). Decide assessment criteria for the forms using the points mentioned above (eg marks out of 10 for good layout, clear instructions, etc).

   Then assess each form and see how each scores. Analyse the main strengths of the best form and the main weaknesses of the worst.

2 Try to design a form yourself – you will find that it is not as easy as you may think! Ask your tutor for all the essential data he or she needs on students during a year and design a form to obtain this information.

   Make three photocopies and ask your colleagues to check your form and score it in the same way as above. Organise a group feedback session when you discuss the easiest and hardest aspects of designing forms.

Failure to meet targets

In this chapter you have read about planning work carefully, coordinating the efforts of a team, monitoring and controlling work so that output is achieved, to the correct standard and within the time scale allocated. If you have done all this, then what can possibly go wrong?

The answer is 'plenty' – and several sections of this chapter have given indications of the areas which can contribute to problems. They relate to

- unrealistic targets, standards and deadlines – no linking of targets to length/complexity of task or source documents/information available, unclear or unsuitable quality standards for different jobs, too short deadlines for achievement bearing in mind quality targets

- problems with staff – from carelessness to inexperience, from tiredness to stress, from demotivation to personal problems

- problems with management – including lack of training for staff, poor staff selection, lack of consideration of individual strengths and weaknesses, poor organisation, demotivational management style, complicated work systems, poor or ambiguous communication, constant interruptions

- difficulties with equipment – insufficient or unsuitable resources and equipment for individual staff, breakdowns and lack of maintenance, equipment outdated or slow to operate, manual systems used which could be mechanised (eg collating documents)

- poor working conditions – poor lighting, cramped conditions, no consideration of workflow, too hot/cold/stuffy, noise levels too high, inappropriate furniture causing fatigue, dreary decor.

 Discussion point

1   Discuss as a group, and with your tutor, what remedies could be taken to improve each of the problems listed above.

2   Decide the extent to which you think payment incentive schemes linked to output might help – and what their limitations may be.

A final word – the importance of administration

You may have watched the programme 'Men Behaving Badly' on television and laughed at the antics of Caroline Quentin, Helen Lederer and Leslie Ash. However, none of them were laughing very much in June 1995 when their agent went into liquidation owing up to £1 million to about 100 actors.

The agency – Sharon Hamper Management Ltd – went into liquidation with a net deficit of £645,000. In the account to pay clients there was only £85,000 – far too little to pay everyone who was owed money.

According to Miss Hamper the business collapsed because of 'the failure to install adequate accounting and administration controls'.

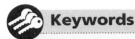

Keywords

The main keywords and terms you have met in this chapter are listed below. Some you have met before, such as planning, though in this chapter they relate directly to administrative work. Check that you understand the meaning and concept of each one.

action plans	inputs
activity sampling	lateral structure
centralisation	monitoring
checking	objectives
checklists	observation
communication process	office services
computerisation	organisation and methods
control	organisation skills
coordination	outputs
costs/benefits	planning
customer service	prioritising
decentralisation	procedures
delegation	productivity
effectiveness	profitability
efficiency	proof reading
estimating	quality
ergonomic design	resourcing
feasibility study	standards
feedback	systems
flow chart	systems audit
formal structure	targets
forms control	team working
forms design	time scale
Gantt chart	time management
informal structure	work completion sheets
information flows	workflow
infrastructure	work measurement

Examination practice

Short-answer questions

1 State three purposes of devising clear procedures for staff.

2 Give six examples of basic administrative functions.

3 Suggest four reasons why information flows and communication are essential to administrative efficiency.

4 State three factors you would bear in mind when delegating work to staff.

5 Suggest four strategies you would employ to foster team work in your staff.

6 Identify three aids to planning and give an example of when each may be used.

7 State three benefits of using a flow chart to illustrate a procedure.

8 State three ways in which you could measure the output of work.

9 Identify six reasons why standards may not be met.

10 State four characteristics of a well-designed form.

Definition questions

1 Explain clearly the difference between each of the following terms.
   a forms design and forms control
   b accountability and responsibility
   c long-term plans and short-term plans
   d checklists and action plans

2 Write clear notes to explain each of the following terms.
   a feasibility study
   b activity sampling
   c organisation and methods
   d systems audit

Essay questions

1 Explain the importance of coordination in an office and the role an administrator can play in achieving this.

2 Describe the relationship between the physical organisation of the workplace and efficient workflow.

3 Describe appropriate methods which can be used to set standards of output and quality within an office. How and why should these standards be monitored by an administrator?

4 'Team work can achieve more than two or three people acting independently.' State why this is the case, making clear reference to the motivation of staff.

5 Suggest reasons why the performance of staff may be below standard and suggest remedies to improve the situation.

6 Explain the importance of up-to-date and effective systems and procedures in an office. In your answer, describe the circumstances under which a systems audit would be undertaken.

Case study

Online Systems is an organisation which has grown rapidly over the past five years. It is particularly concerned with electronic information and communication systems, and offers a range of software programs for computer users. Unfortunately, its own systems are less than perfect. Its rapid growth has resulted in overcrowded offices, rapidly changing systems and procedures and a huge increase in the number of administrative staff employed.

Recently, Gerry Davies, the MD, decided a complete reorganisation was essential. He employed consultants who recommended a relocation to expanded premises, a review of the information systems to enhance coordination and an in-depth O & M study to highlight particular areas where office procedures should be reviewed.

a Explain how the review and subsequent relocation should influence the physical working environment in the new premises.

b Explain the importance of information systems to office efficiency and describe one type of system or procedure which may be improved as a result of the review.

c Describe the steps which the O & M specialists are likely to take and explain why this study is considered necessary.

● Introduction

This chapter is only short, but is crucial to your success in studying for level 3 examinations. Many students who progress to this level are constantly worried about their ability to cram all the information they think they need into their heads before the examination. They also worry and fret that there will be a question on the examination paper which has not been covered or which they cannot answer.

Stop! The huge difference between a level 2 and a level 3 examination is that you are not expected to try to learn lots of information off by heart, or to spout it back like a parrot. There is *no way,* for a start, that any book or tutor can cover every combination of possible questions which may be asked in this type of examination. Why not? Because this would mean covering something like the total combinations which could come up in the National Lottery – and would take half a library to fill or 10 years to teach!

The approach you need to develop is two-fold.

- The ability to think *across* all the areas which have been covered – and relate information from one section or chapter to another.

- The ability to be able to **analyse** and **evaluate** issues – rather than just list or describe them.

This chapter gives examples of strategies you can use to develop these skills. The better you become at them, the more successful you will be in any examination you take – and any higher level course of study you follow.

● The skill of integrating knowledge

Questions which ask you to integrate knowledge are normally those which, at first sight, you think you cannot answer! Virtually all students almost subconsciously 'compartmentalise' their knowledge, not just into subjects but into topics. How much, for instance, have you linked the information you have received in other subjects on your course to this one? Health and safety, for instance, is the same no matter which lesson you learn it in! One piece of information should build on another – not replace the first.

More precisely, how often have you consciously tried to link the information given in one chapter of this book with that provided in another? It is more than likely that the examiners will expect an answer which draws from several areas, not just one!

There are some useful techniques you can use to help. Before we discuss how you can use these to help you, let us examine the type of integrated questions you may be asked.

 Questions to consider

In each case read the question below and then discuss your reactions to them as a group and with your tutor.

1   Identify the factors which can lead to the growth of organisations.

2   Conflict at work can cause stress for all types of employees. Give examples of issues which may create conflict between managers and staff.

3   Give examples of strategies you could introduce to improve productivity in an office.

4   Explain the relationship between economic growth, business investment, interest rates and employment levels.

5   How might a review of employment legislation affect company policies and the systems and procedures which are in force?

6   Explain the importance of good communication in an organisation.

Strategies to adopt

What you might – or should – have noticed is that there is not one page in this book to which you can turn for the answer! This does not mean to say the answer is not to be found anywhere in the book, it simply means that you have now read several questions which are designed to make you **think** – and **apply** the knowledge you have learned.

On many occasions during this book discussion points have been included to give you practice in doing this. Hopefully, you have used some, if not all, of these opportunities to develop this skill. If not, then the time to begin is now!

Start by having a complete change of attitude towards all the information you have received. Think of putting it all into a huge cauldron, stirring it around and then, when you dip a ladle into it, you will get a variety of information! If you want to control the contents of the ladle, then try adopting one of the techniques below.

The brainstorming technique

This is something you should practise in a group. Think of a topic. Then everyone comes up with as many ideas as they can which are in any way related to the topic. The next stage is to group the ideas into themes. Sometimes other ideas will come up whilst you are doing this – you may also decide to reject some of the more outrageous ones. However, do bear in mind that no ideas should be criticised or excluded at the outset – often if the idea itself seems ridiculous to some people, it can lead to other thoughts which are not.

Try this now as a group on question **1**. Allow about 15 minutes to write down all your ideas – preferably on a flip chart – and then try to refine them. You may be amazed at how much you know.

The lighthouse technique

If brainstorming does not work for you, or if you cannot possibly see how you could do it on your own in an examination room, then try this technique instead.

Think of yourself as a lighthouse scanning sectors of the sea. Instead of the sea, however, your scanning sectors are related to the chapters of this book, eg

- the types and forms of private- and public-sector organisations
- their external environment
- outside agencies
- their management and objectives
- the internal structure of organisations

- the functional areas and the role and integration of each

- the people at work

- administrative duties, systems and procedures.

You can now look at each sector in turn to see what it contains – to help, if you wish, you can write down some of the key headings in each chapter to remind you of the areas which were covered.

In each sector you are looking for anything which relates to the topic under consideration.

Try this now for question **2**. If possible, do not check with any of the text in this book until later – see how many ideas you can have without help.

Focusing in-depth
Possibly this is related to scanning the surface using binoculars! Use this approach if a question asks for your own ideas related to a more specific area. Look at question **3**, for example.

This question is concerned with productivity, which is covered in chapter 8. You would need to think about various issues – standards, workflow, organisation of the office, planning, communication, quality of information, things which can go wrong, and so on. However, you can also link it to areas covered in other chapters, eg motivation in chapter 7 and delegation in chapter 4.

Now try one of the techniques you used above to see if you can come up with 10 ideas (on your own) for improving productivity. Then compare your answers with other members of the group to create a joint list.

Finding the thread
Some parts of a question are joined by a thread – it is then a case of identifying where the thread starts and ends. Use this approach if you are asked to state what links there are between one thing and another.

In question **4** the links can be inserted as follows.

- Economic growth – means the country is getting richer – measured through increases in National Income.

- Components of National Income – include investment. The more investment, the greater National Income

- Businesses invest money when interest rates are low and they have confidence in the future.

- Investment can be used for expansion which creates employment opportunities.

You now have a reasonable structure for an essay.

Try using this approach on question **5**. Part of the outline has been done for you – but only part!

- Employment legislation – examples include...

- Leads to human resources policies such as ...

- Systems and procedures to ensure policies are followed include ...

- A change or review may therefore have the following effect ...

Practise yourself

Use any technique you think is appropriate and which suits you to answer question **6**. Then discuss your ideas with your tutor.

● Analysis and evaluation

All tutors know these as 'higher order skills'. In other words, asking you to analyse or to evaluate something is harder than asking you to describe or explain something.

If you can analyse or evaluate, then you are usually awarded a higher grade in the examination than if you keep to standard descriptions or explanations. If these are correct, you will be awarded a pass – but nothing higher.

So what is meant by these terms?

You were **analysing** when you identified the links in relation to question **5**. Analysing means dividing into smaller components and tracing the argument from the beginning to end.

Evaluating means weighing up the advantages and disadvantages of a course of action. Therefore, you could be given a problem and asked to do an evaluation in your answer. Compare the question below with question **2** on page 378 (which asked for skills of analysis rather than evaluation).

 Question to consider

> As a result of a recent restructure, there has been considerable dissatisfaction and unrest shown by members of staff. Suggest how this may have been caused and what action management should have taken to avoid it.

In this case, you need

- to understand the topic (ie restructure, change, staff motivation)

- think about the problems of restructure and change and their effect on staff (both good and bad)

- consider how such changes *should* be managed (but obviously were not in this case)

- and then give your recommendations.

The level of argument you use will influence your mark, so will the degree to which you develop the argument. You must also avoid sweeping statements, generalisations or assumptions! And do not feel you have to identify only one area where a recommendation can be made.

Here are some examples.

- Do not assume that the change is all bad, that staff will have to work longer or harder or that everyone is dissatisfied. *Qualify* such statements, eg 'Some staff may be dissatisfied because ...'

- You would obviously gain more marks through bringing up the topic of communication (which is a broad and important issue) than you would for a basic comment such as staff will have to do different types of work.

- You must then *develop* the idea, eg of communication – state the importance of communicating important changes, how fear can be intensified otherwise, how the grapevine will operate and so on. Link this to management style and corporate culture and lines of communication.

- Make suggestions based on all the ideas you have developed, not just one. Do not say that managers should do this *or* that, often a range of improvements can be made over several areas.

Practise this now by trying to answer the question above. Then compare your answer with some of the others in your group. Ask your tutor to let you see the very best one and see if you can identify where this differs from yours.

A final word – on different perspectives

There are often two (or more!) sides to a story – such as the good and bad effects of change. A perspective is simply a way of looking at something. For instance, you could view change as being beneficial to the organisation but detrimental to the individuals within it. If you look at it from the perspective of the company, you therefore come up with different ideas and a different argument to considering change from the point of view of the employees. You may think of other ideas again if you consider change from yet another perspective, eg the point of view of other stakeholders such as shareholders or customers.

In several places in this book you have been introduced to different perspectives, eg

- Monopolies – one view is that monopolies are always bad because they have too much power and set high prices; another is that no monopoly lasts forever – if a market is profitable other firms will be attracted to it. The biggest problem then is if other firms are not allowed to compete (eg Camelot has a legal monopoly to run the National Lottery).

- Appraisals – one view is that pay should not be linked to appraisals; another is that this is unfair on high performing staff.

- Human resources – one view is that personnel issues should be decentralised because human beings are an important resource, better managed by their own line manager; the other is that the only reason this has been done is to save money and it reduces support to employees.

The key things to remember are that *no perspective is wrong* – though one perspective may be more useful or apply to a greater degree at certain times than others. The second is that by arguing both cases you will always gain more marks.

A final exercise. Try the following question on your own and see how well you can analyse and evaluate the different perspectives outlined.

 Question to consider

The facilities director in your organisation is new and very keen on improving efficiency. She wants standards introduced and monitored in all administrative areas as quickly as possible. Your boss, the human resources manager, is concerned that this approach will destroy the cooperative and friendly atmosphere in the office.

As administrator in charge of this area, what strategies would you employ to help you in this situation?

Index